Tell me where is fancy bred,
Or in the heart or in the head?
How begot, how nourishèd?
        Reply, reply.
It is engendered in the eyes,
With gazing fed; and fancy dies
In the cradle, where it lies.
    Let us all ring fancy's knell;
    I'll begin it—Ding, dong, bell.

—*The Merchant of Venice,* Act 3, scene 2, 1597

Photography by
JASON FULFORD & TAMARA SHOPSIN

BROOKS HEADLEY'S

FANCY DESSERTS

The Recipes of Del Posto's James Beard Award–Winning Pastry Chef

BROOKS HEADLEY
with **CHRIS CECHIN-DE LA ROSA**

W · W · NORTON

NEW YORK · LONDON

Page 162: *Sweet Science* cover design: www.aulicinodesign.com.

Page 163: Pages from *The River Cafe Cookbook* by Rose Gray and Ruth Rogers, published by
Ebury, reprinted by permission of The Random House Group Limited. Photographs by Jean
Pigozzi and Martyn Thompson, copyright © 1996 by Jean Pigozzi and Martyn Thompson;
from *London River Cafe Cookbook* by Ruth Rogers and Rose Gray. Used by permission of
Random House, an imprint and division of Random House LLC. All rights reserved.

For information about permission to reproduce selections from this book,
write to Permissions, W. W. Norton & Company, Inc.,
500 Fifth Avenue, New York, NY 10110

For information about special discounts for bulk purchases, please contact
W. W. Norton Special Sales at specialsales@wwnorton.com or 800-233-4830

Manufacturing by Asia Pacific Offset
Book design by Tamara Shopsin
Production manager: Julia Druskin

Library of Congress Cataloging-in-Publication Data

Headley, Brooks.
Brooks Headley's fancy desserts : the recipes of Del Posto's James Beard
Award-winning pastry chef / Brooks Headley with Chris Cechin-De la Rosa ;
photography by Jason Fulford & Tamara Shopsin. — First edition.
    pages cm.
Includes index.
ISBN 978-0-393-24107-5 (hardcover)
1. Desserts. 2. Pastry. I. Cechin-De la Rosa, Chris. II. Title.
TX773.H345 2014
641.86—dc23
                                                                2014020584

W. W. Norton & Company, Inc.
500 Fifth Avenue, New York, N.Y. 10110
www.wwnorton.com

W. W. Norton & Company Ltd.
Castle House, 75/76 Wells Street, London W1T 3QT

1 2 3 4 5 6 7 8 9 0

THIS BOOK IS DEDICATED TO MY MOM,

Barbara. A super-feminist bad-ass schoolteacher. She is not around any-more, and I miss her every day. She once visited New York to accompany me at an event, and as she arrived in a taxi a nice elderly man grabbed her gently by the arm and escorted her to the front door. It was Juan Mari Arzak. "Who was he?" she asked. "He was so nice!" Years prior she had a screaming match with a police officer over a noise complaint filed during one of my band practices. "Who the hell called the cops on these kids?" She was in her nightgown on the sidewalk. This whole book is for you, Barb.

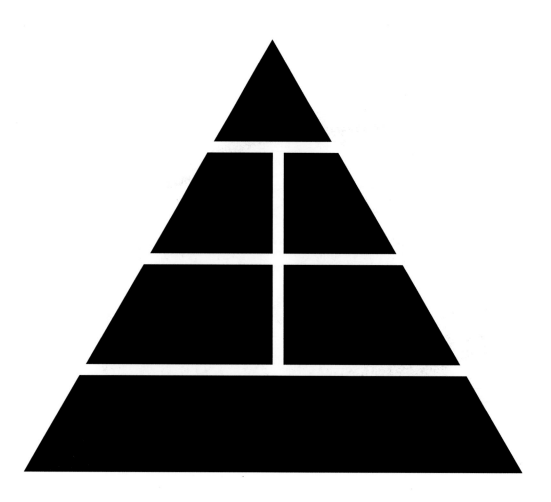

CONTENTS

FOREWORD by Steve Albini

Brooks Headley is my favorite kind of artist. He does his thing, his beautiful, unique thing, and presents it to you with no fanfare. You're going to love it of course, but what he's doing isn't only for you. He does it because he's found his thing, the thing that animates him uniquely, and screw it, might as well devote his life to it. Other people—you—get to enjoy it, and he takes his responsibility to you seriously. But this isn't showbiz.

It is a reflection on our culture, not on the profession, that there are plenty of cooks who are in showbiz, and fuck them. Brooks doesn't pander, or leap on the latest thing. His food doesn't come in costume. It is common today for chefs to insult the palate in a parody of whimsy, forcing you to learn by experiment what should have been self-evident, that snails aren't suited to ice cream. As a pastry chef Brooks has his creative crutches, but they don't include bacon.

They say that all arts aspire to music, but that's a con. Music wishes it was food. Music cries itself to sleep over not having been born a ripe fig or a shank of lamb. No song, no painting can come close to a perfect meal with friends. I would happily trade the best blow job of my life to relive the best steak or bowl of soup. It is the only art without which we die.

Cooking starts with learning to boil water, but you have no idea how difficult it is to boil water. First, you have your heart broken, and then you revel in the natural wonder of a fresh peach straight off a tree. Next, you drive four hundred miles in a van with no heat and one working door to find out the show has been canceled, but you set your shit up and play anyhow, making sure to bolt before the flashing lights get too close. You have to fuck countless people, or one person who really counts. You need to feel your face flush with embarrassment and beam with pride, and freeze in abject boredom between the two. You have to lie shivering and exhausted in a makeshift bed someplace filthy, and retire with a full belly in front of a crackling fire beside the naked body of the person you care for most. You have to build a mountain of broken junk so big you can't see the top, then climb it and beat your chest, shrieking like King Kong at the summit. You need to have your best ideas deemed worthless and exhaust yourself in fruitless experiments that lead nowhere. You have to develop a thick skin, hard with calluses and scars, and with the tips of your hard, callused, scarred fingers, feel the difference between perfect and not quite.

Boiling water is a bitch.

All art is an effort to express the creative impulse, and each discipline uses a different craft to make it tangible. You can get by in some situations without the craft, and in others you can pick it up along the way, but being good at things makes a difference. Don't let anybody tell you otherwise. You get good by trying things and failing, and in the process you develop the skills and calluses and scars that are the shibboleth of any profession. They are not enough, the calluses and scars, but they are part of it.

It's easy with cooking to be dazzled by the process and to give an uneven amount of credit to the recipe. Or the technique. Or the stick blender. But what you're eating is actually the totality of the life experience of the cook, paired with what he knows about history, the ingredients, his kitchen. He needs to be in command of all of those things, not least himself. You're tasting the whole of the dude, and this particular dude has lived enough to be delicious.

Brooks circa 1996 (*Crimewave* E.P.).

BROOKS HEADLEY'S

FANCY DESSERTS

INTRODUCTION by Chris Cechin-De la Rosa

One late night at the end of summer, Mark Ladner and I arranged to meet at a Japanese bar in the Chelsea area of New York City. He'd just finished a dinner shift at Del Posto, where he is executive chef and Brooks Headley's boss. When Ladner arrived, the bartender knowingly placed a big yellow draft beer in front of him with a smile.

Ladner is charming and calm, tall, with short hair and big perfect teeth. He speaks just softly enough for you to realize that you talk too loudly. His tone is measured and serious, but he is darkly comedic. If Ladner is less than a full-blown celebrity, it is by his own design. He has the bearing of a cook from some other time.

Del Posto is a modern relic, too: huge, ornate, massively expensive. As an Italian restaurant, it stands alone in its fine-dining aspirations. The food is astounding but comforting, quietly complex but honest, committed to flavor above all else, including ego. Philosophically, Del Posto speaks to Brooks.

Ladner and I ordered food and a bottle of sake and I asked him how Brooks, then a nobody on the Manhattan food scene, landed the pastry chef job at Del Posto, the crown jewel of the vast Mario Batali and Bastianich family empire.

"Brooks wrote me a letter that was very compelling," he said.

In 2008, Brooks sent Ladner a 570-word e-mail at 3 o'clock on a Saturday morning asking for a shot at the job. He was drunk, but the note was surprisingly lucid. It was at least a little inappropriate, but it was enough to land an interview and afterward a chance to present a tasting. Things went well. Ladner invited Brooks back for a private dinner, where he offered Brooks the job.

"I wore a tie under a sweater and I was terrified," Brooks once told me. "Ladner gave me a bunch of books. I don't remember saying anything except *OK*." They had a lot to drink because there was a lot for Ladner to cover.

"When you work closely with someone in a certain way, you have to know their guts at least a little," Ladner said, like he and Brooks were starting a band. The bet was that Brooks fit the psychological profile. The recipes would come.

"His cooking today is nothing like it was back then," he said.

Between then and now is what is in this book, mostly. The majority of the recipes belong to Brooks. There are several he has inherited, cribbed, or stolen outright. A handful belong to people who work for him and there's one on loan from Ladner. Many of them appear seasonally in one form or another on the Del Posto menu.

There is the celebrated Celery Sorbet, acidic and bright, and the magically cryptic Eggplant and Chocolate. There are eleven gelato recipes—from strawberry to olive oil to oatmeal—and a lot of vegetables used in ways few people are accustomed to. There is the exemplary Butterscotch Mascarpone Semifreddo that evolved out of his inability to steal one of chef Nancy Silverton's trademark desserts. The Bastoncino from the Del Posto dessert box is here, as are several subtle but striking sorbets. Polenta is everywhere. There's also a Pasta Frolla, a cheesy Italian s'more, and the constant threat that Brooks is going to have you soak something in verjus. It is the most unintentionally contrary dessert book you own, which will aggravate Brooks to hear. He isn't out to trick anyone and he isn't hiding anything. His middle name is Oliver.

There is nonetheless something masochistically methodical in getting at dishes as simple as Brooks's. His recipes are a hybrid of childhood ephemera, lessons from time spent cooking with underpaid and overtalented immigrants in DC, and mangled reworkings of the American pastry masters. It is baffling how many screw-ups land on the Del Posto menu. With Brooks, it's all a series of in-jokes, and maybe you never laugh. But by the time the plate is placed in front of you, it contains the most explosively flavored, most biographically layered plum you've ever eaten.

Condensed, the biography is simple. Brooks was born in 1972 in Towson, Maryland, where he was raised by his mom. His family's roots are in the Calabria region of Italy and like with many Italian American families, kitchen work came naturally. He started playing drums in punk bands as a teenager and, along with much of the scene back then, became vegetarian. He started college, dropped out, played in more bands and toured, returned to school, learned how to make desserts, and then won the James Beard Award for Outstanding Pastry Chef in 2013. It is a story that is as endearing to some as it is infuriating to others. In a lot of ways, the schizophrenic career arc is the allure of the food.

Brooks spent what would have been his cooking school years on tour playing drums in obscure but beloved punk bands instead: Born Against, Universal Order of Armageddon, Wrangler Brutes, Skull Kontrol. These names mean a lot to people who may never—or *would* never—step foot in Del Posto. As bands, they have some things in common musically, but more important, they share the unique ideology of an era from the early 1990s to early 2000s punk rock: independent but communal, honest but sarcastic, earnest but often deeply self-conscious. Brooks eventually got a degree in literature from the University of Maryland, but he mentions school once in this book—to explain that he dropped out to join Born Against, then his favorite band.

There are annoying things to be said right here about the artistic connection between playing the drums and pastry cheffing. Each is exacting and rhythmic and you use two hands and both legs. Both require commitment and focus and are physically exhausting. True, all of it. But with Brooks it's simpler: They are service jobs, largely selfless. You are as likely to see Brooks play a complicated drum solo as you are to visit his personalized dessert truck—neither will ever happen. Brooks is collaborative at the core.

"At Del Posto, Brooks instantly made a conscious effort to assimilate," Ladner told me. It's hard to imagine it any other way. The Del Posto kitchen—sprawling, impeccable, systematic, industrial—comes across as maybe the most deferential place in Manhattan.

"And it continues today," Ladner said. "When Brooks hires a new cook, he brings them quietly over to watch the savory side of the kitchen and explains things to them: 'The reason we do *this* is because these guys do *that*.' It's so respectful. That thing just doesn't happen in a professional kitchen."

I asked if what Brooks does was off-putting at first.

"I didn't know how to handle it," Ladner explained. "It's just so unusual. But the more he did that the more I reciprocated and it allowed us to become a seamless expression. Stylistically, we started to create in the same ways."

It makes sense that this book is also collaborative. In a turn that is both ego free and egocentric, Brooks sought out people and ideas to fill pages in ways he couldn't. Contributing writers include three punk icons: engineer and musician Steve Albini, author and musician Ian Svenonius, and novelist and vocalist Sam McPheeters. He commissioned an essay on chocolate from Brad Kintzer, the esteemed head chocolatier at TCHO, and an explication of olive oil from Nicholas Coleman, probably the nation's leading olive oil expert. Essayist Sloane Crosley delivered a personal story about taste buds, food writer and musician Robert Sietsema wrote about where punks ate in New York City in the eighties, and artist Cali Thornhill-DeWitt recounted the horrors of Del Posto's neighborhood before it was recast as a fashionable destination for people with a lot of money. Journalist Katie Parla underscores the macabre side of Italian pastry. In a recurring series cribbed from a Born Against flier from the early nineties called Profile in Courage, Brooks collects portraits of seven people he admires, mostly chefs plus one legendary punk singer, in a way that both sublimates and illuminates his own story.

Taken together, the book is Brooks in full: serious but not, studied but accidental, respectful but ridiculous, approachable yet quietly insular. The book is self-effacing and open and honest. It is slapstick but also massively sincere. There are references you'll latch on to immediately and others you won't get even after an hour of research. In ways, it's novelistic—it doesn't require that you get every allusion. (Although, if you don't know what Joy Division is, you might be in the wrong place.) As with Brooks's food, the book is at once entirely about the thing and entirely not about the thing.

It's been more than five years now that Ladner and Brooks have worked together, and in that time Del Posto has earned four stars from *The New York Times*—tenuous but deserved praise that both Ladner and Brooks know may well be stripped by the time you read this. In the restaurant review, Brooks was given an uncommon amount of coverage for a pastry chef—a testament to Ladner's idea of a "seamless expression."

When Ladner and I finished the sake, it was somewhere approaching 1 a.m. He fielded a message from Brooks, just finishing *his* dinner shift, and we made plans to meet him for a beer. Before we left, I asked Ladner if there was anything else I should know about Brooks.

"It's not about us," he said softly. "You want to express yourself as a chef, but you want your food and your plate to speak in ways that express soul. It's not that you especially want to show how creative you are, but that you have a soul. Brooks does that exceptionally well. It's disarming."

I looked at him, and maybe he felt as if I didn't believe him.

"He's managed a way to express himself," he said. "But it's not exactly punk."

He smiled.

"Maybe it is, though."

Ladner.

THINGS YOU NEED, THINGS YOU MAY NOT RECOGNIZE, AND THINGS I WANT TO EXPLAIN

There are ingredients and tools I use at Del Posto that you may not have. This section is to help familiarize you with a few of them.

INGREDIENTS

ALMOND FLOUR: This stuff is not complicated to cook with, but it is extremely useful. Out of the bag it's just 100 percent very finely ground almonds. But here's a tip: Almond flour is untoasted, and untoasted almonds taste like nothing. Before you use it, spread a thin layer out on a parchment-lined sheet pan and toast it at 325°F for 5 minutes until it browns. Mix it around with a fork and be sure it doesn't burn.

CHOCOLATE: The economic and social impact on source producers of chocolate is usually pretty devastating. There are a few responsible brands, but usually the process is Ronald Reagan meets Ronald McDonald: not cool. Use very good-quality chocolate like TCHO or Amedei. It won't be cheap, but as Flipper (the band) said once: "Life is pretty cheap."

DEXTROSE: I asked Michael Laiskonis, a teacher and a pastry chef in NYC, to explain dextrose. Laiskonis: "Though often referred to interchange-ably with glucose, dextrose refers to a full conversion of starch to sugar, or 100DE (as opposed to partial starch conversions that result in glucose and corn syrups). Roughly three-quarters the sweetness of sucrose, it adds a 'cool-ing' effect due to its high heat of solution. Dextrose increases viscosity and benefits texture in ice cream and sorbet. Because of its low molecular weight, dextrose has a greater effect on freeze-point depression—nearly twice that of sucrose—thus contributing softness to frozen desserts." Dextrose. I use it in sorbet bases.

GRAINS AND FLOURS BY ANSON MILLS: These guys rule. They have high-quality artisanal grains and flours that both restaurants and home cooks can get easily. I am crazy about their Spina Rossa della Valsugana polenta: It is gritty with beautiful little black specks. I also love their buckwheat flour called Grano Saraceno. The grains are milled and stone-ground weekly; these products are highly perishable. Store them in the fridge.

Clockwise from top left: Almond flour, dextrose, buckwheat flour, pectin, nonfat milk powder, polenta.

LABNEH: This is a strained cheese that is pretty much interchangeable with Greek yogurt. I like it because it is really thick and very tart.

MALIC ACID: This is like pastry chef salt, even though I also love actual salt. Find it online. Malic acid adds a beautiful tartness to fruit compotes and jams and sorbets.

NONFAT MILK POWDER: You'll find this at any supermarket. I use it in gelato bases to prevent ice crystals. On the package it says you can mix it with water to make potable milk. Please don't do that.

PECTIN: This white, totally natural, totally powerful powder thickens fruit jams and compotes and creates in them a beautiful shine.

SIMPLE SYRUP: Take equal parts sugar and water and bring to a slow simmer to dissolve the sugar granules. It will keep in your fridge a long time.

SOFT SILKEN TOFU: I make Tofu Chocolate Crème Brûlée (page 147) with this.

TOOLS

BAKING SHEETS (HALF BAKING SHEETS): The gold standard at any restaurant, half baking sheets will fit in your home oven, no problem. They are sturdy sheets with a ½-inch lip on them that won't flex when you hold them. Don't bother with lousy cookie sheets. Go to a kitchen supply place and get a few of these. They'll last forever.

Chinois, *left*; china cap, *right*.

CHINOIS: This is a very fine-meshed, cone-shaped strainer. It'll cost you, even at a kitchen supply store. But it will last you a very long time. Alternately, use a strainer with cheesecloth, or a China cap, which is similar but with larger holes.

COFFEE/SPICE GRINDER: Ideally, you'll have two, unless you are maniacally diligent. Otherwise coffee will taste like spices, and spices will taste like coffee.

CLING FILM (AKA PLASTIC WRAP), 18 INCHES: Sadly, you probably need to go to one of those megalithic corporate shopping warehouse stores—like Costco—to get this. It's worth it. A single roll will last a long time, if you have to replace it at all.

DEHYDRATOR: Get an Excalibur. It is cheap and has trays that slide out. I use one at Del Posto every day to slowly remove liquid from various ingredients. For you holdouts, there is another method: Put your oven on the lowest possible setting, prop the door open slightly, and bake. You'll get nearly the same effect. It'll just clog up your oven for several hours.

DIGITAL SCALE: Unlike other pastry chefs, I hate scales. They aren't necessary for cooking in situations other than the highest of professional kitchens. This will anger some of my closest chef friends, and I have included gram measurements so they'll relax. Julia Child's cookbooks never had weight measurements. But if you must have a scale, get an Escali. It is cheap and lasts a long time.

FOOD PROCESSOR: I'm afraid you need one of these, too. Fancy or unfancy. It's your call.

HUMAN HANDS: If an ingredient can be torn with your hands, put down the knife and tear it with your hands.

ICE BATH: An ice bath is equal parts ice and cold water and will cool your stuff down very quickly and that will make the NYC Department of Health very happy.

IMMERSION BLENDER: Get a good one, something powerful. It blends things. Right around fifty dollars nowadays. Anything cheaper won't last. It *must* detach for easy cleaning.

MANDOLINE SLICER: My mom bought me one for my eighteenth birthday. I got a potato, went to the pantry, and shaved off a big chunk of my thumb and a little piece of potato on the first slice. I refused to go to the hospital, so now I have an oval-shaped divot on my right thumb. Use this to cut all manner of vegetables. Watch your fingers!

MESH STRAINER: You only need a little one—from Bed Bath & Beyond or even the dollar store. It will have slightly bigger holes than a chinois and you'll need it on occasion.

MORTAR AND PESTLE: So caveman. So Pok Pok Andy Ricker. They'll look really classy on your kitchen counter, like you're an Italian grandma. Just keep them clean, OK? Make a pesto with a mortar and a pestle. Ask chef Mark Peel: It is the only way to do it.

NONSTICK COOKING SPRAY: Pam is fine. Ignore the version with the "fat-free" sales pitch on it. It's a fat! It also helps parchment stick to sheet pans. I use it more for sticking than for releasing.

PARCHMENT PAPER: Get a box of the full-sheet pan-style while you're at Costco getting your 18-inch roll of cling film.

RUBBER SPATULA: Buy a professional-grade heat-resistant one from your kitchen supply shop. Get two, actually: one for sweet and one for savory. Tomato sauce and candy don't mix. (Or do they?)

SCISSORS: You need a pair exclusively for food. Wash them once in a while! Same goes for that grimy can opener in your tool drawer. Can you please soak that thing in sanitizer for me, like, *right now?* It's so gross. The peeler, too.

SILPATS: Silpats are indispensable nonstick silicone baking mats that are washable. Use one for any recipe that is too sticky for parchment paper.

SMALL, MEDIUM, AND LARGE STAINLESS-STEEL MIXING BOWLS: These will make your life so much easier and they last forever.

STAINLESS-STEEL SAUCEPANS (ALL-CLAD): It's time. Treat yourself to some nice pans, if you haven't already. You deserve them and they are absolutely necessary.

STAND MIXER: The KitchenAid line does the trick, just don't ever use it to make brioche because you will kill it right away—even before the showroom shine wears off. Whatever brand, make sure it comes with a paddle (for cookies) and a whip (for whisking), and don't worry too much about the hook (that's for bread).

THERMOMETER: This is necessary for making mozzarella, caramels, and other delicate, temperature-based foods. I am addicted to my Thermapen. It ain't cheap, but it is super cool and will last you a very long time. Using it will make you feel very pro.

VEGETABLE PEELER: When I started cooking professionally, I had to peel a lot of apples. Eventually the natural citric acid split open the skin on my index fingers. Nobody cared. I am partial to the Y-peeler. Keep it clean!

WET-SAND METHOD: There are recipes in this book that call for the wet-sand method (Red wine plums and fried Roman artichokes, for example). It's easy: Mix sugar with water in a heavy pot over medium heat until you have a slurry of a consistency a little too gooey to make a sand castle. Put a frying pan or lid on top. The condensation will drip down the sides and clean off any excess sugar that might otherwise cause problems with crystallization. Just watch it closely—peeking is fine. Don't bother with the method of using a brush to wipe down the sides of the pot. Chances are your pastry brush has residual butter or oil in it and that will cause problems later.

WHISK: You probably have one or several already. I'm obligated to be sure.

HOSPITALITY

Brochette.

I am a part of the hospitality industry. Make no mistake about that. But sometimes, as a chef makes his or her way up the professional culinary ladder, the hospitality gets lost in all of the industry. Cooking food for strangers is what I do, and though it's generally a completely different enterprise from cooking at home for friends and family, the ideal is to bring the same feeling to customers. This is why Nigella Lawson is one of my heroes. Her approach is the opposite of a chef's. She cooks for people she knows. And although I do sometimes cook for people I know, on a normal night I'm cooking for strangers. And that's totally cool. That's the job. It's all about the guest. It's all about hospitality. Check your ego at the employee entrance.

I learned true hospitality many years before I started cooking, in an unlikely way. At the time I was a vegetarian in a BBQ joint in Birmingham, Alabama.

It was 1995. Back then I played drums in a band called Young Pioneers. We were based out of Richmond, Virginia, where I worked at a Kinko's making copies, which was the number-one job of choice for a loser in a punk band. My life revolved around not charging friends for copies and stocking reams of goldenrod paper for my personal use. Who could afford photocopying all those show flyers, record covers, inserts, and stickers? These things are critical for a crummy punk band, and they aren't free. Besides, Kinko's was an easy job.

But I've never been a slacker. I worked hard, I was never late, and I didn't complain about getting $6.50 an hour. I was a quiet robot and they loved me for it. My boss was a kindly lesbian named Sue. She promoted her girlfriend to assistant manager (awesome) and chain-smoked in her office. To this day the smell of copy machine toner combined with Parliament smoke is a comfort to me. But most important, Sue always held my job while I went on the road with Young Pioneers. *Hey, Sue, can I have a month off work to go on tour with my band that no one cares about?* The answer was always yes.

On tour that summer we found ourselves in Birmingham, at a record store run by a guy named Russell, who also organized punk rock shows in the area. He knew better than anyone that when a band arrives in a new town, they are confused and hungry. We were no exception. We asked Russell where the nearest health food store was, and he laughed. He said he had a better place for us: Brochette's, downtown. "Tell them Russell sent you," he said.

We parked the van on the street right outside the place. Inside we stared blankly at the menu, displayed on a felt board with plastic grappling letters. There were four of us, including our roadie, Christian. None of us ate meat, and we were bewildered as to why Russell had sent us to a full-on Alabama BBQ that trafficked in pulled pork, burnt-end baked beans, and bacon-fat corn bread. We all looked at one another, glanced again at the menu, turned around, and started to walk out.

"Hey!" a voice called from behind the counter. "Russell send you guys?"

"Uh, yeah. He sent us. . . ."

"So, you all vegetarian?" We looked at one another again. *What the fuck was going on?*

"Gentlemen, please, have a seat."

We walked up to the counter and sat down on the old stools that had puckered, split seams patched with duct tape. Our maroon van parked outside had similar Band-Aids on the seats.

"So," the chef behind the counter said, "Russell sent you guys. Fantastic. You want some lemonade?"

He poured us all glasses and set them on the bar.

"You are in my house now. Get comfortable. Relax. Y'all just vegetarian? Or are you vegan?"

Adam and Christian were vegan. Marty and I were *just* vegetarian.

"Okay, gentlemen. I gotcha," he said, and turned back to his kitchen. And then Brochette (I assume his name was Brochette, because he exuded ownership) began to cook us a personal, off-the-menu procession of plates of food. Technically speaking, it was my first tasting menu. We had no idea what was coming out of the kitchen—or what it was going to cost us. Since that day I have eaten tasting menus at very fancy restaurants—Michelin-starred places—and nothing has ever topped this one.

We were served bread crumb–topped macaroni and cheese (for the non-vegans) and baconless corn bread that Brochette prepared from scratch in a cast-iron pan as we looked on. We had collards sans hocks (he assured us with a grin as he slid our plates onto the counter), and a salad of mixed greens, vinegary and spicy with black pepper. We got drunk on Brochette's hospitality and would have gladly eaten anything he put in front of us—a shoe, maybe, or a piece of cardboard. He was totally showboating, performing. And having a great time. The last course was a banana pudding with homemade vanilla wafers. He explained to the dairy-free members of our party that the fat he used was margarine, even showed us the container.

He charged us twenty dollars. Total. Five bucks a head. Ignorant jerks that we were, we didn't leave a tip. And I really should have, because Brochette taught me what hospitality—real hospitality—is. I took that photo of him on page 12 on our way out. I try to keep him in mind when I'm cooking today.

★ Tubesteak Gazette ★

Vol II NO I
PRE-SPRING 1993 AD

OFFICIAL NEWSLETTER OF SAID ROCK BAND

Born Against

★ NOW FREE IN THE LOWER 48! ★

★ FOR YOU ★

new 10" lp out soon

"BATTLE HYMNS OF THE RACE WAR" DELAYED

SLATED FOR RELEASE SOMETIME BEFORE IT ALL BLOWS UP IN OUR FUCKING BOURGEOS FACES, YET DEFINITELY NOT BEFORE APRIL. TO MEET THE OVERWHELMING DEMAND FOR ROCK MUSIC, ROCK BAND BORN AGAINST HAS PRE-RELEASED ITS "RACE WAR" 10" AS A POORLY PACKAGED, LOW GRADE CASSETTE. PROCEEDS WILL FINANCE THE EVENTUAL VINYL FORMAT. THE RECORDING FEATURES A CROSS SECTION OF MEMBERS PAST AND PRESENT, AND SELECTED HIGHLIGHTS OF THE YEAR IN TELEVISION HISTORY. EVER CONTROVERSIAL, THE BAND WILL PROBABLY TURN THE HEADS OF MORE THAN A FEW PUNKS, SKINS, BANGERS, AND STREET THRASHERS WITH ITS MESSAGE OF AMERIGANE POWER. PRIDE OF IN A PREJUDICED SOCIETIES CANNOT BE DESTRUCTION UNDERLYING THEME MUECID ESTABLIGHMDISM WILL SOON COVER KAN THE STATY WAKY OF NEW JERSEY!!!

NEWS FLASH ✂

A SECRET TREATY BETWEEN THRASH ROCKERS BORN AGAINST AND POETRY BOYS UNIVERSAL ORDER OF ARMAGEDDON HAS BEEN PUBLICLY EXPOSED AS A PLOT TO BEEFEN THE THINNING RANKS OF BORN AGAINST. GYPSY TONIE JOY AND LITTLE BROOKS NOW PLAY IN BOTH GROUPS, VIOLATING INTERSTATE CONFLICT OF INTEREST LAWS. FURTHER ENVELOPING THE TWO IN ETHICAL QUAGMIRE IS THE RELEASE OF SPLIT 7" RECORDS WITH MAN IS THE BASTARD, SCREECHING WEASEL AND A VERY INCESTUOS UOA/BA EP.

★ BORN AGAINST ON TOUR NEAR YOU: ★

FRI JAN 29 BALTIMORE LOFT
SAT JAN 30 WASHINGTON DC MOUNTAIN LODGE
SUN JAN 31 VIRGINIA BEACH KING'S HEAD
MON FEB 1 COLUMBIA S.C. 49 REASONS HOUSE
TUES FEB 2 ATLANTA GA HOUSE
WED FEB 3 PENSACOLA FL SLUGGO'S
FRI FEB 5 NEW ORLEANS LA ABSTRACT BOOKSTORE
SAT FEB 6 DALLAS TX DUNE BUGGY
SUN FEB 7 AMARILLO TX
MON FEB 8 SANTA FE, NM RR PERFORM. SPACE
TUES FEB 9 PETRIFIED FOREST
WED FEB 10 PHOENIX AZ HOLLYWOOD ALLEY
THURS FEB 11 SAN DIEGO, CA CHE' CAFE
FRI FEB 12 HOLLYWOOD, CA MACONDO
SAT FEB 13 SANTA BARBARA, CA ANACONDA
SUN FEB 14 SAN JOSE, CA TREEHOUSE
MON FEB 15 ALCATRAZ

TUES FEB 16 SAN FRANCISCO, CA PRACTICE SPACE
WED FEB 17 OAKLAND, CA YOUR PLACE TOO
THURS FEB 18 SANTA ROSA, CA PRACTICE SPACE
FRI FEB 19 BERKELEY, CA GILMAN
SAT FEB 20 SAN DIEGO, CA
SUN FEB 21 CLAREMONT, CA
MON FEB 22 SMOKIN BOOKS
WED FEB 24 TUSCON, AZ DOWNTOWN PERFORM CTR.
FRI FEB 26 FT WORTH, TX MAD HATTERS
SAT FEB 28 LITTLE ROCK, AR RIVER AMPHITHEATRE
SUN FEB 28 SPRINGFIELD, MO - COMMERCIAL ST.
MON MAR 1 MEMPHIS, TN - ANTENNA
TUES MAR 2 LOUISVILLE, KY - TULIGAN'S
WED MAR 3 HAGGERSTOWN, MD WILSON PURITAN
THUR MAR 4 ANNAPOLIS, MD TONIE'S BSMNT
FRI MAR 5 RICHMOND, VA METRO
SAT MAR 6 WASHINGTON DC - ST STEVENS

IT'S OFFICIAL !!!

LARRY LIVERMORE, MAXIMUMUMROCKNROLL !!! "I have discovered Born Against to be the most important band of our times. !!!!!!!!!!!"

- BORN AGAINST SUPPORTS:

- LEATHER FACE
- INTEGRITY ALBUM
- PANTHER DEMO
- SUPERCHUNK
- "COPS" TV SHOW, NOT REAL POLICE
- UNIVERSAL ORDER OF ARMAGEDDON
- HOWARD STERN
- SEINFELD
- MAN IS THE BASTARD
- TOFUTTI WITH CHOCOLATE FLAVOR

SINGER OF BORN AGAINST EXPOSED!!

their's. That Sam McPheeters guy, I met him a couple of years ago and he seemed like a relatively nice guy, but he's got nothing to complain about. He inherited a bunch of money and blew it all on his fucking record label. Which I can appreciate, getting a whole shit load of money and investing it in something you really believe in, and having it backfire on you, it's sort of poetic justice, there's a beauty to that, the fine art of failure. I can appreciate that... He's another one that came out of the middle of fucking nowhere, and now he's the all-seeing power of New York hardcore, or the geek scene, or whatever. I don't remember seeing this guy in eighty, or eighty-one, or even eighty seven, I don't know who he thinks he is, anyway.

— SHEER TERROR interview, CRUNCHFACE 11

PROFILES IN COURAGE

AN ONGOING UPDATE OF FORMER BORN AGAINST MEMBERS

NEIL BURKE, "Murders" era

AGE: 24
OCCUPATION: MAN
STATUS: MARRIED
NOTABLE QUOTE: "Don't kill you me!"
SHOE SIZE: 8 1/2
FAVORITE DRINK: 7 UP
FAVORITE DRUG: Coke & Heroin... A speedball!!
AMBITION/FUTURE PLAN: TO MAN A VEHICLE
ACCOMPLISHMENTS: DING-DONG SMALLZINE, CONSTRUCTIVE REBELLION FANZINE, LUNG-CAST RECORDS, HELLIVATOR, MURDERS AMONG US, MEN, MENACE DEMENT, LIFES-BLOOD, JOHNSON BROS. RECORDS, UPCOMING TV SHOW, BOOK & SOLO RECORD

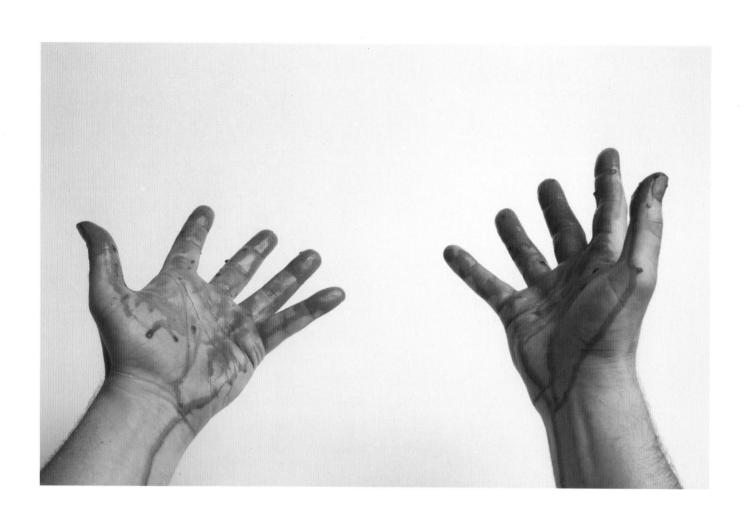

1. FRUIT

This chapter addresses fruit, the most important ingredient in my arsenal. Remember, sweet stuff is still *food*. It needs to be seasoned and cared for; its traits must be championed. Fruit above all must look gushingly embarrassed and red-faced in its plump ripeness. Take care in seeking out the best of the season and your desserts will be wildly flavorful and simple in the absolute best way.

Create a relationship with your local greenmarket. Go and talk to the farmers. Bring them a breakfast taco and a cup of coffee. Befriend them, because they are going to have fruits and vegetables that blow the normal supermarket commodity produce out of the water. Yes, they will be a little more expensive, but you get what you pay for when it comes to fruit. A greenmarket peach in August, warmed by the sun, just picked from the branch, maybe already with a bad spot and having never seen the inside of a refrigerator . . . it body slams even the most tawdry Whole Foods supermodel fruit. The difference is monumental, huge, biblical.

Treat your fruit with respect, coax it rather than manipulate it, and you will reap endless rewards. And don't forget to eat tons of fresh raw fruit. An apple a day . . . that's not a joke.

GREENMARKETS: FOR GOOD AND TERRIBLE

I love greenmarkets. I have a devotion to them that is so deep it's probably killed—or at least maimed—a couple of my relationships.

I started going to greenmarkets long before I ever cooked professionally. The Sunday Dupont Circle market in Washington, DC, was an early favorite. But I was such an amateur back then. I'd truck those plastic bags of pristine mesclun mix and Italian prune plums with fluorescent yellow flesh back to my apartment in Mount Pleasant and let it all rot in the crisper. Oh, how uncrisp that stuff would be by Thursday. But when I started working in local restaurants, my visits to the Dupont market became far more serious. I arrived before anyone else, assuring myself the pick of the fruit litter. It was my mandate—I refused to disappoint my guests. I had to have better produce than everyone else. It wasn't a competition or anything, except that it was absolutely a competition. I'd buy my fruits and vegetables for the week on Sunday, walk them two blocks over to Komi on P Street, unlock the closed restaurant, and lay everything out like jewels on parchment-covered sheet pans.

When I moved to Los Angeles years later, I logged many hours at both the Santa Monica and the Hollywood greenmarkets. Sometimes I was there for work, sometimes for fun. The Hollywood market forms a + shape on Ivar Avenue between Sunset and Hollywood, right by Amoeba Music. Ivar is all stellar produce, increasing in perfection as you travel north. Selma Avenue spears the intersection but is full of delicious prepared foods: *pupusas*, kettle corn, tacos, ice cream, and more. The macho chef types in LA (male and female alike) will tell you that the Santa Monica market kicks Hollywood's ass, but I prefer Hollywood. It's like a Sunday morning party.

When I went to Northern California on vacation a few years ago, I built my schedule around being able to attend the Ferry Building market in San Francisco, where I could get the absolutely killer stone fruit from Frog Hollow Farm. Jesus, have you ever tasted one of their nectarines? I was reduced to a drooling cliché, standing beside the stand with juice gushing down my chin.

Being a devout fan of greenmarkets means I'm also capable of vehemently hating them. In all its posturing, the one in Manhattan's Union Square, for example, strikes me as one of the most joyless places in the entire city. It's infuriating. In the summer I drag myself up there and navigate the sludgy crowds nearly every day, but only because I have to.

It's common at the Union Square greenmarket to spot a camera crew shooting a chef chatting with a farmer. Occasionally, it's someone I know, flaunting a full sleeve of tattoos and hamming it up for the camera. He or she

fondles a tomato, makes googly eyes at a crate of ramps, maybe bench-presses a flat or two of strawberries. His or her hair is perfect. It's greenmarket chef porn, destined for a magazine spread or an online video. It cracks me up. I'm *working* here, for Christ's sake. Get a room.

But in the end it's worth it to brave the vulgarity. I learned this back in 2006, when I was doing a week-long stage at a somewhat prominent restaurant in Manhattan. "Stage" is a French term that means you work for free. But it's usually a win-win situation: The restaurant gets some free grunt work and you, the *stagier*, get to hang out in the kitchen and see how they make stuff. During this particular stint, which was deep into summer, we were seeing a banner season for East Coast peaches. But the cooks at this restaurant were more concerned with technique than flavor. They'd roast a peach in shovels of butter, puree it into submission, and turn it into a pod, or a tube, or a ravioli. Sometimes they'd even *peel* it. *Oh God, no. Please don't peel it. Please? Oh man, all the flavor, wasted.*

They had their peaches delivered from a commercial purveyor rather than walk the seven blocks to the Union Square market, where the peaches tasted better, had ideal texture, and were picked at supreme ripeness. Prematurely picked fruit festers in warehouse chillers, zapping it of all sex and juice gush. I felt sorry for the guys at that restaurant. It wasn't a smug sort of sorry either, which as a chef I am occasionally prone to feeling. I honestly felt bad for them.

For me, a large part of the joy of cooking is witnessing the perfection of nature. These guys deprived themselves of that. And unlike that well-groomed chef hamming it up for a greenmarket photo op, I genuinely love holding a piece of fruit in its perfect state, barely able to contain its own fragile insides, a few hours away from rot. It is magic.

summer schedule
of shows at: **169**

Location: **169 OLD RIVER R... ARNOLD, MD.** (Annapolis)

JUNE 22, TUES.: **RORSCHACH** (NJ.), **UNIVERSAL**

JUNE 14, Mon.: **SINKER** (ca.) + others)

ORDER OF ARMAGEDDON, ASSUCK (FL.)

BONE CLOSET:

Travels to other areas will make it evident to anyone observing that people travel distances of more than an hour (often many hours) to "shows." (example: west coast, mid-west, etc.) Also, where a few of us have our operations base here it is desirable for numerous reasons, but an abundance of active, or atleast interested, comrades is not one of these reasons. There are very few people. Thus we are doing mailings, etc. to invite + encourage our sisters + brothers from anywhere to come to these shows, or just visit. This is an autonomous zone basically, an open space, that won't last too long, so come + take advantage of it now, the time is now! This flyer

JUNE 30, WED.: **ANTIOCH ARROW** (Ca.) + MORE & (SPECIAL GUEST?)

JULY 10, SAT!: **JOHN HENRY WEST** (CA.) + other & maybe UNIV. ORD. of ARM....

contains all necessary info. Over nite accomodations are possible, but please try to call in advance.... It's overall undesirable, but we're utilizing combustion engine transport, currently, so drive here, follow supplied directions, or? Mass transit? - metro to New Carrollton, call us (to pick you up there) in advance. from Balt, #14 bus lets off right at Arnold Rd. (see map). car pool.... call us to offer ride or if you need one, we'll connect the people on both sides. Maybe we'll have vegan feasts too. Call to help....

JULY 13, Tues.: **HELLBENDER** inc, **STILL LIFE** ? (ca.) & ?

JULY 30 or 31, Fri.? sat.: **NATIVE NOD** (nj.), **THE SHIT**

Directions: from Arnold Rd:
follow Arrows,
X marks the spot,
PARK where marked

N
W E
S

↑ To Baltimore

Playground

PARK HERE

Parking Lot

Shell

Arnold Rd.

Exxon

Rt. 2

* Old River Rd. *
169 X

Pool Parking Lot

OR PARK HERE

D.C.

Annapolis

Rt. 50

AUG. 7, SAT!: **HEROIN** (Ca.) & ?

Directions:
From D.C. area: Rt. 50 East, pass all Annapolis exits, take Rt. 2 North. At 1st lite left onto Arnold Rd. Then follow map....
From VA, points South: 95 North to 495 Capital Beltway to 50 East then follow D.C. directions....
From Baltimore area: 695 (Balt. Baltway) to 97 south to 50 East, then follow above directions....
From points between Balt. + Annap.: Rt 2 going south right at Arnold Rd. then follow map
From N.Y., N.J., points north: 95 south (or whatever works) to 695 (Balt. Baltway) then follow Balt. directions
Further directions/info: (410) 757-9226

all shows: 7pm sharp! $3 or 4$ all ages

more to be added....call to verify all dates before traveling

SLOW-ROASTED FRUIT

This recipe celebrates the beauty of hyper-in-season fruit. It exalts pockmarked skin, stems, seeds, blemishes, black spots, zits, boils, and welts. I prefer yellow nectarines (used in the recipe that follows) in the summer and Honeycrisp apples in fall. In the dead of winter, I don't bother. In spring, I hurl myself at the season's first apricot. All you need is a pan, an oven, some lemon juice, and some honey. There are a couple other ingredients, but they're a bonus.
Yield: 4 servings

Nectarines (do not peel!) 4
Honey ½ cup (169 grams)
Lemon juice ½ cup (121 grams)
Salt to taste
Black pepper to taste
Fresh basil 3 leaves, torn
Turbinado sugar

1. Preheat the oven to 250°F.
2. Cut the nectarines in half, discard the pits, and place the fruit in a medium bowl.
3. In a small bowl, whisk together the honey, lemon juice, salt, and pepper. Pour half of the mixture over the nectarines and fold together gently to coat. Add the remaining juice mixture and the basil and combine.
4. Arrange the nectarines in a roasting pan, cut side down, and top with the juice. Roast for 20 minutes, flip the nectarines, sprinkle with turbinado sugar, and roast an additional 20 minutes. Flip the nectarines a second time and roast until the flesh gives to the touch, 10 to 20 minutes. Let the nectarines sit in their own juices until cool to the touch.

To serve: Great alone, with a scoop of gelato (see page 209), or on the Grilled Lemon Pound Cake with Lemon Glaze (page 33).

FAST-ROASTED FRUIT

Sometimes you don't have the luxury of time. In those instances, use this method for fast-roasting fruit. It works beautifully with apples, cherries, and plums. It doesn't work well for nectarines, peaches, or pineapple.

Sugar ¼ cup (50 grams)
Plums, diced 4
Salt to taste
Juice of 1 lemon

   1. Set the oven to broil.
   2. Dust a baking sheet with some sugar, add the diced plums, and top with more sugar and salt to taste. Drizzle the fruit evenly with the lemon juice and stir to coat completely. Broil for 1 to 2 minutes, stirring occasionally, until the plums have charred slightly.
   3. Let the fruit cool on the sheet until ready to serve, and be sure to use the juices in the presentation.

To serve: This works well alone with a scoop of gelato (see page 209). You could also serve it with the Grilled Lemon Pound Cake with Lemon Glaze (page 33).

VERJUS MELON CANDY

Cantaloupe at the height of the hot season is a truly beautiful thing. It drips with sweet summer juice and its fruit is primed for teeth marks. Raw and unviolated is usually the way to eat cantaloupe, but great cantaloupe is a rare and fleeting thing. A few years ago, in the off-season, I became obsessed with the dried version. I was convinced there was a way to give new life to the shriveled form.

Dried melon is typically preserved in sugar, dehydrated, packaged, and sold. I rehydrated the melon in verjus—also known as sour, unripened grape juice—and then dehydrated it a second time. This changed everything. The verjus soak stripped away the acrid sweetness and replumped the fruit into something with an unnatural but intriguing acidity. The melon became tart, like a Starburst or a pickled candy. At the restaurant we serve it with the creamy, rich, caramel-based dishes and its taste cuts through like an acidic jackhammer.

Now I soak all sorts of dried fruit in verjus: raisins, prunes, cherries. My sous-chefs scoff at my reliance on this verjus-soak method, but they eventually come around. When Kim, my current sous-chef, returned from a week-long vacation recently, she went straight for the melon candy ("I fucking missed this so much!").

Josh, another chef, once called to say he'd found my (maxed-out) credit card on the pastry-station floor. He asked what he should do with it. Before I could answer, he said, "Don't worry, Chef. I'll soak it in verjus."
Yield: 1 pound candy

Dried cantaloupe one 1-pound bag
Verjus one 750-milliliter bottle
Sugar 1 cup (200 grams)
Malic acid as needed

1. In a large bowl, add the cantaloupe and pour in the verjus. Cover the bowl with plastic wrap and refrigerate it for 2 days.

2. Drain the verjus and dehydrate the fruit in your dehydrator according to the manufacturer's instructions (see page 9 for an alternate method).

3. In a small bowl, combine the sugar and malic acid until the mixture tastes like the coating on Sour Patch Kids.

To serve: Roll the melon in the sour sugar and eat immediately, before the sugar melts.

RED WINE PLUMS

I discovered dried plums on Houston Street in New York City in the display window of the venerable Russ & Daughters. The plums were placed beside some other, more dramatic dried stuff, looking a bit shriveled and sinewy in comparison. The reality is that they possess more hidden flavor than even those majestically glossy dried pears in the adjacent bin. They are a little more expensive than prunes, but they're worth it. If your local stores don't stock them, you can get them online fairly easily.

As the dried plums sit in the red wine liquid, they plump up and re-create the sensation of fresh fruit. Hit them with freshly zested orange straight from the Microplane just before serving—a blast of citrus freshness to battle scurvy.

Yield: 4 cups

Sugar 2 cups (400 grams)
Water ⅓ cup (79 grams)
Red wine one 750-milliliter bottle
Zest of 1 orange
Dried plums, chopped 4 cups (696 grams)

1. In a large saucepan over medium heat, combine the sugar and water and, using the wet-sand technique (see page 11), cover with a lid to create condensation, and cook until you have a light caramel.

2. When the sugar is a nice light blond, remove the pan from the heat, pour in the bottle of wine, and add the orange zest. The sugar will seize up. Return the pan to the heat and bring the mixture to a simmer over medium heat, cooking until the sugar melts again and the liquid reduces slightly, about 5 minutes.

3. Add the chopped plums and simmer until the plums have absorbed some of the cooking liquid and become engorged, about another 5 minutes—check a plum to see if the texture has changed.

4. In a large bowl, prepare an ice bath.

5. In another large bowl, add the plums and liquid and cool over the ice bath. The plums will keep in an airtight container in the refrigerator for several weeks.

To serve: Red Wine Plums go with the Spezzata di Castagne (page 194).

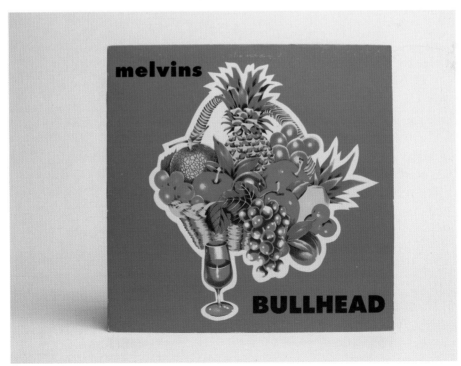

See page 61.

27

TANGERINES

Really good tangerines seem fake. They are too tart, too sweet, too juicy, too texturally perfect. They are more sour patch kid than Sour Patch Kids, more jolly rancher than Jolly Ranchers. I would say they are *nature's candy*, but that would be really dumb. It's not far from the truth, though.

The best tangerines are extremely difficult to cook with: Why screw with something that's perfect already? The zest alone, grated with a Microplane, is intoxicating.

At the restaurant, tangerine season is the time of ego annihilation. It comes in the dead of winter, when there's no fresh fruit available and I've spent the past months manipulating ingredients like crazy—a God complex has set in. *I am the chef! Look at what I can do! I'm definitely a genius!* I'm filled with all sorts of empty, puffy-chested bravado. But then the really good tangerines come in season, innocently, coyly. I fall instantly in love (again, just like I did last year). And I know I have to honor them as they are. See ya later, ego.

I serve them on a bed of cracked ice in a bowl. At the table, guests peel and eat them on their own. The tangerine skin releases aromatic oils into the air and perfumes the dining room. I love how completely Italian it is. All I did was crack up some ice! I know this type of thing makes some of my peers really upset. I love that, too.

SUGARED GREEN STRAWBERRIES WITH TOASTED FENNEL CAKE, CANDIED FENNEL, AND MINT GELATO

The band Dead Kennedys are polarizing, hugely influential, and totally un-rip-offable. Singer Jello Biafra's voice is too distinct, guitarist East Bay Ray's guitar work too deceptively simple. The album covers are works of art. You can't do a band that is anything like the Dead Kennedys. It's not possible. They can't be copied. Don't even try. If you are in possession of the band's first record, *Fresh Fruit for Rotting Vegetables*, I suggest you play the first song on Side Two. This tune is also known as track 8 on your CD, or as the popular one with a German title about the Zen fascist California police state. Let us begin.

There is a restaurant in Copenhagen called Noma. I've never eaten there; I've never been to Denmark. In 2010, Noma was anointed the best restaurant *in the world*, which is a pretty crazy thing to wrap your head around. *Best restaurant in the world*? There are something like twenty-four thousand restaurants in New York City alone.

Noma is miniscule—you could fit four or five of them inside Del Posto. But the moment the *best restaurant in the world* thing happened, fancy restaurants of every size started ripping it off, much in the way El Bulli was targeted a few years prior. But with Noma the shtick was so specific—Nordic cuisine based on foraged ingredients found within miles of the restaurant—that any time it was aped, it was beyond comically obvious. But it went on, and on, and on. For years. The movement is actually still filtering its way down the food chain. For a long time, seeing sorrel and sea buckthorn berries on fine dining menus really

pissed me off. (*You can't rip off the Dead Kennedys, man!*) But then I realized I was doing it, too. I was so guilty, and I didn't even realize it.

Noma was one of the first (if not *the* first) restaurants to use underripe green strawberries. They are slightly inedible raw, so Noma pickled them. Yes: genius. Chef René Redzepi at Noma finds the most perfectly *not* ripe strawberries and figures out how to get them on his menu. OK, that rules.

So now I do green strawberries, too. They are lightly pickled and rolled in citrus sugar. You need to eat them immediately, before the sugar melts and there's still a crunch. I pair it with a mint gelato. The taste it leaves on your palate veers dangerously close to drinking orange juice after brushing your teeth, but it works beautifully.

Yield: 4 to 6 servings

"Copycat."

TOASTED FENNEL CAKE

Fennel seeds 1 tablespoon (6.5 grams)
Extra-virgin olive oil 1 tablespoon (13.5 grams)
Fennel bulb 1, cut into ½-inch cubes
Salt 2 teaspoons (8 grams)
Eggs 6, separated
Sugar 1 cup (200 grams)
Almond flour 1 cup (95.5 grams), toasted
Pistachio flour 1 cup (75 grams)

1. Preheat the oven to 350°F. Line a baking sheet with parchment paper and set aside.
2. In a dry sauté pan over medium-low heat, toast the fennel seeds until they're hot, about 1 minute. Add the olive oil, chopped fennel, and 1 teaspoon of the salt and stir. Cook until the fennel is soft and translucent, 10 to 15 minutes, and set aside to cool.
3. In a small bowl, whisk together the egg yolks and ½ cup of the sugar and set aside.
4. In a large bowl, whisk together the egg whites and the remaining ½ cup sugar. Pour in the yolk-sugar mixture. Add the almond flour, pistachio flour, and the remaining 1 teaspoon salt and fold together gently with a rubber spatula.
5. Pour the batter onto the prepared baking sheet. Bake until set, 25 to 30 minutes. The cake will soufflé up as it bakes and then fall down as it cools (this is good).
6. Allow the cake to cool completely in the pan.

PICKLED GREEN STRAWBERRIES

Rice wine vinegar 2 cups (477 grams)
Sugar 2 teaspoons (8 grams)
Salt 2 teaspoons (8 grams)
Coriander seeds 2 teaspoons (6 grams)
Underripe green strawberries, hulled and cut in half lengthwise 2 cups (304 grams)

1. In a large bowl, whisk together the vinegar, sugar, salt, and coriander seeds until the sugar and salt are dissolved.
2. Place the hulled strawberries in a separate bowl. Pour in the sugar mixture and combine gently. Refrigerate in an airtight

See page 98.

31

container for at least 2 hours—if you can wait 2 days, I recommend it.

CANDIED FENNEL

Water 1 cup (237 grams)
Sugar ¾ cup (150 grams)
Salt to taste
Fennel bulb 1, cut into thin strips

1. In a small saucepan over high heat, bring the water, sugar, and salt to a boil. Add the fennel strips, reduce the heat to low, and cook until translucent, about 4 minutes. Set aside and let cool.

CITRUS SUGAR

Sugar ½ cup (100 grams)
Zest of 2 oranges

In a small bowl, combine the sugar and orange zest using your fingers and set aside.

SEASONED PISTACHIOS

Good-quality unsalted pistachios ½ cup (62 grams), shelled
Egg white 1 (30 grams)
Salt ½ teaspoon (2 grams)
Sugar ½ teaspoon (2 grams)

1. Preheat the oven to 350°F.
2. In a small bowl, toss together the pistachios and egg white until the nuts are coated and sticky, but not too thickly coated. Add the salt and sugar and toss gently. Spread the nuts out evenly on a baking sheet. Bake until they have dried out, about 5 minutes.

FOR SERVING

Mint Gelato (page 210)
Extra-virgin olive oil

To serve: Cut out a chunk of fennel cake. Top it with a scoop of mint gelato. Garnish with strips of the candied fennel, several pickled green strawberries immediately after you've rolled them in citrus sugar, and a few seasoned pistachios. Drizzle with some nice extra-virgin olive oil and serve immediately.

See page 205.

GRILLED LEMON POUND CAKE WITH LEMON GLAZE

Don't bother firing up the Weber for this cake. That would be ridiculous. Instead, keep the recipe in mind for when you know there's a BBQ ahead. If it's winter, all the better! When I was a kid, nothing jazzed me more than grilling outside when there was snow on the ground. It always felt like I was doing something illegal. I pictured neighbors peering out from behind their curtains. *You can't grill in the winter . . . you can't do that! What does that kid think he's doing? The nerve!*

This citrus syrup–drenched lemon cake grills up especially nicely, kind of like French toast. The sugars caramelize over the flame, but the cake is sturdy enough that it doesn't crumble apart. At Del Posto, this cake is a base for a slow-roasted nectarine, when the nectarines are at their absolute peak, near the end of summer.

Yield: 4 to 6 servings

LEMON GLAZE

Sugar ½ cup (100 grams)
Juice from 1 orange
Juice from ½ lemon

In a small microwavable bowl, whisk together the sugar, orange juice, and lemon juice and heat in the microwave for 20 seconds. Stir the mixture until the sugar dissolves and set it aside. (If the glaze gets too hot, the flavors of the juices change; be careful.)

LEMON CAKE

Sugar 1⅓ cups (230 grams)
Almond paste ½ cup (100 grams)
Zest of 1 lemon
Zest of 1 orange
Unsalted butter ⅓ cup or ⅔ stick (75 grams), plus more for the pan
Pure vanilla extract 1 teaspoon (4 grams)
Eggs 4 (200 grams)
Cake flour ⅔ cup (86 grams)
Baking powder ½ teaspoon (2 grams)
Salt to taste

1. Preheat the oven to 350°F. Grease a 12 × 4½ × 2½-inch cake pan with butter and set aside.

2. In the bowl of a stand mixer, using the paddle attachment, combine the sugar, almond paste, lemon zest, and orange zest on medium speed. Mix thoroughly, but don't expect the mixture to come together. Add the butter and vanilla and cream together until light and fluffy.

3. Using a rubber spatula, scrape down the sides of the bowl. Add the eggs, one at a time, and mix, incorporating each one fully before adding the next.

4. Into a large bowl, sift together the flour, baking powder, and salt.

5. Add the flour mixture to the batter and mix until everything is just incorporated; do not overmix. Remove the bowl from the stand mixer and finish mixing with a wooden spoon.

6. Pour the batter into the reserved cake pan. Bake for 20 to 25 minutes, or until a toothpick comes out clean when inserted into the center of the cake.

7. Run a knife around the edge of the cake and flip it over onto a cooling rack. Place another cooling rack on top.

8. While it's still warm, poke holes in the cake using a toothpick and pour the glaze over it *through* the cooling rack, which will help distribute the glaze evenly. Let the cake cool for at least 1 hour.

FOR SERVING

Slow-Roasted Fruit (page 22)
Basil Gelato (page 210)
Extra-virgin olive oil

To serve: Slice the cake into ½-inch slices and cook each piece on both sides on a hot grill for 30 seconds. Serve with slow-roasted fruit, a scoop of basil gelato, and a drizzle of olive oil.

JAMS, FRUIT SPREADS, MARMELLATA

Here are some jams, fruit spreads, and a marmellata. They are good on all sorts of things and are made with a few different techniques.

HUCKLEBERRY MARMELLATA

HUCK-UL-BERRY: It's a dumb-sounding name, but these berries aren't dumb. They are Mickey Rourke playing Charles Bukowski in *Barfly*. They taste a bit like dirt, the way beets do, but not quite that much dirt. They grow in the mountains but are suave and sophisticated, like a grown-up version of blueberries—like blueberries smoking a cigar. Blueberries are children who just learned to walk, cute but sheltered, bouncing around and looking for mommy. Huckleberries are teenagers from Bay Ridge, Brooklyn, or downtown Baltimore, Maryland, or Whittier, California. They know what's up.

Huckleberries freeze well. (Blueberries do not.) This recipe utilizes the frozen kind, which can still be pricey. But they are worth it in the winter months when you are sick to death of apples and pineapple. Do you have any vanilla ice cream or can you get some? Now is a good time for it.

Yield: About 2 cups

Huckleberries, frozen 2 cups (300 grams)
Sugar ½ cup plus 2 teaspoons (108 grams)
Juice of 1½ lemons
Pectin 1 teaspoon (1 gram)
Zest of 1½ lemons
Citric acid ½ teaspoon (2 grams)
Salt to taste

1. In a small saucepan over medium heat, combine the huckleberries, ½ cup of the sugar, and the juice from 1 of the lemons, and stir until the sugar has dissolved. Bring the mixture to a simmer and cook until the berries release some liquid, about 5 minutes. Strain the berries and place them in a medium bowl. Pour the juice back into the saucepan and return it to a simmer over low heat.

2. In a large bowl, prepare an ice bath.

3. In a small bowl, mix together the remaining 2 teaspoons sugar and the pectin. Add the mixture to the berry juice, stirring occasionally, until it dissolves, about 2 minutes. Add the juice of the remaining ½ lemon to thicken the berry liquid.

4. Pour the berry liquid over the reserved berries, stir, and season with lemon zest, citric acid, and salt.

5. Chill the bowl over the ice bath to stop the berries from cooking further. The marmellata will thicken as it cools. Store in an airtight container in your fridge for up to 3 days.

To serve: This goes great with the Polenta Crêpes (page 116). Rub one side of a crêpe with the marmellata, fold, and eat as fast as possible in one bite.

Passion Fruit Gloss.

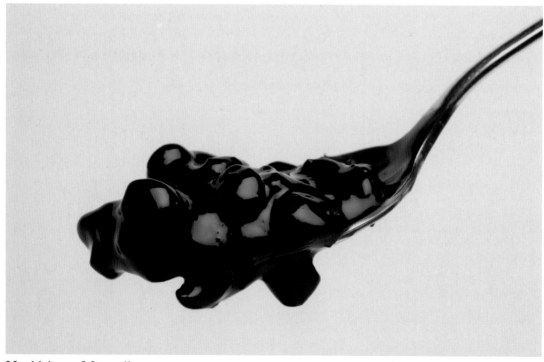

Huckleberry Marmellata.

STRAWBERRY QUICK JAM

Yield: 2 cups

Strawberries 4 cups (608 grams)
Sugar 1 cup (200 grams)
Juice of 1 lemon
Salt to taste

1. Preheat the oven to 200°F. Line a baking sheet with a Silpat and set aside.

2. Remove the tops and cut the berries into irregular chunks. In a medium bowl, toss the chunks with the sugar, lemon juice, and salt.

3. Pour the berries and the juice onto the reserved baking sheet. Bake until the fruit is dehydrated slightly and the juices have turned into a sticky glaze, about 1½ hours.

4. Let the berries cool on the sheet. They will be gooey and jam-like.

To serve: Use this with the Hand-Pulled Stracciatella (page 228) and whatever else seems interesting. It is versatile.

STRAWBERRY SAUCE

Yield: 2 cups

Sugar ½ cup (100 grams)
Water ¼ cup (60 grams)
Strawberry puree (see note in Glossy Fruit
    Sauce), cold 2 cups (464 grams)
Salt to taste
Lemon juice to taste

1. In a small saucepan over medium-high heat, combine the sugar and water and bring the mixture to a boil without stirring (just swirl the pan). Continue cooking until the mixture becomes a light amber color, about 5 minutes.

2. Immediately add the cold strawberry puree, stir, and bring back to a boil. Adjust the consistency by cooking longer if desired.

3. Season with lemon juice and salt.

To serve: You'll need this for Lidia's Sweet Pea Cake with Macerated Strawberries, Strawberry Gelato, and Candied Split Peas (page 61).

GLOSSY FRUIT SAUCE

Few things in life are truly, perfectly shiny. A brand new pair of Vans, purchased at some sketchy place on 14th Street from a salesperson unhappy with life's trajectory—those shoes are very shiny, blindingly so. The keys to your new apartment in New York, too: really shiny. The keys you acquired by putting $7K on your girlfriend's credit card. Jingly and musical and emitting light beams like the Lost Ark of the Covenant. *Holy shit, we got it!* And this sauce. Gleaming and bright. It winks at you if you look at it right. It's all about the pectin—get to know this ingredient. It's less scary than it sounds. Passion fruit works best (see left), but strawberries work great, too.

Note: For 2 cups of puree, you'll need 4 cups of fruit. For a smooth puree, pass it through a chinois or fine-mesh strainer.
Yield: 1½ cups

Fruit puree 2 cups (weight varies by fruit)
Sugar ½ cup plus 2 teaspoons (108 grams
    plus 8 grams)
Pectin 1 teaspoon (1 gram)
Juice of ½ lemon
Zest of 1 lemon
Citric acid ½ teaspoon (2 grams)
Salt to taste

1. In a small saucepan over low heat, bring the fruit puree and ½ cup of the sugar to a simmer.

2. In a large bowl, prepare an ice bath.

3. In a small bowl, mix together the remaining 2 teaspoons sugar and the pectin. Add the mixture to the puree, stirring occasionally, until it dissolves, about 2 minutes. Add the lemon juice to thicken the berry liquid. Season with lemon zest, citric acid, and salt.

4. Chill the bowl over the ice bath to stop the cooking. The sauce will thicken as it cools. Store in an airtight container in your fridge for up to 3 days.

SMOKED APPLESAUCE

Applesauce makes me think of three things: *The Brady Bunch* pork chop episode, pierogi at Veselka in New York's East Village, and my tenure as pastry sous-chef at Campanile in Los Angeles in the mid-2000s. Dahlia Narvaez, my boss there, taught me how to make it. She preferred Granny Smith apples and will frown at me for using multiple varieties. *Dude, it's gonna be brown! They are going to oxidize! Some are gonna be squishy! Did I teach you nothing?!* She will have my neck in a noose for asking you to smoke it.

And she'll be right. This sauce is just as good unsmoked, maybe even better. Equally troubling is that there are tons of sketchy ways to rig a backyard or home-kitchen smoker, none of which I will personally vouch for. But here it is anyway, the way we did it at Del Posto in a dish called *crespelle d'Autunno,* when I was in a phase of saying goofy things at the preservice staff meeting like, *The smoked-apple puree induces the sensation of autumn, burning leaves, the scent of October, the crackling of leaves underfoot.* I'm surprised (and mildly disappointed) no one walked over and drilled me right in the face.
Yield: About 3 cups

Apples, assorted varieties 6, peeled, cored, and roughly chopped
Juice of 1 lemon
Sugar ¼ cup (50 grams)
Salt to taste
Water ⅓ cup (78 grams)
Vanilla bean ½, scraped

1. In a deep-sided saucepan over low heat, stir together the apples, lemon juice, sugar, salt, water, and vanilla bean scrapings until the apples are fully coated in the sugar. Wrap the top of the pot with plastic wrap and cook for 20 to 25 minutes more, or until the apples are soft but still hold their shape. Some will break down more than others, and this is good.

2. Pour the apples into a deep pan, pop into the smoker of your choice, and smoke until the apples have a pleasant, smoky aroma. This will take 5 to 10 minutes, depending on the smoker.

3. Stir the applesauce around a bit and refrigerate in an airtight container for up to 1 week.

To serve: Smear some smoked applesauce on a plate and scatter some Candied Squash (page 74) around. Add a folded Buckwheat Crespelle (page 114) and top with a scoop of Ricotta Gelato (page 213). Drizzle with maple syrup and serve immediately.

See page 239.

BAND TOUR FOOD DIARY: BORN AGAINST

I went on tour with a band for the first time in January 1993. I had just joined Born Against on drums and was excited beyond belief. I hadn't traveled much before then, and I was about to see most of the country in a tour van, playing shows along the way. So I did what any normal twenty-year-old punk kid would do in that situation: I kept a tour diary of the food we ate.

I kept it a big secret from everyone in the van. There were six of us squished together for four weeks, and secrets weren't exactly easy to keep. But writing down what we ate made perfect sense to me: I was being introduced to local delicacies every twelve hours and it was exciting. We were all vegetarians, so every meal was a new regional adventure. But it was the most uncool thing I could have done. I kept it under wraps.

I logged only the food. I didn't mention the shows, which were great, weird, and often mind-blowing. We played a living room in Atlanta, where we Sharpie-d on fake moustaches before performing to sixteen people, and Sam, our singer, called the cops to try to get the show shut down. There was a show in Dallas at an airplane hangar set up by a woman who ran a record store there called Direct Hit Records (the logo was JFK in crosshairs). And another at an abandoned storefront next to a bail bondsman in Amarillo with a band called Slit Throat. The singer was a tiny, shy girl in a hooded sweatshirt with a voice that sounded scarier than a train derailment. She went by Mary Slit, of course. None of it made it to the pages of my diary.

Instead, I scribbled about the time we cooked tortillas and peanut butter at an empty mansion in San Diego rented by twenty kids. There was no furniture, but the place had nice carpets and a gas stove. I detailed the miserable burritos we had just off I-95 in South Carolina at South of the Border amusement park (the least amusing, most casually racist amusement park in the world). I logged an entry about a meal at a vegetarian café in Pensacola, Florida, where we senselessly but happily blew all our show money from the night before: *Sure, let's get another round of soy milk coconut smoothies, hell yeah!* We had perfect homemade enchiladas in Santa Fe, New Mexico, served to us by the mom of some guy we'd just met. I wrote about that, too.

I was known as The Squirrel. It's difficult playing drums in a punk show if you're full, so I usually skipped dinner. By midnight I was famished. I'd learned to squirrel away baked tofu packets, Odwalla juices, and Ak-Mak crackers under the van seat for after shows. Eventually my stomach became inured to the potential fallout of unrefrigerated and improperly stored food.

(Not Born Against.)

We had a six-dollar-a-day food allowance, and back then few parts of the country were vegetarian friendly. But Northern California—Berkeley and San Francisco, especially—was the promised land. Our collective sense of excitement on entering the Bay Area could have generated the electricity needed for the next show. Places like Springfield, Missouri, were more sobering in terms of fake meat and packaged hummus. In places like those, we'd often spend a couple hours finding the one health food store and then proceed to buy out as much of their vegetarian junk food as we could afford.

On that first tour we picked up two hitchhiker skater kids in baggy pants and gave them a ride from Phoenix to San Diego. All they had with them were a bunch of Phil Collins CDs to hock and a plastic bottle that they used to squirt salt water into Coke machines—an early nineties trick that no longer works but which used to relieve the machine of its quarters and soda cans, which they could later sell or drink. One kid had a crude jailhouse-style tattoo of serial killers' faces across his stomach, à la Mount Rushmore. When Christina, our roadie, asked him if hitchhiking around the Southwest increased his chances of running into an actual serial killer, he looked up and without a drip of irony, said, "Oh man, it would be my honor to be murdered by a serial killer."

One Born Against tour ended in Baltimore, near enough to my mom's house that we went there after a show. When we arrived at about 1 a.m., there was my mom, Barbara, waiting for us with a 100 percent vegan spaghetti and red sauce spread. She sat us down at the dining room table and served us in her bathrobe. It was Sunday night and she had to work in the morning. She was the coolest mom, and her unconditional support of all the stupid band stuff I was involved in was truly selfless. That night Sam mined the fridge for (and found!) a Fresca that I swear was four years old.

I destroyed my tour food diary in the mid-nineties. I was embarrassed by it. A food diary was most certainly *not punk*. I wish I still had it. *(Continued on page 96.)*

LEMON GRANITA

A version of this recipe was published in *People* magazine a few years ago. Why the editors asked *me* for a recipe and why I agreed to give them one remains a mystery. They found the most ridiculous photo of me online and printed it beside the recipe. My friend Nastassia spotted it and immediately e-mailed me a photo of the spread: "What are you, a mixologist?" Carlo, the chef at Blanca, in Brooklyn, texted me the exact same photo, with an exasperated "?????".

There wasn't much I could say in my defense. But there is an equal, or perhaps even greater mystery: What were they doing reading *People* magazine in the first place?

Note: The grappa will keep this recipe from freezing entirely, plus it will potentially inebriate you.

Yield: 4 servings

Sugar ¾ cup (150 grams)
Water 1 cup (237 grams)
Juice from 8 lemons about 1¼ cups
   (305 grams)
Grappa 1 cup (222 grams)

1. In a small saucepan over medium heat, combine the sugar and ½ cup of the water and simmer until the sugar dissolves, about 5 minutes. Remove the syrup from the heat and let it cool to room temperature.

2. Add the lemon juice, grappa, and the remaining ½ cup water to the cooled syrup and stir. Pour the mixture into a metal baking sheet and place it in the freezer.

3. Stir the granita every 40 minutes for about 3 hours, until it is slushy.

To serve: Scoop the granita into a frozen bowl and serve immediatel

See page 98.

PHILADELPHIA BELLINI

Ladner developed this Bellini after visiting Harry's Bar in Venice, Italy. He'd never been a fan of the classic drink of prosecco and white peach puree, but he fell in love with the version at Harry's.

Venice is outrageously beautiful. It is also completely, ridiculously, built *in* water. It shouldn't exist. Anyone who's been there knows that the place has an amazing art scene (old stuff *and* weirdo modern stuff), but mostly it's a tourist hub filled with restaurants designed to strip you of your money as fast as possible. Harry's is no exception. It's a lot more formal than you'd expect after a sweaty walk over a thousand footbridges, and when you order a Bellini (everyone orders a Bellini), it's a glorified shot glass that'll run you twenty dollars.

There are a few hard-to-get ingredients in the Del Posto version: citron vinegar (find this online), peach liqueur (this, too!), and dry ice (careful!). The result is closer to a smoothie accented with booze than a cocktail. It's perfect for serving when you have lots of people over. In fact, Ladner's original version was for a two-thousand-person party in Philadelphia, hence the name. The dry ice is the real hero.
Yield: 5 servings

White peach puree 4½ cups (1,000 grams),
    about 8 to 10 peaches
Citron vinegar ¼ cup (60 grams)
Peach liqueur ⅓ cup (80 grams)
Salt 1 teaspoon (4 grams)
Dry ice
Prosecco 1¾ cups (400 grams)

1. In a large metal bowl, combine the peach puree, citron vinegar, peach liqueur, and salt. Whisk to incorporate.

2. Fold the dry ice into a towel neatly, crush it into a powder, and add the powder to the mix. Stir until the dry ice has melted completely—it will bubble up and become slushy. Do not serve until the dry ice is all gone!

3. Add the prosecco just before serving, and whisk gently so that the carbonation remains intact.

To serve: Serve smugly in a miniature shot glass and charge a lot of money.

NELSON JUICE

I love lemonade. Especially really sour lemonade, with barely any sugar in it. Ice, too. It's one of my favorite things. One of the reasons I work in a restaurant is the unlimited availability of ice—I go through quarts of the stuff every day. Europe is aggravating on many levels, but mostly because there's no ice. Whenever I return from Italy, my first stop is a random bodega. I buy ice. A big bag.

Nelson is a cook at Del Posto, on the risotto station at the end of the pasta line. Risotto takes time and love to prepare, and Nelson is the absolute master. His eyes move around the kitchen stealthily as he coaxes the starch out of each grain of rice mystically. Stare secretly at Nelson long enough and he'll find your eyes—without fail. He's always taking on special projects in the middle of his workday that a lesser cook could never manage without botching their actual job. We call one of those things Nelson Juice, and it is the most refreshing, delicious lemonade in creation. It's almost a dessert.

Yield: Enough for you and some other people

Lemon juice 1 pint (488 grams)
Sugar ¼ cup (50 grams)
Fresh mint 5 leaves

1. In a food processor, combine the lemon juice, sugar, and mint and as many ice cubes as you can fit. Pulse until you have a slushy mess that is full of tiny pebbles of crushed ice. You might have an outlier big ass chunk of ice. That's fine. It's still going to be delicious. Don't pulse it too far or you will end up with something like a 7-Eleven Slurpee.

You don't want that. Too fine. You want chunks, so it's more like a Slush Puppie. You need to simultaneously drink and eat it.

To serve: Get this into people's hands as quickly as possible. Sometimes Nelson puts ours in a metal bain-marie and stashes it in the walk-in, where it remains slushy for a few hours.

THE HISTORIC ROLE OF SUGAR IN EMPIRE BUILDING by Ian Svenonius

As much as oil or columbite-tantalite in the modern era, sugar has historically been a diabolical commodity, the cultivation of which precipitated genocide, slavery, and ecological devastation. Not only because sugar is delicious, physically affecting, addictive, and profitable, but because whichever nation ran the sugar supply would rule the world.

What gave the sugar-sprinkled peoples of the world a historic advantage over their foes? Sweetened tea, coffee, chocolate, pastries, trifles, crumbles, and cookies assured a workforce that was more amphetamined, more delusional, and had a greater ability to endure industrial privations. Sugar eaters' dreams were bolder and more vivid, but the complacency of these addicts was assured via strategic control of the precious treacle. Sugar was a magic potion that manufactured, out of mere mortals, a super race of psychotics, capable of stranger thoughts and grander ideas, who were less prone to moral hygiene and more capable of utter brutality.

When Europeans first discovered sugar, during the so-called Middle Ages, they recognized it as a dangerous and possibly "supernatural" material, best kept under lock and key. Sugar was the first of the "controlled substances." It traveled north with the Arab conquest of the Middle East, north Africa, and southern Europe—the "mad" stimulant that rode on the heels of the heretic. In modern times, Muslims are characterized as austere, ascetic, and fun hating, but for a millennium they were portrayed by resentful, sweets-starved Christian Europeans as profligate, sin-loving, licentious, and effete, having scented hookahs and rugs on the walls of their harems. The Arabs spread sugarcane—*Saccharum barberi*—so avidly that it was said "Where the Koran goes, sugar follows."

In seven years the Iberian Peninsula fell to the Muhammadans. It took more than seven hundred for the Christians to get it back. Why were the interlopers so intransigent? Why, in that era of fluid borders, great migrations, and topsy-turvy alliances, could Spain's new Muslim rulers not be ousted? Because they had sugar on their side.

By the time the "Reconquest" was finally realized, the Portuguese, Spaniards, and Azoreans had mastered the cultivation of sugar, making the Muslims' expertise redundant and their presence unnecessary. In the final year of the Reconquest, 1492, Columbus made the first of his historic voyages to the Americas—primarily to find a place to grow sugar for Spain, which he managed to do in spades. Indeed, for centuries the Americas and the Indies were a massive slave plantation utilized for the cultivation of confection. The Arabs were outmatched—the Ottoman Caliphate receded steadily on the world stage until its eventual dismemberment by European imperialists at the end of WWI.

In the sixteenth and seventeenth centuries, the European colonists fought an arms race of ambrosia, which the British ultimately won, first with their invasion of Jamaica and, after the abolition of slavery, with the possession of India, where the process of crystallizing sugar was born. With the Monroe Doctrine (1823), the United States entered the contest. The end of the Spanish-American War (1898), which secured sugar-rich Cuba and Puerto Rico for the *Yanquis*, initiated the "American Century" of global preeminence for the United States. The annexation of Hawaii and the occupation of Haiti and the Dominican Republic made the United States a "sugar superpower."

In the first world—perhaps due to the rabid insanity and addiction caused by the pastoral pre-confection—sugar became a ritual sacrament of a religious-spiritual sort, whether as a magical invocation of mythological or theological creatures (for example, Santa Claus, the Easter Bunny), or as a reward for ingesting ho-hum food in the form of "dessert," the post-meal high. Sugar, formerly the unholy destroyer of worlds, was dressed up as a bunny rabbit, candy corn, bonbon, candy cane, and used as consecration for weddings or given cutesy, infantilized titles.

The covert drugging of the world's population over the centuries is a powerful component in the illogical insanity of the systems such as capitalism and its out-of-vogue, statist brother fascism, that have taken root since sugar's widespread introduction.

When revolution occurred in Cuba, the country was providing America with more than one-third of its sugar market. When the CIA's Bay of Pigs invasion to regain the island for American plantation owners was thwarted by communists, the reality of a sugar-free United States became something to consider.

When Lyndon Johnson was inaugurated, he allayed these fears with a corn syrup substitute that was sweeter than sugarcane and absolutely plentiful. By 1966, midway through Johnson's presidency, sugar consumption stood on the precipice of decline, replaced by corn syrup. The sugar drought sent the empire on its mad descent, marked by calamity, total corruption, general idiocy, an epidemic of political assassination, and surrender to degeneracy. The naked cruelty of the sugar years segued into the depression and flatulence of a corn-syruped nation, to disastrous results.

Initially, corn syrup wasn't considered a suitable alternative and social planners attempted to replace sugarcane with other narcotics. The "lifestyle revolution" promulgated by the mid-sixties drug culture—supposedly a grass-roots rebellion—was their desperate attempt to mollify the public's seething hunger for the sugar high, which was being sadistically withheld (albeit under American embargo) by the damned *barbudos* of Fidel Castro's Cuba.

The CIA fed the population LSD, cocaine, peyote, marijuana, pharmaceutical pills, crystal meth, belladonna, mandrake, ayahuasca, mushrooms, airplane glue, and gave the Mafia a free hand to sell heroin—anything to placate the population and compete with the other sugar-rich economies. Drugs were ubiquitous in the sixties and post-sugar years of the seventies, promoted heavily in all media to both children (*H. R. Pufnstuf,* "Puff, the Magic Dragon") and adults (Miles Davis, *Playboy* magazine, and so on). A "health food" craze was contrived to persuade people that sugar-free diets were "cool." But illegal drugs, though effective as antidotes for sugar withdrawal, were problematic for mass assignation because their role for government was more prescriptive (that is, destroying radical groups and political movements, undermining class consciousness, etc.) and not intended for everyone.

The true solution was a souped-up and muscular version of corn syrup called high-fructose corn syrup (HFCS). In 1977, HFCS went into heavy production as a sweetener and by 1984 had replaced cane sugar in Coca-Cola and Pepsi. HFCS led to epidemic obesity, acne, and insanity (Pepsi drinker Michael Jackson, for example). But it also sweetened more efficiently than sugar ever had, inducing a giddy, manic high in the user, usually followed by severe episodes of withdrawal marked by fatigue, depression, and nihilism.

HFCS was soon added to everything from bread and marinara sauce to beer, peanut butter, cereal, crackers, chips, lunchmeat, hamburgers, hotdogs, ketchup, pickle relish, and Miracle Whip. Even after the dissolution of Soviet power and the end of the confectionary cold war, the USA shirked the sugar that had made it great. HFCS was a heavier narcotic and American palates were now inured to the old-fashioned flavor of cane sugar. For manufacturers, HFCS was so profitable that they lobbied for a continued embargo and the political isolation of Cuba so as to effectively outlaw "the white lady."

Still, warily, sugar started to reappear in outlaw kitchens and cupboards. Old-timers remembered the high it gave them, the illicit joys from their youth spent wandering the streets as addicts, hooked on the delightful residue of the cane plant. Mexican Cokes, still supposedly flavored with sugar, became highly sought vestiges of an underground connoisseurship, a badge of esoteric knowledge. Some chefs started producing food that utilized the arcane sweetener for a small, louche audience of culinary perverts.

Whether these new sugar users can repeat the terrifying feats of their addict forebears remains to be seen.

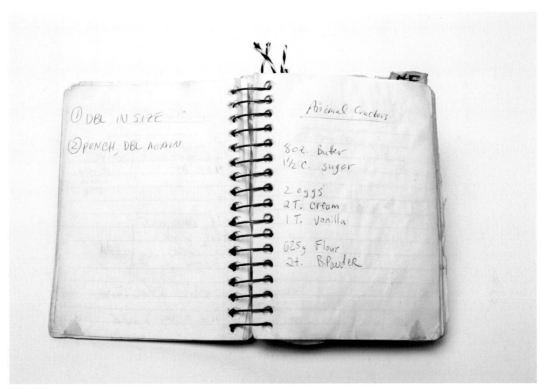

Pasadena, CA, 2004. Needs salt.

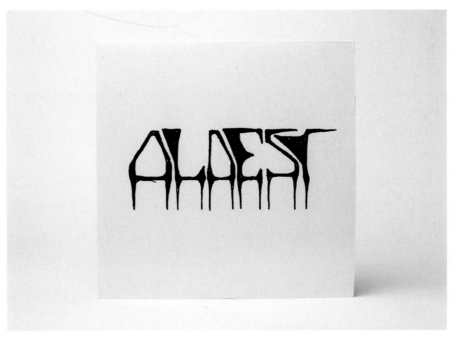

See page 239.

PROFILE IN COURAGE:

David Kinch

Born: April 4

Occupation: Chef and owner of Manresa in Los Gatos, California

Status: Longtime partner, still in love

Notable quote: "There will be a time and a place to finally leave the professional kitchen, though folks say I could or would never do it. 'Watch me,' I say."

Shoe size: 11½

Lunch food: Oysters

Beverage: I'm flexible. Champagne will almost always work, though.

I Heart NY: Lived and worked there as a young man. Many memories, few regrets.

First time: There is, for everything. It is deciding whether to do it again.

Accomplishments: Still in business and can go to the beach

Ambition/Future plan: To not die in the kitchen

LES DEUX CAFES: BUILD YOUR RÉSUMÉ LIKE A PRO

In 2003, I moved from DC to Los Angeles for two reasons: to start a new band with some friends and to try to weasel my way into a pastry job at Campanile. Nancy Silverton was still in charge there, and as a newly minted pastry jerk, I just *had* to work there. Nancy was my idol. I had all her books. I eventually did log some time working under her, but not before doing time at a signless joint with a silly French name on a block just south of Hollywood Boulevard.

Les Deux Cafes had expired as a celebrity nightclub, and its restaurant was completely inconsequential. I can tell when I am in a serious, professional kitchen, because it *always* smells good, no matter if there's farty tripe bubbling away in a pot, whole pigs broken down into little chunks on the countertop, or plastic containers brimming with prepped onions. At least 95 percent of the time hotel kitchens smell like a hospital cafeteria. It's a smell that clings to you—your nostrils, your clothes, your shitty paper toque. It is gross and demoralizing to everyone involved. The kitchen at Les Deux Cafes did not smell good. Of my closely guarded and checkered employment history, rife with embarrassing résumé entries, this is a particularly nasty blight.

They didn't need a pastry chef. None of the patrons ate the food, and certainly not the desserts. But they paid me handsomely to *act* like a pastry chef, so goddamnit, I acted away. It was fine with me, since it afforded me plenty of free time to practice and record with Wrangler Brutes, my new band. I could work two hours a day or twelve, depending on my band schedule or mood. *That* part was cool. Once we flew to the East Coast to do a ten day tour, so I made ten days' worth of desserts and packed the freezer and fridge with *mise en place*. I returned to an apocalypse of melted ice cream containers, shattered *pâte sucrée* shells, and a sink overflowing with week-old crusty and fermented sheet pans. There were stale cookies tangled loosely in shredded plastic wrap. It was like an episode of *Life After People* at a crummy culinary school commissary. I was the only one horrified. *Welcome back! We missed you!* Not my finest moment, but Wrangler Brutes got to play a Halloween show with Lightning Bolt at a warehouse in Providence, Rhode Island, where the floor nearly collapsed, and another great show in DC, where I received the highest drum compliment of my life from my friend Lili: "Your drumming totally induced my period!"

The owner of Les Deux Cafes was a sheepish Woody Allen type and he appointed his daughter, a creepy LA rich-kid, phony-artist type, as the manager. She lived in a room behind the pastry kitchen and woke up at 11 a.m.

every day, walked into our shared bathroom in her boxers, and took a vicious narcotics-induced dump while I taught myself Pierre Hermé *macaron* recipes in the adjacent kitchen. When one of the head chefs quit, she was crowned executive chef. She created a menu that was mostly vegan, but it had a bunch of random veal dishes on it. One day, stoned out of her skull, she asked me to use more "granola" in the desserts. To this day, I can't look at granola without getting a cold, clammy feeling in my soul.

In late December of that year, I asked if there were any plans for a New Year's Eve menu. Everyone shrugged their shoulders and said, "Uh, maybe. We dunno. Maybe we'll just be closed." It seemed weird that a nightclub would close on New Year's Eve, but I was kind of relieved and set out on a series of Wrangler Brutes shows from Los Angeles to San Francisco to Portland to Seattle instead. I came back to find the locks of Les Deux Cafes changed and a note on the door saying the place was no longer in operation. My cookbooks and tools were locked inside and management was already delinquent on my last two paychecks. I scaled the wall, retrieved my cookbooks and crappy knives from the unlocked kitchen, hurled them into the parking lot, and hoisted myself back over the wall.

I applied again at Campanile the next day, desperate to put this dark era behind me. Luckily, the restaurant just happened to need a pastry sous-chef, so I took the job and learned more than I ever had. The nightclub wasn't on my résumé, so mid prep a few months in, as we were making one of Nancy Silverton's classic sorbet bases, Dahlia, the pastry chef, asked me, "So what the fuck were you doing for that first year you lived here?" I told her, looking down shamefully into my bowl of strawberry puree. Dahlia erupted in fitful laughter and couldn't stop. It was the cherry on the fuck-you sundae.

The bird, the dog, and the shirt are attacking the skinhead.

SORBETS

Everyone likes sorbet. It sidesteps nearly all dietary restrictions: no eggs, no dairy, no gluten. But a good sorbet is hard to find. It needs to be extremely creamy—as creamy as gelato. You should have to ask, Is this gelato? There can be no iciness, no crumbliness. Never.

A spoonful of sorbet should feel like you are biting into the fruit's most perfect form: raspberries from the field next to your grandmother's house in the country, peaches straight off the branch in Sicily. The acidity and sweetness must be laser-focused, but in the most natural and organic way possible.

For these reasons and others, sorbet has no ironclad recipe at Del Posto. Fresh, beautiful, fragile fruit picked at its peak is always subtly different. A recipe of exact measurements in grams would be both irresponsible and wrong. All my cooks make sorbets with their palate, tasting constantly at every stage of the process. Find really good fruit. Quality can't be fudged in any kitchen, professional or otherwise.

SORBET SYRUP

Commit this to memory and save yourself the worry. It's easy and you'll need it often.
Yield: 2 cups

Water 2 cups (473 grams)
Sugar 2¼ cups (450 grams)
Dextrose ⅓ cup (120 grams)

In a small saucepot over high heat, bring the water to a full, rolling boil and whisk in the sugar and dextrose. Bring the mixture back to a boil and remove from the heat. Let cool. You can store this mixture in an airtight container in your fridge indefinitely. Please: Make sure the sorbet syrup is *very* cold when you use it to make your sorbets.

FRUIT SORBET

You can use pretty much any dense fruit that purees well: strawberries, peaches, plums, and the like. Don't use lemons or limes. Don't use any citrus for that matter. Note: You will need about 4 cups fruit for 2 cups puree.
Yield: 1½ quarts

Fruit puree 2 cups (weight varies by fruit)
Sorbet Syrup (above), chilled 2 cups (500 grams)
Lemon juice to taste
Malic acid to taste
Salt to taste

1. Make a decision: Do you want really smooth sorbet? If you do, run the puree through a chinois or fine-mesh strainer. (If you don't, don't.)
2. In a medium bowl, combine the puree, sorbet syrup, lemon juice, malic acid, and salt

and stir. In an airtight container, refrigerate the sorbet until cold, about 3 hours.

3. Spin in an ice cream machine according to the manufacturer's instructions. In a prechilled container, freeze the sorbet for at least 2 hours before serving. This will store well for 1 month.

To serve: There are few limitations on when or how you can serve this.

CELERY SORBET

For the celery juice in this recipe, you can do one of three things: buy the juice; use a juicer (pretty easy!); or chop up a bunch of celery, completely eviscerate it with an immersion blender, and pass it through a chinois (discard the pulp).
Yield: 1½ cups

Celery juice 2¼ cups (550 grams)
Sorbet Syrup (above), chilled 2 cups (500 grams)
Salt to taste
Malic acid to taste

1. In a medium bowl, combine the celery juice and sorbet syrup. Season with salt and malic acid. It will take a fair amount of salt. In an airtight container, refrigerate the sorbet until cold, at least 3 hours.
2. Spin in an ice cream machine according to the manufacturer's instructions. In a prechilled container, freeze the sorbet for at least 2 hours before serving. This will store well for 1 month.

To serve: This accompanies Sfera di Caprino (page 94).

RHUBARB SORBET

Yield: About 2 cups

Rhubarb, unpeeled and chopped 2 cups
   (274 grams)
Sugar 1 cup (200 grams)
Juice from 1 lemon
Water ½ cup (118 grams)
Dextrose ½ cup (200 grams)
Salt to taste

1. In a medium saucepan over high heat, combine the rhubarb, sugar, lemon juice, water, and dextrose and bring to a boil. Reduce the heat to low and cook until the rhubarb breaks down completely, about 10 minutes. Remove from the heat, let it cool, puree, and strain through a chinois or fine-mesh strainer. In an airtight container, refrigerate until cold, at least 3 hours.

2. Spin in an ice cream machine according to the manufacturer's instructions. In a prechilled container, freeze the sorbet for at least 2 hours before serving. This will hold in the freezer for 1 week in an airtight container.

To serve: Present as part of Lemon-Ginger Curd with Rhubarb and Polenta Chips (page 91).

YOGURT SORBET

Yield: About 3 cups

Labneh 2 cups (500 grams)
Simple syrup (see page 7) 1¼ cups (418
   grams)
Salt to taste

1. In a medium deep-sided bowl, using an immersion blender, combine the labneh, simple syrup, and salt.

2. Spin in an ice cream machine according to the manufacturer's instructions. In a prechilled container, freeze the sorbet for at least 2 hours. This will store well for about 1 month.

To serve: Present as part of Cucumber Creamsicle (page 69).

SOUR APRICOT SORBET (THE DRIED FRUIT METHOD)

Yield: About 2 cups

Dried apricots 2 cups (226 grams)
Verjus one 750-milliliter bottle
Sugar 1 cup (200 grams)
Sorbet Syrup (page 56), chilled
   approximately 2 cups
Salt to taste
Lemon juice taste

1. In a large bowl, combine the apricots and verjus and let soak for at least 48 hours. Drain the verjus, puree the apricots in a blender with a little water, and pass the puree through a chinois or fine-mesh strainer.

2. In a large bowl, measure in the apricot puree. Add in one-half that amount of sorbet syrup (for example, for 2 cups of apricot puree you add, 1 cup of sorbet syrup). Add salt and lemon juice to taste.

3. Spin in an ice cream machine according to the manufacturer's instructions. In a prechilled container, freeze for at least 2 hours before serving. This will store well for 1 month.

To serve: Present as part of Sour Apricot Sorbet and Cashew Gelato Coppettina (page 59).

THE AGGRAVATING ORIGIN OF THE BEAUTIFUL SOUR APRICOT SORBET AND CASHEW GELATO COPPETTINA

Sometimes having garbage thrown in your face really gets the creative juices flowing.

My dry goods purveyor, a big company with lots of big trucks that clog up the streets of Manhattan, has a rep who likes to send me the wrong stuff all the time. His name is German (pronounced *Herrr-maaan*).

A few years ago, in the middle of a screaming phone call with German, I said, *"Herrr-maaan, your phone number is the only one I have memorized* in the world. *I don't even know my girlfriend's number! If I ever get arrested, you're the only guy I can call!"* German seemed touched.

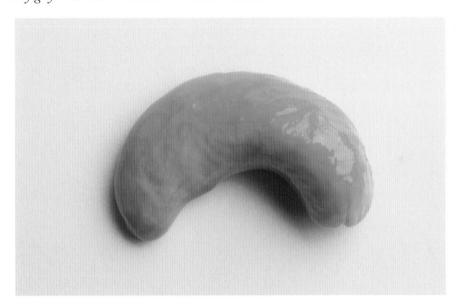

German once sent me fifty pounds of cashews I didn't order. Cashews are not even vaguely Italian. I called to have them returned, but nobody ever came to get them. They sat in the box in the storage room and collected dust. My e-mails were not returned either. My follow-up calls went unanswered. So to spite German, I started making cashew gelato. And goddamnit, German: It's delicious.

We toasted the nuts until nearly carbonized and then used them to infuse the milk. Unlike with other nuts, the buttery, burned richness of the cashews really came through nicely into a gelato base. It was a victory. We made the gelato really salty and it was exciting. And there was some textural bite added by tossing salted, toasted cashews with olive oil and folding them into the finished gelato. It was like the snap of that fantastic autumn special Quarterback Crunch ice cream from Baskin-Robbins that got me so psyched as a little kid.

The sour apricot component of this dish is a sorbet made with dried fruit that's been soaked in verjus. This is a hobby of mine (see page 25), done in small doses. But then one day the meat line unloaded fourteen quarts of unrequested dried apricots soaked in verjus on me: *Hey, pastry boy, use this shit up. We changed the menu. This is left over from the last duck prep. Make some fucking ice cream or whatever. How should we know?* Sorbet, it turned out, works like a charm with verjus-plumped apricots, which are tart and juicy, and in some ways better than fresh apricots, which are in their prime in New York for only a few weeks every year. Another victory.

Because both of these frozen confections were born as refuse, as castoffs, I figured pairing them up might make sense. And, Jesus, did it. I serve these together as Sour Apricot Sorbet and Cashew Gelato Coppettina as a pre-dessert at Del Posto, and I have for many years now. In all this time I haven't been able to come up with a combo quite as wonderful. We serve it in an impossibly tiny cup. Two quick bites and you are done. I describe it as our fake Italian Creamsicle made out of a bunch of stuff I didn't want.

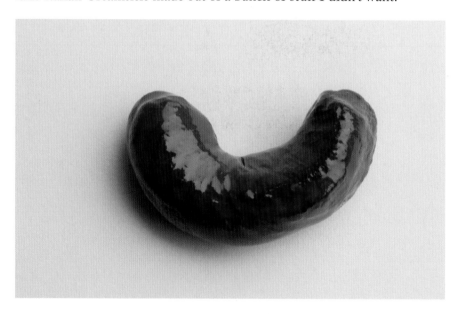

Here's how you do it: Make a batch each of Sour Apricot Sorbet (page 58) and Cashew Gelato (page 216). Put a spoon of each in a small bowl and dress them with freshly Microplane-d orange zest and a splat of extra-virgin olive oil.

LIDIA'S SWEET PEA CAKE WITH MACERATED STRAWBERRIES, STRAWBERRY GELATO, AND CANDIED SPLIT PEAS

"You have to be really good at hiding who you are stealing from."

—Buzz Osborne, Melvins, 2008

Buzz speaks the truth, and for the most part I live by this mantra. But there are times that I want to be perfectly clear about what I'm stealing and from whom.

I knew about this dish. I'd read all about it. Originally on the menu at Lidia Bastianich's restaurant Felidia, the sweet pea cake was fabricated by Lara Brumgnach, Felidia's former pastry chef. She taught me how to make it. We call it "Lidia's" because it is a variation on Lidia's white bean cake from her first cookbook. Somehow the pea version is slightly less weird.

I started making a pea version at Del Posto the second summer I was there, in 2009. I would have put it on the menu immediately, but I was too busy cleaning house of whiny, pouty cooks to get my creative groove working. Whenever Lara comes around and notices it on the menu, she rolls her eyes at me and shakes her head, like a disappointed dad. I suppose I changed her version around a little bit, but not all that much: She invented it, and I just make it.

The key here is to use the best strawberries you can get your hands on. In New York City, we restaurant folk and early-rising home cooks are blessed to live adjacent to the Hudson Valley, where Tristar strawberries flourish in the mid to late summer. In other parts of the country, strawberry season is fleeting (except in California, but that doesn't count—California is a sovereign state in terms of fruits and vegetables), but Tristars are resilient; they just keep on producing fruit until October, when I finally stop buying them because, well, it's October! They kick the ass of just about any other strawberry I have run across. Those creepy little *fraises des bois* the Frenchies love? No, thanks: seedy, flavorless, expensive. Plus their carbon footprint is insane. But Tristars? My god, I have a big, big crush on them. They are so one-of-a-kind crazy and scream New York City summer (even though, yes, they overstay their welcome into fall), and yet we can still hang out and watch *Jackass 3D* together because they are so down to earth. They are tiny and red all the way through. They have a scandalous backstory that involves being stolen from the side of a mountain in Utah and then smuggled back to upstate New York, where they took over like the "meteor shit" in the first *Creepshow* movie. They burst forth with crazy strawberry flavor. And they are a local product of New York. Talk about warming the cockles of my punk rock heart. And they're called Tristars. That could easily be the name of a Kraftwerk song, and there's probably no higher compliment.

But let's talk about the peas, because I know what's happening: You live in Brockport, New York, or Washington, Pennsylvania, or Salina, Kansas, and the strawberry tirade is pissing you off because there's not much chance of your finding Tristars. The peas are frozen, OK? Always and forever. You can find the peas anywhere.

Fresh peas are a pain in the ass anyway, and unless you are serving them barely cooked in the style of Dan Barber at Blue Hill, not a soul on earth is going to be able to tell if you're serving frozen peas. Fergus Henderson of St. John in London has one of my favorite quotes of all time: "Wait until fresh peas are in season, and then use frozen." Genius. So look at it like this. Get some beautiful local strawberries when they are in season and have some frozen peas waiting in the freezer. It'll work. In any case, the strawberry gelato tastes so much like summer and childhood and innocence, even the grumpiest grouch bitching about peas being on a dessert in the first place will be won over.

Yield: 6 small cakes

CANDIED SPLIT PEAS

Frozen peas ¼ cup (36 grams)
Turbinado sugar
Extra-virgin olive oil
Salt

1. Thaw the frozen peas. Using a paring knife, make a slit in the pea skin and gently press out the interior peas. Discard the wrinkly exteriors.

2. In a small bowl, combine the split peas, sugar, olive oil, and salt and toss until the peas are thoroughly coated.

SWEET PEA CAKE

Whole milk ¼ cup (60 grams)
Sugar ⅓ teaspoon plus ¾ cup (5 grams plus 150 grams)
Active dry yeast 1¼ teaspoons (5 grams)
Eggs 3, separated
Peas 12 ounces (217 grams), pureed
Bread Crumbs ½ cup (page 133), for the pan

1. Preheat the oven to 350°F.

2. In a medium microwavable bowl, zap

the milk in the microwave for 30 seconds. (It should be warm; if it's too hot, it will kill the yeast you are about to add.) Add ⅓ teaspoon of the sugar and the yeast and stir once to dissolve. Let the mixture sit for 10 minutes.

3. In the bowl of a stand mixer, using a whip attachment, combine the egg yolks and ¼ cup of the sugar on medium speed until pale yellow, about 3 minutes.

4. In a medium bowl, mix together the yeast mixture with the pea puree. Fold in the yolk mixture and set aside. Clean the bowl and whip attachment of the stand mixer.

5. In the clean bowl of the stand mixer, using the whip attachment, beat the egg whites on high until they aren't getting any taller and have reached stiff peaks. Turn the speed down to medium and slowly add the remaining ½ cup sugar. With a rubber spatula, gently fold the egg whites into the pea mixture.

6. Spray a 6-cup cupcake tin with nonstick cooking spray, sprinkle the bottom of each cup with plain bread crumbs, and fill each halfway with batter. Bake for exactly 16 minutes. The cakes will double in size, and then fall when removed from the oven. It's OK; this is how it's supposed to be.

7. Allow the cakes to cool in the tin and separate them from the sides with a butter knife. Gently remove when ready to use.

FOR SERVING

Strawberry Sauce (page 37)
Strawberry Gelato (page 212)
Macerated strawberries

To serve: Smear some strawberry sauce on a plate. Tear the pea cake into 3 pieces and top with macerated strawberries, a scoop of strawberry gelato, and a few of the candied split peas.

2. VEGETABLES

These days using vegetables in fancy desserts is commonplace. There is even—awkwardly, inexplicably—a backlash. When my sous-chef did a tasting for a potential job at a new restaurant recently, he made a roasted apple dish with candied fennel, caramel, and chunks of toasted sesame semolina bread. I helped him craft it. I was sure it was going to kill.

The young owners smirked: *We have moved beyond savory desserts.* I pictured this as a *New Yorker* cartoon, the owners as bespectacled, turtlenecked bohemians and my sous as a walrus or a cow in a chef's coat doing a "Wha' happen?" à la Fred Willard.

I use vegetables because I like vegetables. I have exactly no interest in appearing "edgy" or avant-garde. I'm more grandma than crazy scientist guy, I assure you. But, yes, there is no denying that I use a lot of savory stuff in my desserts. Beyond vegetables, I also overuse olive oil, bread crumbs, and vinegar. Those are some of the best things in the kitchen. It's weird *not* to use them.

Being referred to as a savory pastry chef used to irritate me, but that's basically what I am, so I wear it proudly now. Really, I'm just the guy who makes the stuff that comes at the end of the meal. (I have included tomato recipes in this section because after much waffling, I realized that putting tomatoes in the fruit section was even more pretentious.)

AVOCADOS AND STRAWBERRIES

Pity the avocado. As guacamole, it is persistently violated and sullied stateside as the plaything of frat boys, sorority sisters, and grotesque American chain restaurants. Too often plowed with soapy cilantro and sarcastically aggressive raw red onions, American guacamole can be a disservice to the avocado's nature. It's shameful the things we do to the noble avocado sometimes.

Avocado is not Italian. But it's a fatty fruit (fattier than . . . all the fruits?), and as such it is at home in my version of the Italian kitchen, despite what some authenticrats are feeling. It is strange and awkward, bulbous and delicate, the Rocky Dennis of fruit. Avocado is mildly sweet, green, and creamy, not that weirded out by being the accidental star of a dessert. So here is avocado in a hotel bathrobe, fresh off the set, filming an independent film destined for basic cable. It's a cool movie, one that won't make any money, but one that will be championed by the punks long after everyone else has forgotten about it. Think *Over the Edge* or *Desperate Living*.
Yield: 4 servings

Avocado scooped out of the shell ½ cup
   (75 grams)
Sugar (100 grams)
Water 2 tablespoons (30 grams)
Extra-virgin olive oil 2 tablespoons (27
   grams), plus more for serving
Lemon juice 2 teaspoons (10 grams), plus
   more to taste
Salt ½ teaspoon (2 grams)

Chocolate mint 5 nice leaves, plus more for
   serving
Tristar strawberries, quartered 1 cup (152
   grams)
Croutons (page 132)
Maldon salt for serving

1. In a large deep bowl, combine the avocado, ¼ cup of the sugar, the water, olive oil, the 2 teaspoons lemon juice, the salt, and chocolate mint and puree using an immersion blender.

2. In a small bowl, combine the strawberries, the remaining ¼ cup sugar, and lemon juice to taste and let sit for about 10 minutes, until the strawberries are slightly macerated.

To serve: Spread the avocado puree on the bottom of a bowl you like. Top with strawberries. Landscape with toasted croutons. Drizzle with olive oil and sprinkle with Maldon salt. Garnish with a few pieces of torn chocolate mint.

See page 114.

CUCUMBER CREAMSICLE

The key to making great food is to get the best possible stuff and avoid fucking it up. I say this to every cook who comes to me looking for a job. If they crack a smile, I know I *probably* have someone I could work with. If they remain expressionless or, worse, if they smirk and roll their eyes, I have them coat truffles for a couple hours to finish out their trial shift and bid them adieu.

Cucumbers are usually terrible, bland and seedy, tasting of a lawn-clippings-and-wet-dog cocktail. In the past I avoided them unless I could get my hands on really good ones at the greenmarket during the summer. But then I had a cucumber epiphany in Italy in the summer of 2013.

I'd been shipped to Friuli–Venezia Giulia, to the outskirts of the city of Cividale del Friuli, to help open up a new restaurant on a secluded winery funded by my bosses Joe and Lidia Bastianich. There I found the best-tasting cucumbers I had ever bitten into. They were so delicious and crisp, so full of explosive cucumber flavor, that they needed almost no seasoning, only a sprinkle of salt. They tasted like a laboratory rendition of a cucumber. When I was a kid, my mom bought a brand of super-cheap imitation blueberry muffin mix that had a tagline on the box: "Blueberrier than real blueberries!" I tell you, these cucumbers were so good they were fake. Only they were real.

Brand me a hopeless romantic, call me out for being spoiled by the summer produce of the Italian peninsula, but I assure you, these cucumbers were cantankerous in their deliciousness. They seemed to look up at me and smirk with their beauty: "Go ahead, jerk. I *dare* you to not fall in love with me."

I recalled an article in *The Washington Post* from right around the time I started cooking in a professional kitchen. It was one of those articles that gets recycled by a newspaper food section every few years about how some restaurants' sorbet survives as the platonic ideal of a certain type of fruit. So my staff and I made cucumber granita. And I swear to you it was like biting into the platonic ideal of a perfect cucumber. Easy. Blitzed cucumbers (skin on), lime juice, sugar, salt. Really easy.

I've always loved the blue raspberry Slushies topped with vanilla soft-serve that were an off-the-menu specialty of the stoner teenagers who manned the ice cream counters in Ocean City, Maryland, where I vacationed as a youngster. For this dish, I added yogurt sorbet to mimic the ice-cream-colliding-with-ice memory fixed inside my subconscious. I definitely have a Creamsicle fetish.

The fake-real cucumbers are diced and salted before getting a quick roll in crunchy turbinado sugar. They deliver textural pop and are camouflaged perfectly by the matching dull-emerald color of the granita. You know, like that soil-colored snake hiding in the dirt that kills you when you accidentally step on it? *Yield: 4 servings*

CUCUMBER GRANITA

Cucumbers 4, peeled and seeded
Juice of 3 limes
Water 1 cup (118 grams)
Fresh mint 5 leaves
Sugar ½ cup (100 grams)
Salt to taste

In a medium deep-sided bowl, combine the cucumbers, lime juice, water, mint, sugar, and salt using an immersion blender. Strain the mixture through a chinois or fine-mesh strainer and freeze in a shallow pan until slushy, stirring occasionally, about 3 hours in a freezer.

CANDIED CUCUMBER

Cucumber 1, peeled, seeded, and cut into
    small cubes
Turbinado sugar 4 teaspoons (16 grams)
Extra-virgin olive oil a tiny glug
Salt to taste

In a small bowl, combine the cucumbers, sugar, olive oil, and salt and toss to coat the cucumber.

FOR SERVING

Yogurt Sorbet (page 58)
Extra-virgin olive oil
Maldon salt to taste
Fresh mint 4 leaves, torn into pieces

To serve: Place a bowl in the freezer and let it chill for at least 10 minutes. Using a fork, break up the granita into irregular shards and place in the bottom of the well-chilled bowl. Top with a scoop of yogurt sorbet. Add several pieces of the candied cucumber on top (you want the sugar to be unmelted and crunchy, which is why you prepared the cucumbers last, just before serving). Drizzle with the olive oil and sprinkle with a few large grains of salt and a few pieces of torn mint.

Sam McPheeters and I have been in two and a half bands together. He can be a difficult character, but he writes incredible lyrics. His novel, The Loom of Ruin, *is a brain-melter that should be made into a movie by John Carpenter. Sam hates food.*

THE FAILURE THAT FORGED BROOKS
by Sam McPheeters

As the man who made Brooks Headley, I am often asked to divulge my methods. How did I turn the boy from Towson, Maryland, into the master chef of Manhattan? Did I impart a love of fine cuisine? Hardly: I find food inconvenient. Did I bequeath a tireless work ethic? Absolutely not: I prefer a life of scholarly indolence. Was it a philosophy, or an attitude, or a significant personal loan? No, my contribution to history runs deeper. I provided Brooks with his first failure.

Failure is the fuel that propels great men. It is also the furnace in which those great men are forged. It's a simple recipe: Take a regular man, load him into the Failure Furnace, squirt in a bunch of Failure Fuel, and presto! Out pops a great man. Ask Lincoln (lost like ninety elections) or Twain (curb-stomped by debt collectors) or Spielberg (ridiculed by every film school in America).

Brooks's failure involved a concert. In 1995, I launched the world's first micro show, in Richmond, Virginia. The idea was simple, as were the rules. Bands were to play for 1 minute. An emcee would keep time. The audience would provide enforcement, storming the stage for any performance running even 1 second over. In the years since, my concept has been cheapened, downgraded into a feel-good statement about youthful exuberance. In the twenty-first century, micro shows—a weekly event in most American cities—are just one more live event. The original micro show was a tribute to efficiency, nothing more or less.

Doors opened at midnight. The venue, Hole in the Wall, quickly filled to capacity, and we all found ourselves packed into a hot holding cell of a nightclub. I assumed that such stress would work to the show's advantage. I certainly wanted out as quickly as possible. Why would any musician spend more time here than they had to?

And yet the opening band ran a full 30 seconds over. The second band, Action Patrol (performing with plastic bags over their heads), went 49 seconds over. Worse, the audience seemed baffled by its duty. No one ejected anyone. It was the disastrous flip side to the infamous Milgram experiment on obedience to authority: Charged with maintaining order, the howling mob dithered.

Brooks's band, Young Pioneers, charged through its song. I studied my watch. As the second hand zipped past sixty, heads in the crowd parted in such a way that I momentarily had a view of Brooks on drums. Our gazes met for an instant and he seemed to say with his eyes, *What is this? What is this new feeling?*

I said, with my own eyes, *This is failure. You and your band have shamed yourself with your over-long performance.*

Brooks's eyes continued, *How do I undo this shame?*

And my eyes replied, *Keep this shame in your heart for all your days. Never forget this night. Learn from your past. Go forward from this place and bring great pastries to mankind.*

KABOCHA CAKE WITH SAGE GELATO AND CANDIED SQUASH

"Trick or Treat?"

I have always been a fan of the iconic flavor combination of pumpkin, brown butter, and sage that exists as a classic Italian pasta dish. It is sweet (the pumpkin or squash filling), savory (the salty pasta dough, the grippingly near-burned brown butter sauce), and oddly floral (the striking sage, like an evil shiv of whittled Christmas tree branches).

Turning pumpkin ravioli into a dessert was both inevitable and scary. Especially at a restaurant where *actual* pumpkin ravioli would be served, with identical flavors, in the meal's opening courses. Thomas Keller would not approve of such duplication. It reveals weakness. It confesses a lack of imagination.

I went for it anyway. I tried to keep an eye on each table's progression during service to make sure that no one who had ordered the pumpkin ravioli dish got the dessert version, but Del Posto is big, so I often failed. *So, uh, like, well, this is the same thing you had an hour ago. Only now it's dessert.*
Yield: 4 to 6 servings

KABOCHA CAKE

Unsalted butter 1 cup, or 2 sticks (225 grams)
Granulated sugar ¼ cup (50 grams)
Light brown sugar ½ cup (100 grams), packed

Extra-virgin olive oil ¼ cup (54 grams)
Eggs 2 (100 grams)
All-purpose flour 2 cups (280 grams)
Instant polenta ½ cup (115 grams)
Baking powder 2 teaspoons (9 grams)
Baking soda 1 teaspoon (7 grams)
Salt ½ teaspoon (3 grams)
Kabocha squash, shredded 3 cups
    (340 grams)

1. Preheat the oven to 325°F. Line a baking sheet with parchment paper and set aside.

2. In the bowl of a stand mixer, using the paddle attachment, combine the butter, granulated sugar, and brown sugar on medium speed until light and fluffy. Drizzle in the olive oil, add the eggs, and continue mixing.

3. In a small bowl, sift together the flour, instant polenta, baking powder, baking soda, and salt. Add the flour mixture to the butter mixture and mix until incorporated. Fold in the shredded squash.

4. Pour the batter onto the reserved baking sheet. Bake for 20 to 25 minutes, or until golden brown.

5. Let cool in the pan for at least 10 minutes.

CANDIED SQUASH

Kabocha squash 1 cleaned and cubed
Extra-virgin olive oil as needed
Salt to taste
Freshly ground black pepper to taste
Turbinado sugar ¼ cup (50 grams)
Zest of 1 lemon
Juice of 1 lemon

1. Preheat the oven to 400°F.

2. In a medium bowl, combine the squash, olive oil, salt, and pepper and toss to coat the squash. Spread the squash evenly on a baking sheet and roast until golden but not mushy, 10 to 12 minutes.

3. Sprinkle the squash with the turbinado sugar, lemon zest, and lemon juice and toss to coat the squash.

BROWN BUTTER SAUCE

Unsalted butter ¼ cup, or ½ stick (57 grams)
Salt a pinch
Fresh sage 1 leaf
Honey ½ teaspoon (2 grams)
Water ¼ teaspoon (2 grams)

1. In a small saucepan over medium heat, melt the butter with the salt. The butter will froth up after about 1 minute and when it does, begin whisking constantly. The butter will darken and become nutty and fragrant, about 1 more minute. When the butter is dark brown, add the sage and remove from the heat.

2. Let the butter cool for 5 minutes, then whisk in the honey and water. The sauce is ready to use immediately.

FOR SERVING

Sage Gelato (page 211)
Sage leaves, torn

To serve: Tear the squash cake rebelliously into irregular chunks and put them on a plate. Scatter the candied squash across the plate and add a scoop of sage gelato. Drizzle the brown butter sauce all over everything and add a few pieces of torn sage leaves.

ERROR CARROT CAKE

Perfection is overrated. A little sloppiness is reality. It shows vulnerability. But screwing up has actually saved my ass on countless occasions, in the studio and in the kitchen.

An early Universal Order of Armageddon recording from 1992, when I still lived with my mom, was rife with mistakes. I tried to record a drum part that I had no business attempting, one that I maybe got right *once* at practice. There was no chance under the pressure of expensive studio time that I was going to nail it. Recording songs is stressful enough as is. You go into some sterile environment during the day and try to document something that requires the energy of a crowd to support it. Those same songs you nail triumphantly *at night*, at shows, in awkward and uncomfortable venues, can't always be replicated when you are wearing headphones in a soundproof studio. (Note: The more cramped and uncomfortable you are *as an attendee*, the smaller the venue, the more fun it is for me *to play*. It just is. Always.)

So I left a big botched drum part in one of the UOA songs, because I couldn't play the rest of the song any better either. I started playing the error at live shows, too, but intentionally. Cross-pollination.

I refuse to play songs live unless they are so practiced that I don't have to think about them during the show. I have always preferred to go on autopilot and dream about pizza like Homer Simpson. People say I look intense when I'm playing live: It's because I'm picturing a pie from Di Fara, or maybe the floppy slice that Mr. Hand steals from Spicoli in *Fast Times at Ridgemont High*.

Do I think about drumming when I am in the heat of dinner service? No, it doesn't work backward (see page 77).

The Error Carrot Cake is a mistake we kept. We overfilled the pan our first couple tries. It made a mess of the oven with crunchy overcooked cake spewing everywhere. Everyone on the kitchen staff who walked by grabbed a handful of the crunchy bits. I thought it was so obviously trash. But it was delicious trash. And then, as if we were planning it all out (I can assure you there was no plan), we decided to at least look into the center of one of the screwed up cakes. It was light, as full of air and as moist as a cake could possibly be. So in the end the cake was both crunchy and soft. It was a botched riff. *Screw it, leave it in.*

Here's how you do it: Replace the kabocha squash with an equal amount of carrots in the cake recipe. You also need to chill a mortar and pestle, along with ½ cup sugar and ½ cup fresh parsley, in the freezer for at least 8 hours. Crush the sugar and parsley together in the mortar with the pestle and sprinkle the mixture over the cake when serving. Garnish with cured lemon from the Tartufo al Caffè recipe (page 165).

RECORD REVIEWS

UNIVERSAL ORDER OF ARMAGEDDON - "The Switch Is Down" 12"
    Well, disappointed once again by UOA. For a band that does so well when they actually play, they certainly manage to kill themselves with all the time wasted in self-indulgent artiness. Making a record sound like a mastering fuck up is called 'experimental', not punk. (TM)
(Kill Rock Stars, 120 NE State Ave, Olympia, WA 98501)

UPFRONT - "Spirit" CD
    Aww yeah!!! I have to admit it, I loved this record, so

song
then,
more
(Des
4020

WIL

the n
many
band
like I
and tl
to th

Maximum RockNRoll, August 1994.

NO MUSIC IN THE KITCHEN

I don't listen to music in the kitchen. It distracts me. Music is sacred. Cooking is, too. Mixing them is unnecessary and confusing. It bugs me out.

The ambient sounds of a restaurant kitchen are important and soothing. The dot matrix whir of the ticket machine; the airplane-like howl of an industrial blender going full blast; that beautiful hiss of a screamingly hot pan dropped into a full sink of water; the crash of a huge quantity of ice dumped into a plastic container; the quiet scrape of a peeler against the skin of an apple; that wrenching chug of the enormous dishwasher. It's like house-made Einstürzende Neubauten. I love it.

My prep team listens to music downstairs during daytime production. When I am occasionally forced to invade their space, I'm always the jerk who lowers it to a whisper: *My god, it's so loud!* I say, like a cranky grandma. *How can you hear yourself think?* As I stomp off, they blast it. Once someone had a mix playing and a Bikini Kill song came on as I walked by. I stared at the speakers, mesmerized. I forgot what I was doing and where I was going. I don't listen to music when I cook at home, either. The one exception was several years ago, when I ingested a large quantity of marijuana and prepped Thanksgiving dinner by myself. I listened to *Paul's Boutique* five times in a row.

Carrot cake with parsley gelato and candied carrots.

CARROT SAUCE

I went through a splat phase. Lots of chefs do. It's an awkward time in a cook's career, when suddenly spooning sauce onto a plate is no longer good enough. Instead, you hurl it full force in the general vicinity of a plate. You whip it violently from a spoon. It *looks* cool. It just isn't. This sauce used to be served with the carrot cake, and it utilizes a technique of cooking carrots *in* carrot juice, which is among my favorite tricks. With a little tweaking, this could be made into a very decent homemade baby food. Leave the splatting to the kids.

Yield: About 2 cups

Carrots peeled and diced 2 cups (244 grams)
Carrot juice 2 cups (480 grams)
Salt to taste
Sugar to taste
Lemon juice to taste

1. In a medium saucepan over medium heat, combine the carrots and carrot juice and bring to a boil. Reduce the heat and simmer the sauce until almost all the liquid has disappeared, about 5 minutes.

2. Remove the sauce from the heat and blend using an immersion blender until smooth. Season with salt, sugar, and lemon juice.

CANDIED CARROTS

This recipe is inspired in part by the *Looney Tunes* episode where Bugs Bunny buys carrots out of a vending machine. Even as a kid I was obsessed with food, but this image struck me especially: *He bought carrots out of a vending machine!* At eight years old, to me carrots (historically boring, healthy, a drag) were granted the same status as candy, then the most important thing in the world.

Kim Janusz, one of my long-standing sous-chefs at Del Posto, came up with this method for candying carrots. My single contribution, as usual, was to suggest adding salt. It is likely this is going to set off your home's smoke alarm. Don't disable it! Do you know how dangerous that is? Instead, do as my mom used to and stand on a chair and use a dish towel to wave the smoke away from the alarm. That's fun! It means you're really cooking.

Yield: 3 servings

Extra-virgin olive oil 1 teaspoon (5 grams)
Baby carrots 6 halved lengthwise
Sugar 2 tablespoons (25 grams)
Unsalted butter ½ teaspoon (2 grams)
Salt to taste

1. In a small sauté pan over high heat, heat the olive oil for 1 minute. Sear the carrots, cut side down, until they've taken on a little color. (Don't cook them through. You want them al dente.)

2. Coat the carrots and the pan with a light layer of sugar, stir, and cook until the sugar darkens to a golden brown, about 5 minutes. Remove from the heat.

3. Add the butter to the pan, toss to coat, and season with salt.

PAPPA AL POMODORO

Pappa al pomodoro is one of my very favorite things to eat. It isn't a dessert, but here it is nonetheless, in my dessert book. It is pizza in stew form: tomato and bread stew. It's a snack I make for my pastry staff each winter. Everyone loves it. One of the issues of working around and tasting desserts all day is that your body constantly craves salty, umami-filled stuff to balance out all that ice cream and cookie dough. This is a perfect example of that.

As a method of using up stale bread, pappa al pomodoro could not be more efficient. Use canned San Marzano tomatoes if you can find them. Massimo, an old coworker from my time in DC and a proud Tuscan, taught me this recipe and said the literal translation means "it's good for your grandfather because he doesn't have any teeth." It's warm and soft and comforting. Pillowy. On the same playing field as Martin's Potato Rolls, chickpea doubles from a Trinidadian take-out spot, or potato gnocchi.

We usually eat pappa al pomodoro straight out of the pot early Sunday mornings, as Saturday night's service winds down. If you plan to go on a dessert recipe bender using this book, for the love of god, please have a pot of this stuff hanging around to temper your sugar high.

Yield: 2 large servings

Onion, white or yellow 1 large, chopped
Extra-virgin olive oil 2 tablespoons (30 grams)
Garlic 2 cloves thinly sliced

San Marzano tomatoes, crushed one 28-ounce can (790 grams)
Sugar a pinch
Salt to taste
Freshly ground black pepper 1 teaspoon (2 grams)
Stale bread, torn 2 cups (274 grams)
Fresh basil a handful torn

1. In a deep-sided saucepan over low heat, sweat the onion in the olive oil until translucent, 8 to 10 minutes.

2. Turn the heat up to medium and add the garlic, stirring regularly. Once the garlic colors slightly, add the crushed tomatoes (including the juice), reduce the heat, and let the mixture simmer for 10 minutes. Season with the sugar, salt, and pepper and add the torn bread and basil. Mix with a wooden spoon until thick and chunky.

To serve: Present in a large bowl to people you really like.

DRIED TOMATOES

Sun-dried tomatoes rate high on the annoyance scale. They're up there with rethreading the string in a hooded sweatshirt and washing Crisco off your hands. The poster child of food in the 1980s, sun-dried tomatoes are insipid, oily, and cloyingly grating. They remind me of boring dinner parties my mom forced me to attend as a kid.

These dried tomatoes are not at all annoying or retro. They are like tomato shells stuffed with tomato paste—wildly delicious. The fresh strawberry variety of tomatoes works best, but grape tomatoes work, too. The result is a sweet and slightly salty half-dehydrated tomato that is savory enough for a winter Caprese salad and sweet enough to flank ice cream. Actually, there's one irritating thing: peeling the tomatoes. But after that, it's pretty much a set-it-and-forget-it activity. Ron Popeil would smile knowingly.

Yield: 15 dried strawberries that won't last (double the recipe at will)

Sugar 3 tablespoons (37 grams)
Salt 1 tablespoon (12 grams)
Freshly ground black pepper 1 tablespoon
    (6 grams)
Extra-virgin olive oil as needed
Strawberry tomatoes 15

1. Preheat the oven to 200°F. Line a baking sheet with parchment and set aside.

2. In a medium bowl, combine the sugar, salt, and pepper, adding one splash of water at a time until the mixture is the consistency of wet sand. Whisk in the olive oil slowly until it becomes a paste and set aside.

3. In a large bowl, prepare an ice bath.

4. In a small saucepan over high heat, bring 3 cups of water to a boil and blanch the tomatoes for 1 minute. Transfer them to the ice bath. With a paring knife, carefully remove the skins and discard.

5. On the reserved baking sheet, scatter the tomatoes and brush them with the olive oil paste until completely covered. Bake for 2 hours. The tomatoes will become wrinkled, sweet, and soft. Store the tomatoes in the refrigerator in an airtight container completely covered in olive oil. They will keep this way for a couple weeks.

To serve: However you'd like.

See page 122.

PROFILE IN COURAGE

Barbara Lynch

Born: Southie

Occupation: Chef/founder BLGRUPPO

Status: Not really sure

Notable quote: "Bon Fucking Jour"

Shoe size: 8

Lunch food: BLT, roasted tomato; shitloads of bacon still warm, fatty, and crispy; and extra mayo

Beverage: Chablis

I Heart NY:

First time: 1986

Accomplishments: Tons

Ambition/future plan: Change the way we produce food in this country!

RED PEPPER JELLY

I met Dario Cecchini on my first trip to Italy. If you've read the outstanding *Heat*, by Bill Buford, you already know way too much about this maniac butcher from the tiny village of Panzano in Tuscany. (If you haven't, get to your local independent bookseller and snag a copy immediately.) Dario is half artisanal champion of Tuscan Chianina beef, and half John Belushi in *Animal House*. If he were a punk guy in Los Angeles in the eighties, he would have been a roadie for Fear—not *in* the band, because he's too smart for that. Dario's a troublemaker. A prankster.

I'm not much for the fetishizing of meat.

I eat animal flesh sporadically and sparingly, and prefer it more as a condiment than the focus of a dish. Nothing bores me more than a big pile of meat. My first published piece of writing was a poem about how a Subway steak and cheese sandwich was weird, confusing, and gray—unfit for human consumption. The poem was for my high school literary magazine in the late eighties. But Dario, a meat guy at the core, is a cool and crazy lunatic. My favorite type of person.

You can drive through Panzano in a couple minutes without knowing you've missed Dario's butcher shop, Antica Macelleria Cecchini. It's so sweetly charming it warms even the tofu- and seitan-lined chambers of my heart. You're greeted with a complimentary tumbler of Chianti. The refrigerators containing the meats of the day usually have a dick joke or two written on the glass. On one of my visits, there was a pig's head molded from lardo and smoking a carrot cigar. Adjacent to the display case is a table with loaves of Tuscan bread. There's a knife and you're welcome to cut yourself a slice, but there's no salt in the bread. It's a weird Tuscan thing; I don't get it either.

There is also the infamous bull-minotaur statue with a boner that juts out from the lower part of its robe. You have to look close or you'll miss it. Dick joke after dick joke.

Above the engorged bull-man are four varieties of jars: a proprietary blend of indigenous fennel pollen, a marinated sliced pepper condiment called *bruciaculo* ("ass burner"), a spice mix with a corny but hilarious rant that claims to invoke nostalgic sensations of Tuscany, and an absolutely killer red pepper jelly. The jelly is slightly spicy, red as the McDonald's strawberry sundae topping. One spoonful of this stuff and I knew I had to make my own version at Del Posto. It's sweet *and* savory. It would work perfectly on roasted or braised pork, or as a dipping sauce for potatoes. I smear it on bread with some ricotta (I'm the weakling semi-vegetarian, remember). At his restaurant upstairs from the butcher shop, Dario pairs the jelly with fried cubes of breaded meat and twirls of orange zest—it's a dish that tastes like the world's best version of an order of General Tso's from a crummy Chinese takeout. Note: Make red pepper juice at home or purchase it at your favorite juice store.

Yield: 1 cup

Red bell pepper, peeled and diced 2 cups (250 grams)
Red pepper juice 1 cup (250 grams)
B&G cherry peppers ½ cup (50 grams)
Sugar ½ cup plus 1 teaspoon (100 grams plus 4 grams)
Salt 1 teaspoon (4 grams)
White wine vinegar ¼ cup (50 grams)
Pectin ¾ teaspoon (2 grams)

1. In a small saucepan over medium-low heat, combine the red pepper, red pepper juice, cherry peppers, ½ cup of the sugar, the salt, and vinegar and stir occasionally, until all the liquid has evaporated, about 20 minutes.

2. In a small bowl, mix the pectin with the remaining 1 teaspoon sugar and sprinkle the mixture over the peppers.

3. Cook the peppers for 1 more minute, remove from the heat, and let them cool in the pan. This jelly will stay in your fridge in an airtight container for several weeks.

Dario's bull-minotaur. Photo by Brooks.

WHERE PUNKS ATE IN NEW YORK CITY IN THE EIGHTIES by Robert Sietsema

Few care to remember the 1980s in downtown Manhattan, but it was the best of times and the worst of times: Crack was replacing heroin as the drug most dogging the neighborhoods, and the colorful caps of drug vials filled every seam in the sidewalk. Children collected them to make 3-D artworks.

But it was also a time when, in the East Village at least, carrying a guitar down First Avenue was a passport to a secret world. You lived in a tenement with crumbling stairways, pennies in the fuse boxes, and a shared toilet in the common hallway, but when you stepped up on stage or into your makeshift rehearsal studio, you were part of a rich and vibrant culture mainly hidden from public view.

Our days may have been spent in Midtown offices xeroxing endless piles of meaningless documents, but our nights were spent in the clubs. The test of your clubbing prowess was if you could put in a full day at work after staying up till 5 a.m. the night before. Clubs like CBGB, Pyramid Club, Brownies, Mudd Club, Tier 3, Club 57, Danceteria, Nightingale Lounge and Continental Divide offered music seven days a week, and if you knew the doorman, you got in free. These places started hopping around midnight and went until 4 a.m., when after-hours clubs like Save the Robots and AM/PM kicked in until dawn and beyond.

Bands tended to load-in and sound-check around 5 p.m., went on stage sometime after midnight, then dragged their equipment home in the wee hours. At that time, the streets were dark and quiet save for the elephantine scream of garbage trucks. There were few places open for a hungry musician to eat. It's hard to imagine now, but in the East Village of the early eighties, most all of the restaurants were closed by 6 p.m. Those that existed—and there were about 95 percent fewer than there are now—catered mainly to a lunch crowd that worked in nearby offices, warehouses, spare-tire shops, and secondhand stores.

An exception was Stromboli. Open late weeknights and even later on the weekends, the pizzeria was located at the iconic corner of First Avenue and St. Marks—beyond which every human being you knew passed at least once every twenty-four hours. It was half the size it is today: a narrow room, a high

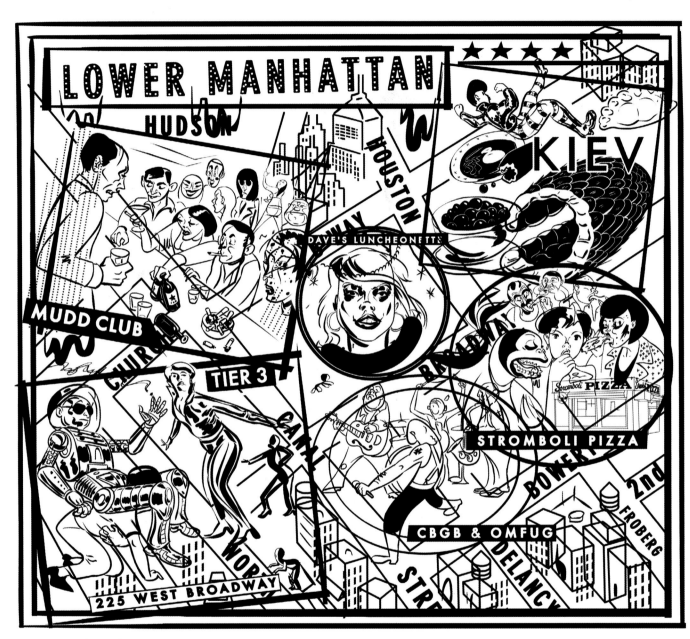

Map by Rick Froberg.

counter, a pizza oven that caused summer customers to swelter, and a shelf for eating while gazing disconsolately out the window and wondering how you were going to make rent. The slices were cheap, and no one had ever been known to order a whole pie. With the thin crust and oven-browned "bone" a given, Stromboli's slice differed from other typical neighborhood slices by sporting a slightly sweeter tomato sauce with no chunks in it, and a modest strew of better-than-average cheese. It was common to see Arto Lindsay of DNA or the Beastie Boys chowing down there.

Many East Village musicians were drawn to the Mudd Club, or its cheaper and less pretentious cousin Tier 3, down near Chinatown. Jean-Michel Basquiat was a bar back at the latter, though he was already famous for his work as part of a three-person graffiti-writing crew, SAMO. Whenever you'd come out of the club, often a bit tipsy from all the free drinks, you'd see a SAMO inscription nearby, the lettering all capitals and the paint still wet. The one that most sticks in my mind was on Franklin Street: LIFE IS CONFUSING AT THIS POINT—SAMO. The Mudd Club paid better, but dates at Tier 3 were more common. It became a kind of obscurely located rock clubhouse for East Village musicians, because Tribeca was even more desolate than SoHo in those days, a neighborhood of broken-down warehouses and small manufacturing facilities, many dating to the nineteenth century.

Most of Chinatown closed up shop around 9 p.m., so the main place to eat in the early-morning hours around Canal Street in the vicinity of Tier 3 was Dave's Luncheonette. I remember seeing Debbie Harry there. The main thing they sold, at a dimly lit, curved formica counter top, was hot dogs. At least that was all we ate there. There may have been more on the menu, but who'd even seen a menu? Coffee was downed in profusion, and those with the scratch would score the occasional chocolate shake or egg cream. Dave's was located right on the southeast corner of Broadway and Canal. What a spot!

Back in the East Village tenderloin, Kiev, at 7th Street and Second Avenue, was open far into the night. Most rockers I knew eschewed it because it was becoming the neighborhood's only bona fide tourist destination—besides CBGB, of course—and we could always be sure of being exposed to some uptowners slumming there. The fare was bland and Ukrainian. We deemed it far better to get Greek diner food, which included flame-grilled hamburgers and decent fries. At that time the closest actual Greek diner was called something like Oak Leaf, and was located on 23rd Street. Going up there we considered an uptown adventure; it was a street famous for being represented in detective fiction. And as you strolled along 23rd Street at 4 a.m. picking hamburger fragments out of your teeth with a toothpick, you'd look up at the second-story lofts and see many privates dicks' shingles. Not anymore.

Really, the only other option we knew about downtown (and none of us had ever set foot in the West Village) was on Mott Street in Chinatown, where the Mayflower Tea Shop was open after midnight. And eating cheap plates of chop suey and egg foo young while drinking steaming glasses of tea drawn from humongous stainless-steel urns was not the worst way to spend your time after a gig, before you went home to your East Village tenement and collapsed.

Xray Spex at CBGB, 1980. Photo by Robert Sietsema.

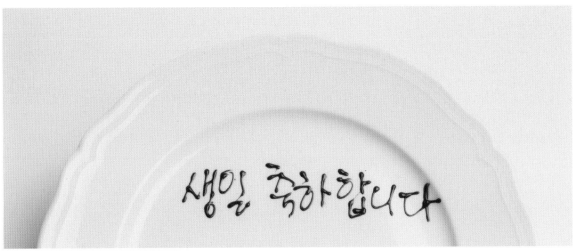

See page 253.

THREE-STAGE HAMMERED RHUBARB JAM

This jam is horribly unstable. You can't jar it. You have to make it and eat it really quickly, but it is extremely flavorful—you won't mind rushing. The instructions that follow apply also to cherries, strawberries, apricots, peaches, and plums. Pineapple, too. As for the recipe's name, look at the method like this: The first stage of cooking is the complete destruction and annihilation of your fruit—nuclear fall-out. No survivors. The second stage is a sword fight during the Roman empire, violent and bloody, but your fruit's still got half a leg when it's over. The final stage presents a sea of beautiful little bobbleheads of barely cooked fruit swimming around in a hammered, drunken daze, about to get rescued from the wing of an airplane maneuvered gently into the Hudson River, probably able to make it to work in the morning. (Smuckers, Polaner's, and all the oversugared stuff you find in the jelly aisle of the supermarket? Fully hammered. It's just a phrase I use to describe something that's been decimated in stages.)

Yield: 1 pint

Sugar 1¼ cups (250 grams)
Rhubarb, cut into ½-inch dice 4 cups
    (548 grams)
Rhubarb, finely diced 1 cup (137 grams)
Salt to taste
Lemon juice to taste

1. In a medium saucepan over high heat, combine the sugar and 3 cups of the ½-inch pieces of rhubarb, stirring regularly until the rhubarb releases its liquid and the water has evaporated, about 15 minutes, maybe more.

2. Add the remaining 1 cup ½-inch pieces of rhubarb and cook until about half of it has broken down, about 10 minutes. You are creating texture.

3. Add the finely diced rhubarb and stir to incorporate. Remove from the heat and season with salt and a squeeze of lemon.

To serve: Use this in the plating of Lemon-Ginger Curd with Rhubarb and Polenta Chips (page 91).

LEMON-GINGER CURD WITH RHUBARB AND POLENTA CHIPS

On May 1, 2002, there was a huge protest in DC for International Workers' Day. The staff at Tosca, where I was working, consisted mainly of El Salvadorean cooks, and it was likely they weren't going to show up for work. The owners of the restaurant were pre-pissed and ready to fire the lot. I was in support of the probably-protesting Salvadorean cooks, who were and are, in fact, the unsung heroes of every kitchen in DC. I sucked it up and got to work really early to compensate for any no-shows.

Rhubarb is the harbinger of spring. The earliest bunches are hothouse grown in either Washington State or Denmark. The stuff that comes from Denmark, Holland, and even Eastern Europe arrives in amazingly artful boxes, as beautiful and thoughtful as the product they carry. One box I received that day—from Poland, I think—looked especially sharp, like Soviet Constructivist art but brimming with glowing pink stalks of rhubarb, stylized into immortality. I cut off the top of the box, thinking I'd use it for something cool some day.

I got out of work at the same time the protests ended, as the cooks who had attended the gathering arrived for their dinner shifts, in a swift display of some serious Black Flag–level work ethic (see page 197)! I was holding my *rabarber* (rhubarb) cardboard lid when I got on the bus. I sat in the back, on top of the heater, the worst seat on the bus, and rode the 42 back to my room in Mount Pleasant. I wasn't part of the protest, but at least I had a sign like everyone else.

I moved that piece of cardboard all over

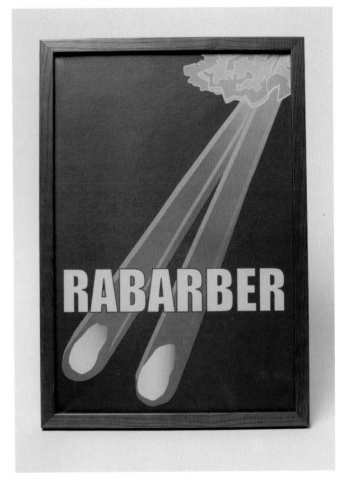

the country, from DC to LA to DC to New York, just *knowing* that one day it would be in the right place. It lay on my floor in New York a long time before Stella, my ex, had it framed for me as a birthday present. It hangs on my wall to this day.

In New York City if you put rhubarb on your menu too early and there's a freak, late-March snowfall, you're going to get laughed off the stage. However, early rhubarb can be difficult to resist. It is particularly beautiful, with lovely pink stalks that cook down into an electric-pink puree that makes the kitchen smell like dirt (in a good way). Rhubarb is one of my exceptions for having produce flown in. The hothouse stuff from out of state is horribly sexy. The local Hudson Valley rhubarb that comes later in the spring and summer is brown, green, and pockmarked. It smells equally of dirt and is exceptional in its own ways, but looking at the two side by side it's hard not to be reminded of a before-and-after methamphetamine-addiction photo essay: *That's the same person? You're kidding.*

This is a plated dessert taken straight from the Del Posto menu. The lemon cream is a variation on lemon curd that we keep in the freezer (does the world really need another lemon curd recipe? Probably not). I really love super-cold lemon stuff. My sous-chef Kim calls this the Barbie Dream House dessert, which initially bummed me out. Now I think it's hilarious. I include ginger because it is spicy and has the coolest Italian name: *zenzero*. ZENZERO. Think about that. That's definitely what I'm naming my kid.
Yield: 4 to 6 servings

LEMON-GINGER CURD
Yield: 1 pint

Ginger juice 2 tablespoons plus ¼ cup
    (12 grams plus 90 grams)
Zest of 1 lemon
Lemon juice ¾ cup (183 grams)
Egg yolks 7 (125 grams)
Sugar ½ cup (100 grams)
Unsalted butter ½ cup, or 1 stick
    (113 grams)
Salt to taste

1. Fill a heavy saucepan with water and bring to a light simmer over medium-low heat.

2. In a medium bowl over the simmering water, whisk together the lemon zest, lemon juice, 2 tablespoons of the ginger juice, the egg yolks, and the sugar until smooth and slightly thickened and glossy. Remove the mixture from the heat and let it cool for 5 minutes.

3. In a large bowl, prepare an ice bath.

4. Transfer the mixture to a deep bowl. Add the butter, the remaining ¼ cup ginger juice, and the salt. Combine using an immersion blender until smooth. Transfer to a freezer-safe bowl and chill in the ice bath.

5. When the curd is chilled, seal it in the container and place it in the freezer overnight to set fully.

RHUBARB STRINGS

Rhubarb 2 stalks
Sugar 1 cup (200 grams), plus more for
    dredging
Water ½ cup (118 grams)
Salt a pinch

1. In a small bowl, whisk together the sugar and water to create a syrup.

2. Using a vegetable peeler, shred the rhubarb into thin strings and soak the strings in the simple syrup for 1 hour.

3. Remove the rhubarb, drain on paper towels, and dredge in sugar.

4. Prepare snakes of aluminum foil (see the photograph) and drape the sugared strings in a free-form pattern on the foil.

5. Place in a dehydrator overnight until crisp (see page 9 for an alternate method). Store in a very dry plastic container for 2 days.

FOR SERVING

Sour cream 2 tablespoons
Rhubarb Sorbet (page 58)
Polenta Chips (page 121)
Three-Stage Hammered Rhubarb Jam
　　(page 90)

To serve: Smear the sour cream on a plate. Top with a scoop each of the frozen lemon-ginger curd and rhubarb sorbet. Garnish with pieces of rhubarb string and some polenta chips. Add a few spoonfuls of rhubarb jam. Serve immediately.

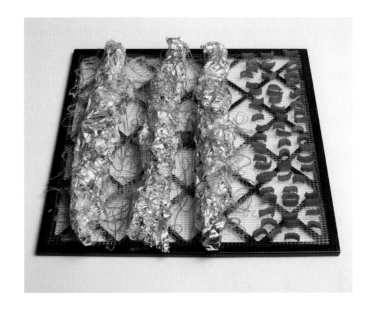

SFERA DI CAPRINO WITH CELERY SORBET

This is a case of me trying to please the chef, my boss. It's no secret that Ladner loves celery. So I incorporated celery into a dessert. I confess I didn't work too hard on this one— it was kind of a B-side.

But then a couple *New York Times* folks (Sam Sifton and Mark Bittman) wrote flatteringly about it, which made me think a little bit harder about what makes it work. Maybe I've always taken celery for granted. Celery, I can admit now, has hidden powers. It is humble but wise. Ladner knows things.

Yield: 6 to 8 servings

GOAT CHEESE MOUSSE WITH FRIED BREAD CRUMBS

Honey 1½ teaspoons (10 grams)
Water 1 tablespoon
Salt a pinch
Unflavored gelatin ½ teaspoon (1 gram)
Cream cheese ¾ cup (170 grams), softened
Goat cheese ¾ cup (170 grams), softened
Crème frâiche ½ cup (115 grams)
Heavy cream ¼ cup (60 grams)
Sugar ½ cup (100 grams)

1. Preheat the oven to 300°F.
2. In a small saucepan over low heat, combine the honey, water, and salt and stir until the honey melts. Sprinkle the gelatin over the honey mixture and whisk until it dissolves completely, about 4 minutes. Turn off the heat.
3. In the bowl of a stand mixer, using the paddle attachment, combine the cream cheese and goat cheese on medium speed

until light and fluffy, about 2 minutes. Add the crème fraîche, cream, and sugar and continue beating until the mixture is smooth and creamy. Add the honey mixture and beat for 1 minute. Transfer the mousse to a clear bowl and cover with plastic wrap. Refrigerate for at least 1 hour. This can hang out in your fridge for up to 1 day.

BALSAMIC FIG COMPOTE

Sugar ½ cup (100 grams)
Zest from 1 lemon, cut into strips
Water 1 cup (237 grams)
Dried Black Mission figs 1 cup (149 grams)
Balsamic vinegar ½ cup (127.5 grams)

1. In a small saucepan over medium-low heat, combine the sugar, lemon zest, and water, stirring occasionally until the sugar is dissolved.
2. In a medium bowl, add the figs. Pour the warm syrup over them and let the mixture cool for 2 to 3 hours.
3. Drain and discard the syrup. Place the figs in an airtight container. Add the vinegar, seal, and refrigerate for 3 hours, or until ready to use. (Use leftover vinegar for drizzling or for vinaigrettes.)

SHAVED CELERY SALAD

Celery 4 stalks, peeled and cut into 3-inch lengths
Gulden's spicy brown mustard ½ teaspoon (2 grams)
Honey ½ teaspoon (3.5 grams)

White wine vinegar 2 teaspoons (10 grams)
Salt to taste
Freshly ground black pepper to taste
Extra-virgin olive oil 2 tablespoons
    (27 grams)

1. In a medium bowl, prepare an ice bath.
2. Using a vegetable peeler, shave the celery into thin strips and soak the strips in the ice bath while you make the vinaigrette.
3. In a small bowl, whisk together the mustard, honey, vinegar, and ½ teaspoon water and sprinkle with salt and pepper. Slowly drizzle in the olive oil, whisking constantly, until an emulsion forms. Taste and adjust the seasoning as needed.

FOR SERVING

Celery Sorbet (page 56)
Bread Crumbs (page 133)

To serve: Dry the shaved celery and dress it with the honey mustard vinaigrette. (This is done immediately before serving!) Using a small ice cream scoop or two teaspoons, shape the goat cheese mousse into oval balls and coat them with the fried bread crumbs. Place a scoop of celery sorbet on a plate, surround with mousse balls, and tear apart the figs and scatter them around. Finally, add the celery salad as garnish.

95

BAND TOUR FOOD DIARY: UNIVERSAL ORDER OF ARMAGEDDON

At the same time I was playing with Born Against, I was also drumming in Universal Order of Armageddon. Tonie, UOA's guitarist, played bass in Born Against and we were a package deal. Back then, Tonie was a crazy vegan macrobiotic hippie nut (I mean that in the most endearing way). We rehearsed at his place, the 169 House, better known as either the Bone Closet or the Total Experience, depending on whether or not there was a show scheduled in the basement. It was in Arnold, Maryland, and there was a single sunflower growing in a big garden on the side. It was mostly a peaceful, well-maintained suburban neighborhood with windy roads. Except for the 169 House, which was dilapidated and falling backward, off a cliff. Sometimes the toilets didn't work. In the small driveway, there was an old VW van that was filled to the brim with the aseptic soy milk containers Tonie saved for recycling. Maybe you know this neighbor.

Tonie liked to cook big, bubbling crocks of cabbage and burdock root in tamari broth. The 169 House always smelled like fermenting cabbage. On tour, he'd fill a Tupperware container with cabbage and brown rice, hide it under the seat, and eat it in the middle of the night as he drove with his knees and listened to dubbed Can and Don Cherry cassettes across some desolate part of the country.

We toured often, and probably played South Dakota six times but never once stopped at Mount Rushmore. The verdict was always the same: too fucked up, too racist. We were regulars at the Rapid City natural foods co-op, though, downtown, on Mount Rushmore Road. We'd sometimes miss a show entirely, having underestimated the time it takes to drive seven hundred miles in one shot. We were booked to play Montana once, but we blew it by strolling around a roadside flea market for an hour we couldn't spare. We played an impromptu set at some house instead. Driving for ten hours and unloading directly into a kid's basement to play for sixteen or seventeen minutes: That's what we did.

If we were lucky enough to find a health food store back then, we would stock up on frozen black bean burritos—the *super*-healthy kind with little salt or seasoning of any kind. We'd toss our stash on the dashboard and let five hundred miles of direct sunlight thaw them until they were edible. The band broke up right before a tour of Europe we'd scheduled. *(Continued on page 125.)*

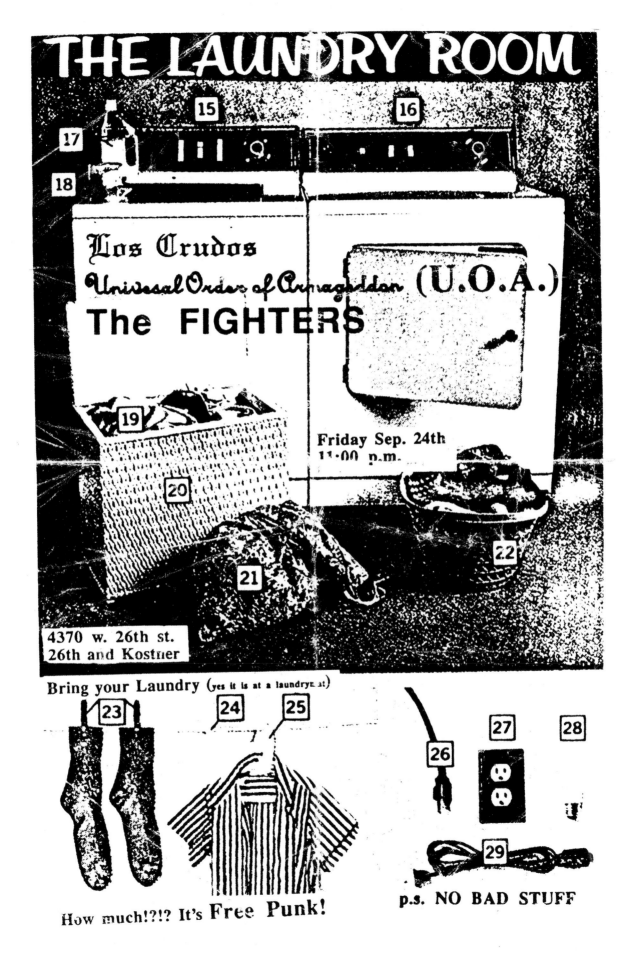

EGGPLANT AND CHOCOLATE

Eggplant in a dessert. Yeah, I guess it's weird. But I'm not avant-garde. I'm not even an artist. Not at all. I'm kind of a dolt, a knucklehead, a wannabe *nonna* cooking while half-cocked on limoncello. I'm also lazy. I didn't want to make this dessert.

But Ladner pushed me hard to give it a try and he can be very convincing. Then Mario Batali came poking around the kitchen one day when we were still in the R&D stage. Ladner was bouncy, giddy, and laughing hysterically, like a little girl: "Mario, dude, check it out," he said. "Brooks is working on a version of that classic eggplant and chocolate dessert. Pretty cool, right?" Mario, not missing a beat, gave us that trademark smirk, a single eyebrow jutting up through ceiling. "Good luck, guys," he said. "I've had the real thing in Italy. It was fucking gross."

And do you know what? At that very moment I became obsessed with making eggplant work in this dessert—and to make it delicious and comforting while remaining clearly inspired by the Italian original.

We did all sorts of wacky crap to try to make this dessert a success. We poached eggplant in a cocoa nib stock (absolutely awful), deep-fried it in a rice flour batter, and drenched it in fudge syrup. We made a sweetened eggplant puree—easily the weirdest, most unpalatable baba ghanoush I've ever had—and then dipped it in chocolate to make a bonbon thing. Terrible.

Eventually, I gave a particularly curmudgeonly sous-chef at Del Posto a taste of one of our experiments, and he looked at me and frowned. "Brooks, this is totally con-fusing on my palate," he said. "It's not bad, just confusing." Italian food should never be confusing. When I was able to sleep, I started having nightmares about eggplant. Horrible nightmares.

It occurred at exactly 3:18 a.m. I was hanging out with some line cooks at a shady Irish bar on 14th Street that we used to frequent after service because it's open late and has cheap beer and the constant potential for an accidental bar fight. "Have you tried cooking the eggplant in a panini press?" one of the cooks asked. I hadn't. *I'm an idiot.* Why were we even talking about cooking eggplant at three in the morning?

I got on the train back to Brooklyn and set my alarm. I woke up the next morning (it was a Sunday) and went straight to Bed Bath & Beyond to buy a George Foreman grill. I carried it back to Del Posto with a shit-eating grin on my face. I knew it was going to work. I didn't need to try it to know. But I tried anyway. And it worked.

The dish wasn't anything like the original version . . . but it was. It went on our since-retired tasting menu and camped there for a year waiting, like a sniper, to pull the chocolate-covered trigger on each unsuspecting guest. Whenever possible, use Fairy Tale eggplant from the farmers' market—they are tiny and austere and look like Rumpelstiltskin shoes. Otherwise, Japanese eggplant will do just fine and is available year-round.

Yield: 4 servings

CHOCOLATE SAUCE

Bittersweet chocolate, very best quality
    chopped 1 cup (313 grams)
Extra-virgin olive oil ½ cup (54 grams)
Salt to taste

1. In a medium microwavable bowl, melt the chocolate in the microwave in 30-second intervals until it is completely smooth. Do not burn it. (If you don't have a microwave, use a double boiler.)

2. Stir in the olive oil. Add salt—a considerable amount. Seriously, more than you think you need. Taste it. It should taste like all three ingredients.

EGGPLANT

Japanese eggplant 1 (or several Fairy Tale)
    peeled
Extra-virgin olive oil 2 tablespoons
    (27 grams)
Salt and sugar to taste
Honey 3 tablespoons (63 grams)
White wine vinegar 3 tablespoons (97 grams)

1. Using a mandoline, slice the eggplant thinly. Coat the individual slices in the olive oil, season with salt and sugar, and grill on both sides in a sandwich press or on a stove-top grill pan, whichever you have, just to soften.

2. In a small bowl, whisk together the honey and vinegar, season to taste, and set aside.

ALMOND SPREAD

Almond flour 1⅓ cups (125 grams), lightly
    toasted

Sugar ⅔ cup (133 grams)
Unsalted butter ½ cup, or 1 stick
    (125 grams), cubed
Eggs 3 (150 grams)
Zest of 1 lemon
Salt a pinch

1. In a medium bowl, whisk together the almond flour and sugar and set aside.

2. In the bowl of a stand mixer, using the paddle attachment, cream the butter on medium speed until softened. Add the almond flour mixture and combine. Add the eggs, one at a time, and continue to mix on medium until you have a batter that looks and feels like unfinished cookie dough. If it's grainy, don't worry about it. Add the lemon zest and salt and mix until just combined.

FOR SERVING

Cream Cheese Crust (page 230)
Ricotta Stracciatella (page 213)

To serve: Cover a cracker-size piece of the cream cheese crust with the almond spread and lay a slice of eggplant on top. Put it on a plate. Add a scoop of the ricotta stracciatella, and drizzle the plate with the chocolate sauce, making sure to avoid the gelato.

SUNCHOKE CRUDO WITH YEAST GELATO AND CANDIED WALNUTS

Sunchokes are not part of the Italian diet. I'm not sure if they are a part of any indigenous cuisine. Native American? European? People also call them Jerusalem artichokes, so maybe that means something.

They are knobby, dirty roots—somehow dirtier than carrots, and even potatoes. They are the crust punks of root vegetables: They *can* bathe, they just choose not to. There is something alien and appealingly prehistoric about them, too. Weird patches of hair sprout from them at random, like in your grandfather's ears or Lemmy Kilmister from Motörhead's mole. And like your granddad and Mr. Kilmister, they are total sweethearts with tons of great stories under that pocked, patchy skin. Sweet and a little bit off. Drunk, maybe, or in need of a nap. They smell musty, like the Egyptian art exhibit on permanent display at the Metropolitan Museum of Art or a thrift store in Baltimore. All winter long at the Union Square greenmarket in NYC it's apples and sunchokes and the weird dudes selling hard pretzels.

Flavorwise, sunchokes remind me of sour potatoes sprinkled with dirt and Splenda. I enjoy them roasted into submission and also nearly raw. In this dessert I serve them both ways and paired with yeast gelato, bread crumbs, citrus, and candied walnuts. For the yeast gelato, I was trying overly hard to be weird, which in 2011 was very trendy. I apologize. But I ended up keeping it because it works so well with the other stuff on the plate. *Yield: 4 to 6 servings*

CURED SUNCHOKES

Lemon pulp, pureed ¼ cup (61 grams)
Sugar ¼ cup (50 grams)
White wine vinegar ⅓ cup (78 grams)
Water ⅓ cup (78 grams)
Extra-virgin olive oil 1 cup (216 grams)
Salt ¼ teaspoon (1 gram)
Sunchokes 3 peeled and scrubbed

1. In a small bowl, whisk together the lemon pulp, sugar, vinegar, and water. Slowly drizzle in the olive oil, whisking constantly, until an emulsion forms. Season with the salt and set aside. This vinaigrette can be stored in an airtight container in the refrigerator for up to 2 weeks.

2. Using a mandoline, slice the sunchokes thinly. Add the sunchokes to the lemon vinaigrette and let them sit until seasoned yet still slightly crunchy, about 5 minutes.

HAMMERED SUNCHOKES

Sunchokes 5, unpeeled and scrubbed
Extra-virgin olive oil ¼ cup (54 grams)
Salt ½ teaspoon (2 grams)

1. Preheat the oven to 400°F.

2. Chop the sunchokes into irregular chunks. In a small bowl, toss the sunchokes with the olive oil and salt. Pour the sunchokes onto a baking sheet and roast until very soft and slightly blackened, about 20 minutes, checking halfway through.

3. While the sunchokes are still warm, use your fingers to crush them slightly.

CANDIED WALNUTS

Walnuts 1 cup (117 grams)
Sugar 1 cup (200 grams)
Water 1 cup (237 grams)
Cayenne pepper 1 tablespoon (5 grams)
Peanut oil ½ quart (432 grams), for frying
Salt to taste

1. In a small saucepot over high heat, add the walnuts, sugar, water, and cayenne and bring to a boil. Reduce the heat to medium and cook until thick and syrupy.

2. Drain the liquid from the walnuts and fry in the peanut oil until shiny. Salt the nuts heavily and immediately, while they are still warm. These keep for a week in an airtight container in your pantry.

FOR SERVING

Yeast Gelato (page 211)
Bread Crumbs (page 133)

To serve: Lay some cured sunchokes on a plate. Garnish with pieces of walnut and the bread crumbs. Add chunks of the hammered sunchokes and finish with a scoop of yeast gelato.

102

FRIED ROMAN ARTICHOKES WITH RICOTTA GELATO, HONEY, AND MATZO CROCCANTE

A few years ago, Dave Arnold gathered a bunch of local chefs to each present a dish at a large lunch he'd organized at Del Posto. Dave is New York City's food-world mad-scientist-lunatic (if he ever offers to show you his rigged "puffing gun," *run away fast*), and the gimmick, the prank, was that he'd personally assign each chef a theme for his or her dish. Momofuku's David Chang got "American Food, 1491." Wylie Dufresne, of wd-50, was given "Caveman Food." Ladner did a whole roasted ostrich in honor of his theme, "Ancient Rome." Each concept was intentionally ridiculous and aimed at playing into, or sometimes, more comically, *against* each chef's strengths and reputation.

The topic for my dessert was "Jewish Food in Italy, pre–World War II." It made me feel more than a little uncomfortable. Everyone else got comedy routines. Mine was both intensely historic and somber. *Thanks, Dave.* I called Nastassia, Dave's right hand, and asked if I could have something funny instead. She said no.

Carciofi alla Giudea (fried artichokes) are one of my favorite Roman snacks. There is something so satisfying about a crisp, oily, salty artichoke. I like to eat them blazingly hot so there's a little bit of hot oil dripping down my forearm. For the Dave Arnold experiment, I decided to turn fried artichokes into a dessert. They met the guidelines. In my research I also found a lot of baked goods with honey from that time period. I fried some artichokes, salted them heavily, and doused them in honey. Delicious, but a bit too sweet. I cut

the honey with some white wine vinegar: perfect. I finished the dish with a scoop of ricotta gelato and a candy-brittle-nougatine thing made with caramelized matzo. It was tasty and fun, but in no way traditional. It was also just this side of Milk Bar boss Christina Tosi's dessert at the same event, which included a meringue made with powdered Tang drink mix. Her topic: "Space Food."

A few days before the lunch, I received a call from the *Forward,* a Yiddish newspaper covering Jewish news—the oldest of its kind in the nation. When asked about my intended dish, I told the reporter why I picked carciofi alla Giudea. "But are you Jewish?" she asked. *No, that was just the topic given to me.* "But, *you* are not Jewish!" I explained again that I wasn't. In the article I was referred to as "the non-Jewish Headley."

Yield: 4 servings

MATZO CROCCANTE

Sugar 1 cup (200 grams)
Matzo, broken into small pieces
    1 cup (50 grams)
Salt 1 teaspoon (4 grams)

1. Line a baking sheet with a Silpat and set aside.

2. In a small saucepan, caramelize the sugar using the wet-sand technique (see page 11), until it gets pretty dark. Add the matzo and salt and swirl to coat the matzo in the caramel. Pour the mixture out in a fluid motion onto the prepared baking sheet.

3. Let it cool on the countertop until hard and then break it apart like peanut brittle.

HONEY VINEGAR GLAZE

Honey 3 tablespoons (63 grams)
White wine vinegar 3 tablespoons (97 grams)
Salt to taste

In a small bowl, whisk together the honey and vinegar. Season with salt and set aside.

FRIED ARTICHOKES

Peanut oil for frying 1 quart (864 grams)
Baby artichokes 8
Lemon juice for the holding water
Salt to taste

1. In a large deep-sided saucepan over high heat, bring the peanut oil to 275°F.

2. Trim off the exterior leaves of one of the artichokes until you see the pale yellow flesh—the color of the artichoke will change, moving from yellow at the bottom to dark green at the very top. Lay the artichoke on a cutting board and cut off the top, at about where the pale flesh meets the dark green.

3. Using a paring knife or peeler, trim the base of the artichoke and stem to remove the fibrous material, moving from top to bottom and revealing the tender interior.

4. Continue in this manner with all 8 artichokes, cutting each in half and placing it in a bowl of cold water with lemon juice, which will keep the artichokes from oxidizing until ready to use.

5. Strain the artichoke and blanch in the preheated oil until tender, 3 to 4 minutes. Remove from the oil and cool on a paper towel–lined cooling rack.

6. Once you have blanched all the artichokes, increase the frying oil temperature to 350°F. Fry the artichokes for a second time, until the leaves are golden and crispy, 4 to 5 minutes, turning occasionally.

7. Remove the artichokes from the oil and place in a paper towel–lined bowl. Season with a little salt while still warm.

FOR SERVING

Powdered sugar
Ricotta Gelato (page 213)

To serve: Drizzle the freshly fried artichokes with the honey vinegar glaze, lightly dust with powdered sugar, add the matzo croccante, and serve immediately with a scoop of ricotta gelato.

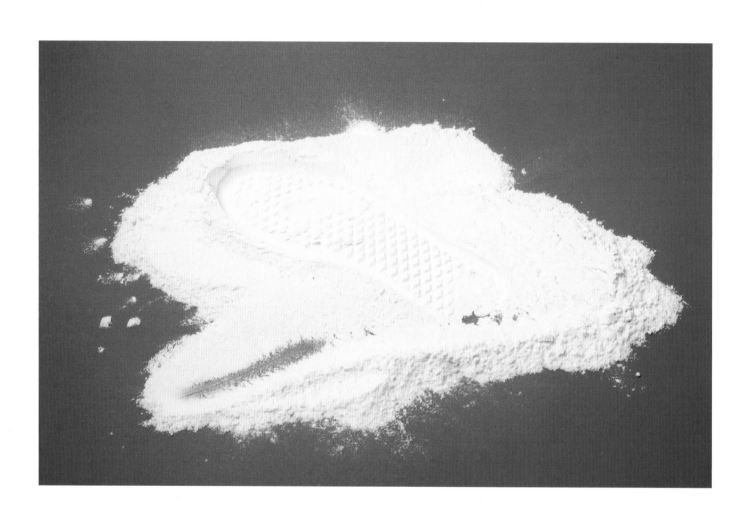

3. GRAINS & FLOURS

"Quit School Join the Band"—vinyl matrix inscribed on Born Against's *Industrial Relations* 7-inch, 1990

I can think of only one time when Ladner asked me do something I was not *entirely* keen on. He wanted a selection of cookies made of all different grains. It was conceptual. I dug the idea, but the problem was that I couldn't get my head around it. I kept putting it off, and Ladner kept prodding. *Are you gonna do the fucking grain cookie thing or what?* When I finally figured out what the selection could actually be, I realized that he wasn't asking me to prepare anything I wasn't up for. It was *exactly* what I wanted to do.

Babbo, near Washington Square Park in Manhattan, is a key restaurant in the Batali-Bastianich empire. I had its namesake cookbook branded into my subconscious from repeated readings years before I ever stepped foot in Del Posto. I knew all the words. I'd ingested all the book's ideals and propaganda, had stared at its pages and studied them for hours. And not just the desserts. The whole damn thing. In a way, joining the staff at Del Posto was like getting to join my favorite band. It was eerily similar to when, several years before, I got to join Born Against, at the time my favorite band, as their seventh drummer. I had pored over their lyric sheets in the same way I'd obsessed over the Babbo book. I listened to their records incessantly. It was ludicrous that I got to join that band. I had to quit college to do it. My mom was not pleased.

The record that everyone in Born Against obsessed over more than any other was *Flex Your Head,* a compilation LP on Dischord Records. It was an album that made you want to DO shit: start a band, make some art, anything creative. I knew it backward and forward, way better than I knew anything else in my vinyl collection. We all did. It represented everything we believed in, even though the record was already eleven years old by the time I joined Born Against. It was a *statement* on the state of DC punk rock in 1981, compiled by Dischord boss Ian MacKaye, exactly as the Babbo cookbook was the definitive doctrine of New York Italian food innovation in 2003, brought together by boss Mario Batali.

The really rare early pressings of *Flex Your Head,* the ones still on the wall at record shops sporting disproportionate price tags, have a generic stock photo of wheat grains as an in-joke. *Just give this thing we care about so much whatever bullshit cover.* Later pressings revealed the now-iconic blurry dude in a hat. But those wheat grains tilting in the wind: That was the picture, man. We all wanted that copy. Amber waves of grain. Inspirational.

When we did finally figure out the cookie plate of multiple grains, I took ownership of it like I'd personally conceived, developed, and accomplished it. It's exactly what I would have done anyway, Ladner.

"We ate sand."

Born Against. Pensacola, Florida, January 1993. Photo by Christina Brown.

CORN-CORN HUCKLEBERRY COOKIES

For these cookies I use a combination of instant polenta and pulverized freeze-dried corn to get a really corn-y flavor. (For pulverizing, pulse the freeze-dried stuff in a clean coffee grinder.) Christina Tosi, the James Beard Award–winning pastry chef behind Milk Bar, taught me how to do this. Freeze-dried corn is available at most health food stores. I love the stuff. Don't ever get a bag near me or I will eat it all in one sitting and get a gnarly stomachache. And blame you.

This is a thumbprint cookie and there is nothing that crazy about it. But the huckleberry jam baked into the cookie halfway through gets even jammier by the time it finishes baking. Right when the cookies come out of the oven, we add a couple freeze-dried corn kernels on top to hammer home the corn flavor, which makes them look simultaneously insanely elegant and totally stupid.

Yield: 50 to 60 small cookies

Unsalted butter 1 cup, or 2 sticks (220 grams)
Granulated sugar ¾ cup (150 grams)
Eggs 2 (110 grams)
Instant polenta ⅓ cup (65 grams)
All-purpose flour 2⅓ cups (300 grams)
Freeze-dried corn, pulverized 1½ cups (70 grams)
Baking powder ¾ teaspoon (4 grams)
Baking soda ¼ teaspoon (1 gram)
Kosher salt 1½ teaspoons (6 grams)
Turbinado sugar to coat
Huckleberry Marmellata (page 35)
Maldon salt to taste
Whole freeze-dried corn pieces as needed

1. Preheat the oven to 350°F. Line a baking sheet with a Silpat and set aside.

2. In the bowl of a stand mixer, using the paddle attachment, combine the butter and granulated sugar on medium speed until light and fluffy. Add the eggs and continue to mix.

3. In a separate bowl, sift together the instant polenta, flour, pulverized corn, baking soda, baking powder, and kosher salt. Add to the butter mixture and mix until just combined.

4. Shape the dough into nickel-size balls and roll in turbinado sugar. Place the dough balls on the prepared baking sheet. Bake for 5 minutes.

5. After 5 minutes, remove the sheet from the oven and make an indentation with your

pinkie finger in the top of each cookie. Fill the indentation with a teaspoon-size blob of huckleberry marmellata and return to the oven. Bake until the cookie is golden and the jam has set a bit, about 4 minutes.

To serve: Top with two ridiculous kernels of dried corn and a piece of Maldon salt and eat immediately or within a few hours. Don't let the cookies sit overnight.

PROFILE IN COURAGE

Erin McKenna

Born: **The tenth child of twelve, female**

Occupation: **Baker, owner of BabyCakes NYC**

Status: **Married with a kid**

Notable quote: **"Pull your own strings."**

Shoe size: **8**

Lunch food: **Kale chips, nuts, seeds, nori, a handful of chocolate chips**

Beverage: **Yerba Mate**

I Heart NY: **My first memory is having a deep desire to live in New York. It's the only place I could have opened an at-the-time bizarre bakery and watch it become celebrated even with all its quirks. I love New York fiercely.**

First time: **The first bar I ever went to was the 500 Club in San Francisco in 1993. I was seventeen. They gave me a Tom Collins and it became "my drink" because it was the only drink I knew other than beer.**

Accomplishments: **Growing a baby.**

Ambition/future plan: **To scrape together enough money to invest in young women and men with great ideas and no funding.**

QUINOA COOKIE SANDWICHES

Quinoa is one of my favorite grains to cook with, but as a chef at an Italian restaurant I don't get to use it very much. I've tried using it in rice pudding, *budino,* but even after I'd laced it with mascarpone and amaretti and orange zest, it just never seemed Italian enough. Quinoa has never made it to the Del Posto menu.

I created these sandwiches for a friend who requested a gluten-free dessert/snack option. It was a one-off. But I kept the recipe in the bank and bring it back every once in a while because it's totally fun to eat, even if you are completely tolerant of ye olde gluten. I like

to think of it as quinoa wrapped in itself. A few years back, I used to taunt the meat-roast cooks at Del Posto when they'd prepare a veal tenderloin wrapped in beef deckle as "a baby wrapped in its own mother." This is the same thing.

The cookie is overcooked red quinoa seasoned with a little honey and salt and then sandwiched between puffed quinoa "crackers" that are less complicated than you might expect. Normally in my life I have always gravitated toward the massive-effort-with-little-payoff-style of things (traveling three thousand miles to play a show in an ice cream

111

shop for no money, working sixteen-hour days for months straight on a set salary, etc.). But the payoff here is huge! You won't regret it. *Yield: 4 to 6 servings (unless you're feeling particularly lonely, in which case 1 serving)*

Red quinoa ¼ cup (46 grams)
White quinoa ¼ cup (46 grams)
Water 1 cup (236 grams)
Salt to taste
Peanut oil for frying 1 quart (864 grams)
Honey to taste
Sugar to taste
White wine vinegar for drizzling

1. Preheat the oven to 200°F. Line a baking sheet with a Silpat and set aside.

2. In a fine-mesh strainer, rinse the red quinoa under cool running water. Swish the grains around with your fingers to make sure they are really clean, about 2 minutes, and set aside. Repeat with the white quinoa.

2. In a small saucepan over medium-high heat, add ½ cup of the water, some salt, and the red quinoa and bring to a boil. Reduce the heat to the lowest setting, cover, and cook for about 15 minutes. Remove from the burner and let stand, still covered, for 5 minutes. Transfer the red quinoa to a bowl and set aside.

3. Follow the same cooking instructions for the white quinoa but *do not* add salt to the remaining ½ cup water. When the white quinoa is done smear it across the reserved baking sheet, and dehydrate it in the oven (see page 9) until crispy, with just a little moisture remaining, about 45 minutes.

4. In a large deep-sided saucepan, heat the peanut oil to 350°F.

5. To the reserved red quinoa, mix in honey, sugar, and salt. Set aside. Line a medium bowl with paper towels and set aside.

6. When the white quinoa is dehydrated, break it into irregular chunks. Deep-fry in the peanut oil, turning occasionally, until extra crisp, about 3 minutes. Transfer each batch of fried chips to the reserved paper towel–lined bowl and salt immediately. Drizzle the chips lightly with vinegar.

To serve: Mush some red quinoa into a ball and smush it between 2 chips. Repeat this over and over again until you run out of chips. Serve immediately.

BUCKWHEAT SHORTBREAD COOKIES

"This is a story, a very special story. It's about Brian Jones, one of the Rolling Stones"
—"Godstar," Psychic TV, 1985

An easy recipe—shamelessly easy—it requires nearly no effort. The cookie is slightly crunchy (the instant polenta) and a little dark (the industrial buckwheat flour). At Del Posto, we cut it out with a cute, fluted cookie cutter. This cookie is Genesis P-Orridge wearing a tutu.

Yield: Depends on the size of the cookie cutters

Unsalted butter 1 cup, or 2 sticks (240 grams)
Sugar ⅔ cup (133 grams), plus more for
    coating
All-purpose flour 1½ cups (190 grams)
Instant polenta 4½ teaspoons (22 grams)
Buckwheat flour ⅔ cup (80 grams)
Salt 1¼ teaspoons (5 grams)

1. Preheat the oven to 325°F.

2. In the bowl of a stand mixer, using the paddle attachment, combine the butter and sugar on medium speed until light and fluffy. Add the all-purpose flour, polenta, buckwheat flour and salt and mix until just combined.

3. On your countertop, place the dough between two pieces of parchment and roll it out to ¼-inch thickness with a rolling pin.

4. Transfer the parchment-covered dough to a baking sheet and refrigerate until firm to the touch, about 30 minutes. Cut the dough into shapes of your choice.

5. Coat each cookie with sugar, place on a baking sheet, and bake for 16 minutes. Cool the cookies on a cooling rack. The cookies will keep for several days in an airtight container.

BUCKWHEAT CRESPELLE

What's the difference between crêpes and crespelle? Nothing. They are exactly the same. The buckwheat flour and brown butter announce that it's autumn—like putting on a camouflage coat with a quilted liner the very second you can see your breath in the air for the first time since March. I like to serve these with Ricotta Gelato (page 213) and some Candied Squash (page 74). If possible, I'll put some maple syrup on there, too. Get some good maple syrup, but not that grade A crap. It's too refined. That's sissy stuff.

Yield: About 20 crespelles

Sugar 2 tablespoons (25 grams)
Cornstarch ¼ cup (28 grams)
Buckwheat flour ½ cup (60 grams)
Salt 1 teaspoon (4 grams)
Eggs 3 (150 grams)
Whole milk 1 cup (244 grams)
All-purpose flour 1¼ tablespoons
(10 grams)

Unsalted butter ⅓ cup, or 1⅓ sticks (90 grams), browned

1. In a medium deep-sided bowl, combine the sugar, cornstarch, buckwheat flour, salt, eggs, milk, all-purpose flour, and browned butter and pulse for 10 seconds using an immersion blender. Cover with plastic wrap and refrigerate for 1 hour.

2. In a small nonstick pan coated with nonstick cooking spray over medium heat, pour about 2 tablespoons of the batter into the center of the pan and swirl to spread it out evenly.

3. Cook for 30 seconds, flip, and cook for another 10 seconds. Remove and let each crespelle cool individually on a parchment-lined baking sheet. Once they are cool, stack the crespelle atop one another and store on a plate, covered with plastic wrap. They will stay in the fridge for a few days, and in the freezer for about 2 months.

SLOW-AS-HELL POLENTA PUDDING

This is the recipe that encapsulates perfectly all I try to do at Del Posto. It's like a rice pudding, but with an exceptional artisanal polenta as the grain. We finish it with a touch of butter, for creaminess, and a splash of olive oil because I put olive oil in everything.

All good polenta takes hours to cook. There are no shortcuts. When polenta is done cooking, it turns into a sweet napalm that splatters boiling hot projectiles all over your arm. Be careful! Don't waste any!

We serve it with a scoop of vanilla gelato and Huckleberry Marmellata (page 35), or sometimes as a miniature bite on a shard of Polenta Chip (page 121) with whatever fruit is in season. Be sure to find a polenta that remains gritty even after you've trounced it into submission with hours of simmering. In the words of Ladner, the goal here is something that is "texturally rewarding."

Yield: 4 servings

Anson Mills polenta ⅓ cup (55 grams)
Whole milk 4¾ cups (1,175 grams)
Salt 2½ teaspoons (5 grams)
Sugar ½ cup (100 grams)
Eggs 2 (100 grams)
Extra-virgin olive oil 2 tablespoons (27 grams)
Unsalted butter 2 tablespoons (28 grams)

1. In a medium saucepan over medium-low heat, whisk together the polenta, milk, salt, and sugar. Once it starts to stick to the bottom of the pan, whisk the mixture even more. It's worth it. You'll know the polenta is ready when it starts to knot in the middle as you whisk. It will be bound and almost dry when it's done.

2. In a medium bowl, whisk the eggs. Add a little hot polenta to the eggs to temper them, otherwise they will cook themselves and it'll be nasty.

3. Add the tempered eggs to the polenta and cook over low heat, just until the polenta has thickened. Pour the polenta into a bowl, add the olive oil and butter, stir, and serve. (If you don't want to eat this right away, you need to press a piece of plastic wrap over the surface of the polenta or a skin will form.) This will last for 3 to 4 days in the refrigerator.

TEMPERED STAINLESS STEEL

See page 172.

POLENTA CRÊPES

I hit rock bottom in Los Angeles near the end of 2004. My band Wrangler Brutes had imploded violently, a gaggle of thirty-year-old men acting like diaper-wearing toddlers (*my caterwauling was particularly WWF meets maternity ward*). I had left my job as pastry sous at Campanile, was flat broke with no girlfriend, and was living in the guest room of my best friend's house. I needed a job.

The funny thing was that I *got* plenty of jobs. They just all sucked. I couldn't rationalize committing myself to a year (at least) at any of these restaurants. This was my era of *the tasting.*

Tastings are miniature stress-filled auditions to get pastry chef gigs. You show up at an unfamiliar kitchen, make some desserts, and present them to the head chef, with maybe a chef de cuisine or a general manager in tow. I was a master of tastings. I loved doing them. They stressed me out and would keep me up at night, but I always knocked them out of the stadium. I was a professional! They would involve several rounds of desserts, some small, some plated; maybe I'd make a loaf of bread if I had time. Preparing tastings, you're always weaving in and out of people and working in a foreign kitchen. Sometimes the people are helpful, and other times they sabotage you. It can be passive-aggressive warfare, for sure. A fresh bag for an adrenaline junkie like myself.

My Babe Ruth–pointing-at-the-bleachers dish is always polenta crêpes, because nearly every kitchen has the raw materials. It helps that it is also a simple variation on Claudia Fleming's cornmeal crêpes from *The Last Course: The Desserts of Gramercy Tavern*, her masterpiece and my bible.

Yield: About 20 crêpes

Whole milk 1½ cups (365 grams)
All-purpose flour ¾ cup plus 2 tablespoons (93 grams plus 17 grams)
Heavy cream ½ cup (119 grams)
Sugar ⅓ cup (66 grams)
Eggs 3 (150 grams)
Salt ¾ teaspoon (3 grams)
Vanilla bean ½, scraped
Anson Mills polenta 5 tablespoons (52 grams)

1. In a medium deep-sided bowl, using an immersion blender, combine the milk, flour, cream, sugar, eggs, salt, and vanilla bean scrapings until smooth.

2. Pass the mixture through a strainer into a bowl and stir in the polenta. Cover with plastic wrap and chill overnight.

3. In a small nonstick pan coated with nonstick cooking spray over medium heat, pour about 1 ounce of the batter into the center of the pan and swirl to spread it out evenly.

4. Cook for 30 seconds, flip, and cook for another 10 seconds. Remove and let each crêpe cool individually on a plate. Once they are cool, you can stack the crêpes on top of one another to store. They will stay in the fridge for a few days, stacked on a plate and covered in plastic wrap, and in the freezer in an airtight container for about 2 months.

Saturday
Oct. 9, 1993
924 gilman street, berkeley

SPITBOY

oakland/san francisco, california

MAN IS THE BASTARD

southern california

UNIVERSAL ORDER OF ARMAGEDDON

annapolis, maryland

QUEEN MAB

east bay, california

all ages: four bands, five bucks (+ membership), nine p.m. pronto

POLENTA SHORTCAKE WITH BLACKBERRY COMPOTE

Even when strawberry shortcake is crummy it delivers, which is something fast-food franchises and commercial manufacturers have known and banked on forever. They pay people good money to know what people like! Good Humor ice cream bars and KFC parfait cups, even the McDonald's strawberry sundae—each flirts with the strawberry-cream construct. But there is a Grand Canyon-esque gap between a perfect strawberry and the strawberry-like flavoring you find in those desserts. Even at the supermarket, those red-skinned, white-fleshed strawberries don't have much to them. Nothing like the sex bombs you find at your local farmers' market in the heat of June. It isn't June right now where I am, and I'll assume it isn't where you are either: Use blackberries instead. They are far easier to manipulate into something delicious when they are not at their peak. A bit of sugar and lemon and you can get an inky purple-black mess that will be great.

If you have kids, put them to work on this one. For once they can earn their keep. The legacy of this recipe should be mini handprints of seedy blackberry goo on the wall of your kitchen and your pant leg. (Or the sticky shortcake wreckage pictured.)

Yield: 12 servings

BLACKBERRY COMPOTE

Blackberries 2 cups (300 grams)
Sugar ¼ cup (50 grams)
Juice of 1 lemon
Zest of 1 lemon
Salt a pinch

1. In a medium bowl, combine ½ cup of the blackberries, the sugar, lemon juice, lemon zest, and salt and mash them together with your hands or your grandmother's potato masher, until you have a gooey mess. Let the blackberries sit for 30 minutes. (Go make the shortcakes.)

2. Press the berry mess through a chinois or fine-mesh strainer to get rid of the seeds. Add the remaining 1½ cups blackberries, stir, and serve.

FOR THE SHORTCAKES

All-purpose flour 1 cup (125 grams)
Instant polenta ⅔ cup (110 grams)
Salt 1 teaspoon (4 grams)
Baking powder 2¼ teaspoons (8 grams)
Granulated sugar 3 tablespoons (40 grams)
Heavy cream 1¼ cups (303 grams), plus
    more for brushing
Maldon salt for sprinkling
Turbinado sugar for sprinkling

1. Preheat the oven to 325°F.
2. In a medium bowl, combine the flour, polenta, salt, baking powder, and granulated sugar. Make a well in the center and pour the

cream inside it carefully. Slowly and gently drag the outsides of the well in together until the dough is just combined.

3. With your hand, divide the dough into 12 irregular blobs and place them on an unlined baking sheet. Brush each lightly with cream, sprinkle with Maldon salt and turbinado sugar, and bake until just set and lightly golden in color, 10 to 15 minutes.

FOR SERVING

Corn Cream (page 205) 2½ cups

To serve: Split each shortcake in half, stuff with blackberry compote, and douse it with corn cream. Serve to eight-year-olds absolutely immediately.

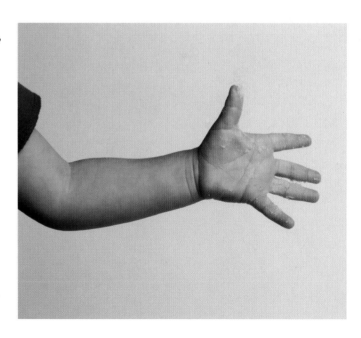

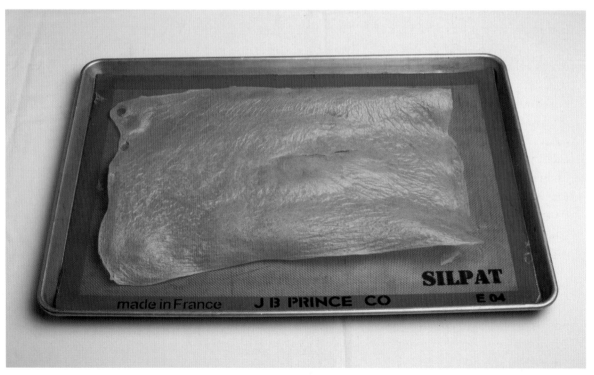

POLENTA CHIPS

Everyone in the kitchen at Del Posto agonizes over polenta. We ship in the best possible stuff from either these crazy folks in upstate New York, or else from a tiny company called Anson Mills in South Carolina that takes the stone milling of obsolete grains to unheard-of levels of obsession. Anson Mills sends us gritty, gnarly product that takes three hours to cook and is still gritty as hell when it's done. I'd never waste that precious stuff on the chips that follow.

Thankfully, a good polenta chip demands something low brow—in fact, the chips I make require that you find the absolute worst dry instant polenta you can get your hands on. Trust me, it's everywhere. The good stuff is hard to find, but this instant junk . . . I guarantee your local supermarket has some dusty nine-year-old packages tucked away in the dry goods aisle somewhere.

At the restaurant I use these chips as a garnish all the time. They are crunchy, contain no sugar, and taste incredible. Nothing is more annoying than when you go to an ambitious modern restaurant and you're served something that is supposed to be crunchy and exciting but is limp and frightening instead. These polenta chips are our crunch mercenaries. Ladner sometimes does a variation for a passed *assaggi* (little taste) that utilizes these chips as the bread in a baccalà sandwich.
Yield: 4 servings

Water 1 quart, plus 1 cup, hot (950 grams, plus 236 grams)
Salt 3 hefty pinches
Instant polenta 1½ cups (250 grams)

1. Preheat the oven to 300°F. Line two baking sheets with Silpats, spray with nonstick cooking spray, and set aside.

2. In a medium saucepan over medium-high heat, bring the 1 quart water and the salt to three-quarters of a full boil. Whisk in the polenta until it thickens, about 1 minute.

3. Add the 1 cup hot water and puree the mixture using an immersion blender until the polenta is a light yellow color, about 3 minutes.

4. Spread the mixture on the prepared baking sheets. Bake until crisp, about 40 minutes. Break the baked polenta into whatever size pieces you prefer.

SBRISOLONA

When I was a kid and I'd make a mix tape (maybe to impress a girl I had a crush on, maybe to impress myself), I would mumble quietly to no one, *Avoid using anything that Ian MacKaye has played on or released.* But then in the end the tape would be 45 percent Dischord Records songs. Every time. I felt compelled by a higher force. And it's the same with *sbrisolona*. Even when I'm consciously trying to keep it to a minimum, I still end up with sbrisolona on every single plate. I use it a lot.

In Italy, sbrisolona is a crumbly cake-cookie hybrid shared among friends while sipping coffee and talking passionately about nothing important. It comes as a single cookie, but as soon as the first person snaps into it the whole thing shatters into confetti all over the table. It's great. My version of sbrisolona is never intact. It is born as a crumble or, more accurately, a streusel topping. I use it to coat balls of strawberry ice cream for a snack that mimics a Good Humor ice cream bar perfectly. I toss it on desserts that are a bit too introspective otherwise, the ones that need to be reminded that everything we do is supposed to be a joyful experience.
Yield: 3 cups

All-purpose flour 1⅓ cups (233 grams)
Instant polenta 1⅓ cups (233 grams)
Sugar ¾ cup (150 grams)
Salt 2 teaspoons (8 grams)
Baking powder 2 teaspoons (8 grams)
Egg 1 (50 grams)
Vanilla bean ½, scraped
Zest from ½ lemon
Zest from ½ orange
Unsalted butter, very cold 1 cup, or 2 sticks
   (233 grams)

1. Preheat the oven to 350°F. Line a baking sheet with parchment or a Silpat and set aside.

2. In a medium bowl, combine the flour, polenta, sugar, salt, baking powder, egg, vanilla beans scrapings, lemon zest, and orange zest and mix by hand.

3. In a food processor, combine the butter and polenta mixture and pulse until the butter is pea size. Do not overpulse; you want there to be chunks of butter. (If you don't have a food processor, you can use a pastry cutter or two knives—just don't use your hands, because the butter needs to be cold.)

4. Sprinkle the mixture out into an even layer on the prepared baking sheet. Bake for 8 minutes, stir with a fork, and finish baking until lightly browned, about 10 minutes more.

To serve: Store in an airtight container for up to 2 weeks. Keep on hand for pretty much anything and everything.

PROFILE IN COURAGE:

Kathleen Hanna

Born: **Star sign Scorpio**

Occupation: **Musician**

Status: **The female version of Ian MacKaye**

Notable quote: **"Girls to the front."**

Shoe size: **7½**

Lunch food: **Leftovers inside a flaxseed wrap, microwaved**

Beverage: **Ice water**

I Heart NY: **Liverwurst toast in the lunch place inside ABC Carpet & Home**

First time: **While eating Ramen in Osaka, 2004**

Accomplishments: **Wrote a catchy song about a Metrocard once**

Ambition/future plan: **Avoid e-mail for an entire year and see what happens.**

POPCORN WITH NUTRITIONAL YEAST PUDDING

For a stretch I lived at a group house in Mount Pleasant, Washington DC, at 1654 Monroe Street. There were four bedrooms, and when I first moved in, I shared a room with my buddy Josh. He hung out there during the day and I slept there at night and the situation worked nicely. It was in the basement, maybe five square feet. I had a backpack and a laptop to my name and I paid $250 a month.

A lot of great artists and musicians did time at 1654 Monroe. Before I lived there, Eddie Janney, of Rites of Spring and Happy Go Licky, and I talked over tea about starting a band we never got off the ground. Mick Barr, guitar guy and my eventual bandmate in Oldest, and I made plans for Oldest there, in the wee hours, when Mick was still wide awake and I'd just gotten home from a restaurant shift. *Hey, Brooks, wanna start a band?*

There was *always* a half-eaten bowl of popcorn on the kitchen table when I came home late after work. Our housemate Justin was vegan and would often snack on stove-cooked popcorn seasoned with olive oil, salt, and nutritional yeast while watching cable. By 2 a.m., when I'd get home, the popcorn was a wet mess. I never bought groceries, so I'd eat the leftover stuff as a late dinner. One night I mashed it up with a fork and made a pudding. When it's that late and that quiet, weird things happen.

Ten years later, I was happily surprised to see a popcorn pudding recipe in an issue of *Lucky Peach,* where Daniel Patterson of Coi restaurant in San Francisco did the same thing, only professionally. There was no nutritional yeast in his version, but the approach was remarkably similar. His is fed to guests seeking a Michelin-starred experience, and mine is drunken leftover mush because I'm too lazy to buy groceries. Food is food. A shameful gag on one coast is the third course of a tasting menu on the other.

Popcorn brand of your choice (no microwave popcorn, please)
Salt to taste
Nutritional yeast to taste
Extra-virgin olive oil about 1 hefty teaspoon

1. In a medium saucepan, make some popcorn per the instructions on the package.

2. Season with salt and top with loads of nutritional yeast. It should taste as sharp as 24-month aged Parmigiano-Reggiano. Add olive oil and mix.

3. Toss with your hands and let the popcorn hang out in a bowl on the kitchen counter for a while.

4. When the popcorn is nice and mushy, mash it up with a fork and push it through a medium-mesh strainer to eliminate the hulls. You can use it as a spread on items of your choice, like old toast or new toast. Or you can eat it when it's still crunchy, like a dignified human being.

BAND TOUR FOOD DIARY: YOUNG PIONEERS

When I'd tour with Young Pioneers, we'd carry pieced-together note-books of where to find health food stores and vegetarian-friendly restaurants. It was rare that we found anything, and we cooked at people's houses a lot. We traveled with a milk crate that held a frying pan and olive oil in case our host was not adequately equipped. My mom's husband at the time was selling crappy Herbalife products, so we made him give us a big bunch of vitamins and elixirs so we would stay healthy on our month-long tours. Jesus, how much healthier could we be? There weren't any drugs on these trips. We never drank or smoked. We all ate vegetarian and every show was a total-body workout. Why we felt the need to be *healthier*, I have no idea. But we ate a lot of falafel and a lot of healthy burritos. There'd be an occasional Buddhist Chinese place with mock duck and we would lose our minds.

But it was the non-Buddhist Chinese spots that were the most unreliable, and our nightmare was mapo tofu. Chinese take-out joints are everywhere, and you can usually craft a vegetarian meal easily enough. But we weren't exactly Chinese food scholars, and someone would always gamble on the mapo tofu, mostly because it *sounds* safe. From the back of the van you'd hear bags of food torn open. And then a defeated groan: *Shit, is that meat? Fuuuuuck!* The mapo tofu risk was high. Why would anyone mix ground pork with tofu? What's the point?

When we'd make food at people's houses, it was usually Adam, our guitarist, who would cook. Most often it was his famous vegan fettuccine: whole wheat pasta drenched in olive oil, garlic, tahini, and clumps of nutritional yeast. Totally satisfying, a complete gut bomb, the perfect sleeping pill for passing out in your sleeping bag, four people deep in a suburban living room in Arkansas. When I first told Ladner of these early, monk-like tours, he looked at me and scrunched his face. *God, that sounds miserable.* But it wasn't. *(Continued on page 168.)*

ALEX STUPAK SCARES THE SHIT OUT OF ME

There comes a point in every cook's life when you realize that it's time to stop ripping people off and do your own thing. You make a Venn diagram. You populate each circle with all the different techniques you have stolen and/or learned throughout the years. You place one hand over your eyes and nose and part your fingers slowly to see if anything in the middle section makes sense. Does it?

In 1988, I started my first band. We were pretty awful, but goddamn we tried. We practiced in my mom's basement in Towson, Maryland, and Barbara, bless her, put up with our lousy noise for way longer than she should have. We were bad and it was loud.

We were all sixteen and we had a vision: sound like Joy Division. We wanted to be gothic and scary and dark. We failed. We sounded like a crappy punk band. Of course, we still ripped off Joy Division, Bauhaus, and Savage Republic, it's just that we sounded like a bunch of teenagers with no chops and absolutely no licks in doing so. We were, in the grandest sense of the term, a "local band." We played one show outside of Baltimore—a gig in DC, thirty minutes down the B-W Parkway in a grim neighborhood (circa 1990), with Neurosis and Filth, both on tour from California. There were twenty paying people in attendance when Neurosis played at the show's finale. Earlier, when we played, there were maybe two, and they were the friends we had brought down with us. They got in for free.

Fast-forward to 2006. I was pulling double restaurant shifts at Komi (morning production) and Tosca (night service) in DC. I wasn't doing it for the money; there wasn't really any money to be had. I mostly just got off on designing dessert menus for two very different restaurants. But I was running out of ideas. So I started stealing recipe ideas from New York City restaurants that I found online. These thieving sessions occurred late at night on a laptop, sitting on the back porch of the group house where I lived in Mount Pleasant, the power cord stretched out the door. The occasional raccoon from the creepy nearby bamboo forest would wander by, but otherwise there was complete silence in total darkness. There were many searches.

I was obsessed with Alex Stupak's work at wd-50. It was pure genius. And I ripped it off constantly in DC. I mean, who would know? I stole Alex's twisty chocolate ganache thing blatantly (mine would always snap and fall limply as it left the kitchen), as well as his liquid shortbread thing (it's a liquid cookie that is frozen so it melts! *What?*).

I had to go work for him. It felt inevitable. My girlfriend then, Stella, was living in NYC, and I was traveling up there a couple times a month, and as comfortable as DC was, I felt the itch to hurl myself into the vortex of the New York pastry chef world. Wd-50 was looking for a new pastry cook, and a couple e-mails secured me a stage. I was very, very excited.

I hopped the Chinatown bus up to NYC on an early Sunday morning, after service, at 2 a.m. The bus driver got lost. We ended up doing a series of unnecessary U-turns just outside Greenbelt, Maryland. Have you ever been on an unlicensed charter bus full of screaming strangers? The driver was besieged by insults and worse. *We can see the B-W Parkway on the left! It's right there! What's this guy doing?*

Stella lived in Bed-Stuy, Brooklyn. It was still dark when we pulled up at 88 East Broadway in Manhattan, the unloading dock for the Chinatown bus. Everyone got off the bus and instantly scattered into the morning darkness. I had no idea where I was. My usual New York City visits centered around St. Marks Place and Williamsburg, and I'd never been this far south on the island. A livery cab picked me up and charged me fifty dollars for the three-mile ride to Stella's place.

The next day I got to wd-50 at 11 a.m., excited beyond belief. I was wearing puffy chef's pants and rubber Birkenstock clogs. When I arrived, I walked downstairs and Alex greeted me. He was not smiling. I later discovered it was his day off and he came in only to oversee my time in his kitchen.

We sat at an empty banquette in the dining room. I told him that I was working at Komi in DC. He was expressionless at first and then half-smiled to indicate that he really did not give a fuck at all: DC was a backwater. NYC was the promised land. I mentioned that I had spent some time at Campanile in Los Angeles. I may as well have said I had worked at the Del Taco drive-through window on Los Feliz Boulevard. His shoulders sagged, deflated.

"Do you know how to make a fluid gel?" he asked.

"Absolutely. I made one last night!" I said.

We went into the basement prep kitchen. I was handed a recipe for a milk sauce. Really just milk sweetened with honey, seasoned with salt, and then set with gellan gum, a hydrocolloid that, as they like to say, is "thermoreversible," or heat stable. *Right on*, I was going to bust this out in a matter of seconds. It took me an hour, and in the end, I had only a clunky, chunky mess of off-white blobs littering a sheet tray. Alex looked at it and grabbed a plastic bowl scraper. He handed it to me, pointed toward the trash can, and walked away. I scraped.

He set me to work making dough for the iconic wd-50 flatbread, which was the job of the pastry department. In the end, it was to be a very thin, nearly see-through lavash cracker pebbled with sesame seeds. *So cool! I'd seen pictures of this on the Internet! Rad! I can't believe I'm getting to make this!*

It took me *way* too long to make and stretch the dough. How did I know? Alex told me. "Listen, man, if I give you this job, I am going to be *on your ass*. You're really fucking slow."

The two other pastry cooks in the basement prep kitchen were Rosio and some guy who didn't offer his name. Rosio was nice, helpful, very sweet, and was working on eight different projects at once. She was probably fifteen years my junior. The other guy called everyone "chef" pejoratively, was prematurely potbellied, and sported heavy bags under his eyes. Had it been New York in 1988, he would have been smoking a cigarette in the kitchen and trading barbs from the *Truly Tasteless Jokes* books with no one in particular. He would have had ninety-eight euphemisms for "vagina," absolutely. He saw me as both a complete hack (he would no doubt have to remake everything I was screwing up) and a guy who could potentially take his job.

Alex called me a few days later and offered me the job. I took the call at a Dunkin' Donuts downstairs from Komi and accepted a job offer from wd-50, surrounded by a display case of old doughnuts and the smell of microwaved scrambled eggs. I said I could start in three weeks.

Then I got cold feet. I turned down the job like a complete coward. All of my credit cards were maxed by this point and I didn't have any mom loans left to take. Without these things, the math didn't make sense. I couldn't afford to move. Plus Alex is intense, and it would have been a daily shakedown. I chickened out.

Even though we had spoken several times on the phone, I e-mailed Alex to decline. It was a weak way to go about it. And he let me know it in a twenty-two word e-mail that I discovered in my Yahoo trash bin a few weeks later. To paraphrase: *You will never amount to anything, and you completely suck*.

I was crushed. The e-mail made me shrivel like a slug freshly sprinkled with salt by a mean eleven-year-old. Humiliating. I was always going to be a local band playing to two people. It was decided.

Alex Stupak has since given up pastry cheffing entirely. He owns two very successful Mexican restaurants in Manhattan, where he is in charge of savory menus. He is no longer merely a chef. He is an operator. Everyone who works in kitchen for extended periods of time dreams of being an operator. I have nothing but complete and utter respect for the man. But he still scares the living shit out of me. I'm a salaried pastry chef. He's a restaurateur.

In 2012, I was invited to present at an international food conference in Mexico City called Mesamerica, one of the many slightly self-congratulatory food conferences that are held all over the world these days. I went on right after the scholar Diana Kennedy, who sat on a couch with a moderator and discussed sustainability and authenticity in Mexican cuisine. Alex was invited to present as well. We flew to the Mexican capital from New York on separate planes. My thirty-minute performance was unintentionally comic and I cooked nothing. I told a story and then played a crappy punk song—in English, in front of fifteen hundred Mexican food-obsessed people. Alex made Mexican food. That took serious confidence and risk and guts. I was just clowning.

After the performances, I was standing outside the venue when some excited Mexican kids asked to take my picture. Alex was a few feet away, and they gestured for him to join me in the photo. We both cringed, and then the kid snapped the photo. A permanent, perfect Venn diagram.

Jennie & Brooks.

CRUSTOLI, JENNIE STYLE

As a kid, I spent a lot of time cooking with my mom and grandmother. It wasn't why I became a professional cook, but it absolutely contributed to the love and respect I have for food and cooking. *Crustoli* were one of the cookies I made with my grandmother, Jennie, each year for the holidays. In Sicily, these are called *chiacchiere*, which conjugated and translated means "purposeless passionate talking, or talking nonsense." They're eaten midday with a glass of wine by gossipy old ladies and shit-talking grandpas as they complain about "everything and nothing." They are dough knotted into an awkward twist, deep-fried, and given a quick shake inside a brown paper bag partially filled with powdered sugar. The bag eventually disintegrates from the heat and oil. That was always my favorite part. Sometimes the most pronounced food memories have nothing to do with what you put in your mouth.

Yield: A big platter that disappears fast

All-purpose flour 2 cups (250 grams), plus
    more for dusting
Sugar ¼ cup (50 grams)
Eggs 2 (100 grams)
Unsalted butter ¼ cup, or ½ stick (57 grams),
    softened
Dry white wine 2 tablespoons (29 grams)
Baking powder 1 teaspoon (3.5 grams)
Zest of ½ orange
Salt to taste
Peanut oil for frying 1 quart (864 grams)
Powdered sugar for serving

1. In the bowl of a stand mixer, using the hook attachment, combine the flour, sugar, eggs, butter, white wine, baking powder, orange zest, and salt and mix on medium speed.

2. Dust a countertop with flour. After the dough comes together, transfer it to the countertop and knead with your hands until it becomes smooth. Form the dough into a ball, transfer the ball to a bowl, cover with plastic wrap, and let it sit on the countertop for 1 hour.

3. With a rolling pin, roll out the dough to ⅛ inch thick. (You can also use a pasta roller if you have one.)

4. In a medium deep-sided saucepan over high heat, bring the peanut oil to between 325° and 350°F.

5. Using a knife, cut the dough into 2 × 4-inch strips. Cut a ½-inch slit lengthwise along the center of each pastry strip. Loop one end of the strip through the slit and pull it through into a little bow-tie thing. Ta-da!

6. Fry the crustoli, a few at a time, for 1 to 2 minutes on each side, or until the pastry bubbles and the crustoli are golden and crisp. Drain them on paper towels on top of a cooling rack.

7. While they are still hot, shake the crustoli in a brown paper bag with some powdered sugar and serve immediately.

CROUTONS

More stale bread: my favorite. At Del Posto we use these often as a crunchy component to plated desserts, a textural bonus that brings the sweet yeast flavor of toast. Making them is really fun. We cut into a large loaf of rustic Italian bread with an airy crumb structure (I prefer *filone*) and pull the innards into free-form tufts of bread. It reminds me of when Han Solo sliced open the Tauntaun and slid Luke Skywalker inside to warm up in the guts after Luke had his ass handed to him by that Wampa.

Yield: About 3 cups

Rustic Italian bread 1 loaf
Sugar about 2 tablespoons
Salt about 1 tablespoon
Extra-virgin olive oil enough to lightly coat
    the bread pieces

1. Preheat the oven to 350°F.

2. Using a knife, split open the loaf, pull it into two halves, and tear the bread out in bite-size pieces.

3. In a large bowl, toss together the bread, sugar, salt, and olive oil to taste. It's up to you how sweet or salty you would like your croutons.

4. Spread the pieces of bread in a single layer on a baking sheet. Bake for 10 minutes, stir, and bake until golden brown throughout, about 10 minutes more.

BREAD CRUMBS

I make these in a very inefficient and time-consuming manner that includes pushing toasted bread through two different-size perforated pans. It's loud and messy. One of our former cooks, Adriana, was so annoyed by the crunching sound that she refused to be in the room during the process. But it's a great way to get the irregular miniature bread chunks that we love so much. A more reasonable and perfectly acceptable approach is to use a regular strainer—like a colander. These bread crumbs are used on Bastoncino (page 217), Sfera di Caprino (page 94), and the Sunchoke Crudo (page 101), among others. They're also just good to have around when you want some nonsweet crunch.

Baguette, day-old 1
Extra-virgin olive oil 5 tablespoons
    (67 grams)
Salt 2 teaspoons (8 grams)

1. Preheat the oven to 300°F.

2. Slice the baguette into ½-inch pieces and scatter the pieces in a single layer on a baking sheet. Bake until dried out and crunchy, about 10 minutes.

3. In a food processor, add the bread and pulse until roughly chopped. (If you don't have a food processor, you can crush the baked baguette pieces using the bottom of a heavy saucepan in a seesaw motion.) Using a medium strainer, sift out the fine bread crumbs (save these for the pea cake coating, page 61) and reserve only the small pieces (they should look kind of like Grape-Nuts cereal).

4. In a large deep-sided saucepan over high heat, bring the olive oil to 320°F. Fry the bread crumbs until golden brown, about 5 minutes. Drain on paper towels and salt heavily. These keep for a week in an airtight container.

Grapenuts & bread crumbs.

BREAD CRUMB–FRIED FRUIT

Fried fruit (*frittelle*) was on the menu a few years back in what used to be the enoteca section of Del Posto, beside the bar near the front window. One Christmas Eve, a night we are always very busy and the stress levels are in the red, I nearly came to blows with Daniel, then the manager of that section of the dining room. Fried fruit was involved.

Daniel and I had conducted a series of heated screaming matches in the kitchen from 11:30 p.m. to 12:20 a.m. (Merry Christmas!) At issue: I'm an adrenaline junkie asshole and Daniel is a stubborn Italian from Friuli. Eventually, I refused to let him serve a fried fruit I'd finished and went to serve it myself. He blocked me in the passageway of the kitchen as I left, creating a wedge with his chest and shoulders. I pushed against him with one forearm, outraged that a waiter would dare take on a chef. In my other hand was a plate of warm, cinnamon-drenched *frittelle* accompanied by soon-to-melt gelato. Flying fists seemed inevitable. The rest of the staff looked on, some horrified, some laughing hysterically. I would have gotten my butt kicked and been disgraced. But I wouldn't have surrendered that plate. Finally, I moved past him (or he let me pass, whatever). Today, Daniel and I are friends, the near-fisticuffs a smudged, if comical, Christmas memory.

Apples and pineapples work wonderfully. Peaches in the summer are the absolute best. It should be a firm fruit. Apple rings are the most forgiving and nonconfrontational.

Yield: 4 servings

Granny Smith apples 2 cored and sliced into
    ¼-inch rounds
All-purpose flour 2 cups (250 grams)
Eggs 2 (100 grams), beaten
Bread crumbs, untoasted (page 133) 2 cups
Peanut oil 1 quart (864 grams)
Salt ½ teaspoon (2 grams)
Sugar ¼ cup (50 grams)
Ground cinnamon ½ teaspoon (1 gram)
Yogurt Sorbet (page 58)
Extra-virgin olive oil for drizzling

1. In medium a deep-sided saucepan over
high heat, bring the peanut oil to between
325° and 350°F.

2. In three separate bowls, place the flour,
eggs, and bread crumbs. Going one piece at
a time, dredge the fruit in the flour, then the
egg, then the bread crumbs and set on a plate
until all the fruit is prepared.

3. Deep-fry the coated fruit pieces, turning occasionally. Don't put too much stuff
in at once. The fruit is done once it is golden
and floating in the oil, about 3 minutes.

4. Remove the fruit from the oil and drain
on a paper towel on top of a cooling rack.

5. In a bowl, combine the salt, sugar, and
cinnamon.

To serve: Drop each piece of still-warm
fruit into the cinnamon-sugar mixture, coat
thoroughly, and serve immediately with
a scoop of yogurt sorbet and a drizzle of
olive oil.

See page 35.

135

PASTA FROLLA

If something is meant to be crunchy, it must be crunchy. I talk about this constantly with my staff at Del Posto. Humidity is the enemy. In the middle of a sweltering New York City summer, I often pine away for the dry heat of Las Vegas or Phoenix, where nothing ever goes limp in their restaurants and bakeries. And then I think back to all the hellacious trips I've made to Las Vegas and I stop pining immediately.

Pasta frolla is my go-to tart dough, and it always does the trick. It isn't persnickety like puff pastry and it can be made start to finish without much thought or preplanning. Perhaps its most important virtues are that it retains its crunchy bite under even the most slobbery of fruits and it isn't too sweet. Bake this dough until it's nearly burned and you won't be disappointed.

Yield: 1 baking sheet

All-purpose flour 2 cups (250 grams)
Instant polenta 1¼ teaspoons (25 grams)
Sugar 3 tablespoons (38 grams), plus more
    for sprinkling
Salt 2 teaspoons (8 grams)
Unsalted butter, cold ¾ cup, or 1½ sticks
    (170 grams), diced
Ice water 1 ounce (43 grams)
Egg 1 (50 grams) beaten

1. Preheat the oven to 350°F.
2. In the bowl of a stand mixer, using the paddle attachment, combine the flour, polenta, sugar, salt, and butter on medium speed. Stop when the butter chunks are the size of peas.

3. Pour in the very cold ice water and combine as quickly as possible, resisting the urge to overwork it, about 1 minute. (Chunks of butter are still good. Embrace them.)
4. Using a rolling pin, roll the dough out on a sheet of parchment until it is ¼ inch thick. Lift the dough by the parchment and transfer it to a baking sheet.
5. Brush the dough with the beaten egg and sprinkle with sugar. Bake until golden brown, 15 to 20 minutes. Cool on the pan on a cooling rack.

Blueberry Crostata—sorry, this recipe isn't in the book.

DOUGHNUTS: THE HARD WAY AND THE LA WAY

Shoving doughnuts into my mouth directly from the fryer is among my favorite pastimes. During dinner service, I often imagine a restaurant so tiny and intimate that the little joys of a restaurant cook's life (eating molten doughnuts, spooning vanilla gelato straight from the ice cream machine while it's still running) could be experienced by the guest. It would be immersive, like an amusement park's hall of mirrors or a haunted house. Moving from place to place, room to room, no barriers, no walls, interacting directly with the chef. Then one day I realized that what I was imagining is everyone eating at their mom's house.

DOUGHNUTS: THE HARD WAY

Yield: As many as you can make

All-purpose flour 4 cups (500 grams)
Sugar ⅔ cup (133 grams), plus more for
    coating
Active dry yeast 1¼ teaspoons (5 grams)
Salt 1¼ teaspoons (5 grams)
Eggs 3 (150 grams)
Water ⅔ cup (158 grams)
Unsalted butter ⅔ cup, or 1⅓ sticks
    (150 grams), softened
Peanut oil for frying 2 quarts (1680 grams)

1. In the bowl of a stand mixer, using the hook attachment, combine the flour, sugar, yeast, and salt on medium speed.

2. In a separate bowl, combine the eggs and water. Add to the flour mixture and continue mixing as the dough comes together.

3. Add the softened butter, a little bit at a time, as the dough continues to mix. Once you've added all the butter, let the dough continue to mix for 15 minutes.

4. Dump the dough into a large bowl and cover the bowl with plastic wrap. Let the dough proof in a warm, dry place until it doubles in size, at least 4 to 5 hours, possibly longer.

5. Place the dough on a well-floured cookie sheet. Press it down with your fingers until it is about ¼ inch thick. Sprinkle flour over the top of the dough and put the dough in the fridge to chill until it becomes firm.

6. In a medium deep-sided saucepan over high heat, bring the peanut oil to 350°F.

7. Remove the dough from the fridge and cut rounds with a 1-inch round cutter. (You can also make full-size doughnuts with this dough.) This dough cannot be rerolled, so work wisely.

8. Deep-fry the doughnuts until golden brown.

To serve: Coat in sugar and eat these right away! You can also fill them with Pastry Cream (page 204).

DOUGHNUTS: THE LA WAY

Yield: As many as you can make

Warm water 1¼ cups (425 grams)
Unsalted butter ⅓ cup, or ⅔ stick (85 grams), melted
Sugar ¼ cup (50 grams), plus more for coating
Salt 1 teaspoon (4 grams)
Active dry yeast 1¼ teaspoons (5 grams)

All-purpose flour 3 cups (382 grams)
Bread flour 1½ cups (220 grams)
Pure vanilla extract ½ teaspoon (2 grams)
Zest of ½ orange
Peanut oil for frying 2 quarts (1680 grams)

1. In the bowl of a stand mixer, using the hook attachment, combine the water, butter, sugar, and salt on medium speed until the mixture just comes together. Add the yeast and mix for a minute or so, until the dough just comes together.

2. Add the all-purpose flour, bread flour, vanilla, and orange zest, and mix for 10 minutes, or until you have a smooth dough. Cover the bowl with plastic wrap and let it sit in a warm, dry place for 3 hours, or until the dough has doubled in size.

3. In a medium deep-sided saucepan over medium-high heat, bring the peanut oil to 350°F. Line a baking sheet with parchment paper, dust it with flour, and set aside.

4. Turn the dough out onto the prepared baking sheet and press it into the shape of the sheet until it is about ¼ inch thick.

5. Cut out the doughnut shapes of your choice and deep-fry them until golden, or until they float to the top. (You can also store the portioned dough in the refrigerator, but you cannot reroll this dough, so what you see is what you get.)

To serve: Coat in sugar and serve hot.

VAN HALEN

The first thing I ever truly loved was Van Halen: Diamond Dave, Eddie, Alex, Michael Anthony (first *and* last name, always). My first love, absolutely.

Van Halen slugged it out in clubs in LA for six years before their first album, *Van Halen*, was released in 1978. I admire their pre-fame work ethic. Whenever anyone brings up Van Halen, I'm always quick to note that they worked really long and really hard before they achieved anything, like I have proprietary ownership of the fact.

There was a book at our house when I was growing up that I assume came as a freebie with a Columbia House offering. It had a blue cover and the title was embossed: *The Year in Music, 1979*. I pored over this thing religiously. Frank Zappa with a rubber cone on his head, Gilda Radner aping Patti Smith, and, of course, Diamond Dave in soft light, shirtless, chest hair aglow, wearing leather chaps and leaping into the air, just completely psyched and at the beginning of his notoriety. I was awestruck.

So as a seven-year-old, I discovered love. And by the time the album *1984* came out, I was an armchair Van Halen scholar, in the way that only a nerdy kid from the suburbs of Baltimore could be. I'd gleaned most of what I knew from *The Year in Music, 1979*, the older brothers of a few friends, and MTV VJs.

In fancy fine-dining New York restaurants, you call the person in charge "Chef." But that goes for almost everyone in any position of authority or management in the kitchen. I had never experienced this until I started working at Del Posto. *Yes, Chef! I got it, Chef!* The formality wasn't part of the kitchen vernacular in the restaurants where I'd worked before. You called the head chef by his or her name. That was normal. That made sense.

People started calling me Chef at Del Posto and it was incredibly weird. If I was standing next to Ladner, Tony (the chef de cuisine), and one of the sous-chefs and someone yelled "Hey, Chef!" from behind, we'd all turn around. It's completely goofy. It's silly.

It was extremely awkward at first—probably for a full year. But I love it now. It's a total New York City thing. Everyone's "Chef." I am 100 percent into it. To this day I find it uncomfortable introducing Ladner to a friend outside of work and I'm forced to say, "Hey, this is Mark." *Goddamnit, he's Chef! That's his fucking name!* It's not unlike when I'd hear "Panama" on the radio while in the car with my mom in 1984 and that part where David Lee Roth sings "Reach down between my legs / Ease the seat back" would make me freeze with embarrassment. It's a great song, though, so I would never have thought to change the station. A little less than a year later, my mother began cranking "Just a Gigolo" from Mr. Roth's first solo endeavor every time it came on the radio.

Van Halen is the reason I could never with a straight face work under the talented chef Michael Anthony, currently of Gramercy Tavern. I don't think I'd be able to introduce him to friends outside of work as either "Chef" or "Michael Anthony" without picturing him with a Jack Daniels bass guitar flying across a stage over Diamond Dave, Alex, and Eddie.

ROSA'S BISCUITS, OR "THE BEST THING I HAVE EVER EATEN IN AMERICA"

I have two rules for my staff at Del Posto.

One: Call your mom. Often. If you need a few days off to go visit her, no problem—I will cover your shift. When was the last time you called your mom? Call your mother, OK?

Two: Do not piss Rosa off.

Rosa is the master of the basement at DP, which is not nearly as brutal as it sounds. The basement houses the prep kitchen below the main dining room, is nicer than most professional kitchens, and is well equipped with all kinds of beautiful appliances. Rosa rules that roost. I suppose an org chart somewhere says that I'm in charge, but that is the most shameless sham: Rosa is the boss.

Rosa started at DP in 2005, the year it opened. Initially, she was the "linen lady," meaning she'd iron tablecloths during the day and clean the bathrooms at night. There are a lot of bathrooms to clean, and tons of linens, too—it's a crappy job. The pastry chefs before me had declined Rosa's many requests to move into the kitchen. *Why would I hire someone with no experience?* It is a perfectly reasonable question.

When I started at DP, I was absolutely desperate for staff. No one wanted to work for me. I was a chucklehead, a beefsteak Charlie, a total loser. I was new to town and didn't have any connections. So one super-depressing day, a day when I was particularly forlorn, a day yanked straight from W. Somerset Maugham

that "broke gray and dull," when "the clouds hung heavily, and there was a rawness in the air that suggested snow," the banquet manager asked, "Hey, do you need people? I can transfer Rosa to pastry."

I said yes and Rosa started working with me. This was in early 2008.

Rosa is from El Salvador. She came to New York to earn money to help her family back home. She lives at the northern-most tip of Manhattan—beyond Harlem, almost in the Bronx, some street in the 200s. Her palate is impeccable. She balances salt and acid seamlessly and perfectly, like an art cultivated in the womb. She just knows.

One gnarly March day a few years ago, the morning prep team called in sick. All of them.

Except Rosa. She showed up. Rosa always shows up. *Always*.

When I arrived at 11 a.m. after a stressful and slow-moving L train voyage from Williamsburg, Brooklyn, the prep list was almost done, and Rosa had no fewer than five massive projects going simultaneously. I was floored. Her commitment to getting the job done, no matter what, is baffling. She consistently schools CIA grads and sous-chefs. Everyone who works at DP loves her to death, and she loves them back.

We don't serve this recipe at the restaurant, which doesn't make much sense because it's probably the best one. For staff meal, Rosa's biscuits are a *contorni* to Meat Loaf Day, Fried Chicken Day, even Veal-Scrap Curry Day. They defy gravity, light and delicious but somehow still hearty. I feel about these biscuits the way I feel about *Black Sabbath, Vol. 4,* and Jim Lahey's pizza Bianca loaf at Sullivan Street Bakery.

But there's a higher compliment. A few years back, one of the restaurant's Italian-national managers—*very* Italian, *very* hard to please—grabbed a couple biscuits off the family meal table, took a bite, and said the most beautiful thing I have almost ever heard within the walls of Del Posto, flakes of biscuit guano spewing from his mouth and in the best Italianate English: "This is the best thing I have ever eaten in America."

Yield: 12 biscuits

All-purpose flour 2½ cups (315 grams)
Baking powder 2½ teaspoons (11 grams)
Salt 1½ teaspoons (6 grams), plus more for sprinkling
Sugar ¾ cup (150 grams)
Unsalted butter, cold 1 cup, or 2 sticks (226 grams) cubed
Buttermilk ¾ cup (183 grams)
Melted butter for brushing

1. Preheat the oven to 350°F. Line a baking sheet with parchment paper and set aside.

2. In a large bowl, combine the flour, baking powder, salt, and sugar. Add the butter and combine using two butter knives or your fingers, being careful not to handle the butter too much. You want chunks of butter to remain. Add the buttermilk and mix with your hands until the batter just comes together, but no further.

3. Gently portion out the dough into twelve 1-inch balls and place them on the prepared baking sheet, evenly spaced. Bake until golden, about 10 minutes.

4. Brush immediately with melted butter and sprinkle with salt.

To serve: Serving them hot is all that matters.

Rosa.

4. CHOCOLATE

I feel bad for chocolate, and a lot of times I feel sorry for people who are obsessed with it. Maybe it's because I am not *that* crazy about it. What can I say? I'm a fruit guy. "Death by chocolate," or whatever the common saying is . . . that just sounds terrible.

It's an intense and complex process to get from cacao bean to ready-to-eat chocolate. It involves fermenting and traveling and roasting and grinding and on and on. I have never thought of dessert making as an art. A craft, for sure. But an art? That's going too far. Manipulating and tempering chocolate into different forms and shapes, *that* is an art. No denying that. But at that point the chocolate's flavor has already been set. That part is not going to change. Chocolatiers are artists and their medium is the chocolate. Few pastry chefs are on that level.

In her brilliant book *The Last Course*, Claudia Fleming created the most iconic chocolate dessert of them all: a chocolate and caramel tart with flakes of sea salt on top. There was a point in the early 2000s when every dessert menu in the world included a cribbed variation of her dish. That's because it is utter genius. The salt tempered the sweetness of the chocolate ganache on top and made the chocolate taste *more* like chocolate. In working with chocolate, I aim toward that end. We all do, or should. (It's her fault if nobody ever quite reaches it.)

FAKE HEALTHY CHOCOLATE CHIP COOKIES WITH LOTS OF SALT

Chocolate needs salt. Like George needed Weezy, like Joey needed Dee Dee, like Stanley needed Christiane, like Axl needed Slash. They complete each other. They can't get anything done without the other. Chocolate without salt, well, you shouldn't bother.

Once we made a batch of these cookies for a family meal and they were scarfed by the staff with the vigor of a pack of violent mountain lions chomping on a lost hiker in Big Sur. It was animalistic, raw, hilarious. And it was all about the salt. Kosher salt in this case. It feels good between your fingertips—granular, exfoliating. Chocolate's best friend.

This recipe is not that far removed from the one on the back of that bag of chocolate chips at your local supermarket. It's just got the salt boosted *to 11.* And you are not using those goddamn chips. You are getting some good chocolate, OK? Good lord, promise me that. Lastly, these cookies have a bunch of whole wheat flour, too, which might lead you to believe that they are good for you. They're not.
Yield: 24 cookies

Whole wheat flour 3½ cups (420 grams)
All-purpose flour ¾ cup (95 grams)
Baking powder 1½ teaspoons (7 grams)
Baking soda 1 teaspoon (4 grams)
Salt 2¼ teaspoons (9 grams)
Unsalted butter 1 cup, or 2 sticks (220 grams)
Granulated sugar 1 cup (200 grams)
Dark brown sugar 1 cup (220 grams), packed
Eggs 2 (110 grams)

Pure vanilla extract 2 teaspoons (8 grams)
Bittersweet chocolate, very best quality, chopped 1¼ cups (225 grams)

1. Preheat the oven to 375°F.
2. In a small bowl, combine the whole wheat flour, all-purpose flour, baking powder, baking soda, and salt.
3. In the bowl of a stand mixer, with the paddle attachment, combine the butter, granulated sugar, brown sugar, and vanilla at medium speed until creamy. Add the eggs, one at a time, beating in the first thoroughly before adding the second. Gradually add in the flour mixture. Stir in the chocolate.
4. On an ungreased baking sheet, portion out the cookie dough with a tablespoon leaving ¼ inch in between the cookies. Bake for 9 to 11 minutes, or until golden brown.

To serve: Encourage your loved ones to eat these warm, directly off the baking sheet. (But if the cookies do cool, you'll be fine—just transfer them to a cooling rack after they've set a couple minutes.)

TOFU CHOCOLATE CRÈME BRÛLÉE

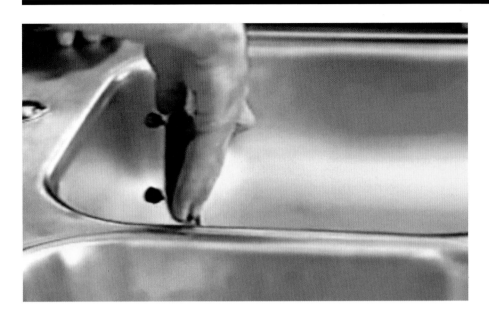

"I'm a future primitive, and I skates to live"
—Bones Brigade's *Future Primitive*

Like everyone, I have iconic things from my youth that are difficult to explain to people who didn't experience them for themselves. In the mid-eighties skateboarding had serious outlaw cachet, and although I was the worst skater to ever grace the planet, I fell in love with the iconography and culture. I pored over each issue of *Thrasher* magazine, soaking up every word, advertisement, and photograph. It was easy for a teenager from the suburbs of Baltimore to idolize professional skateboarders: They were my age and most of them were also suburban kids. Only they had escaped. There is a scene in *Future Primitive* where Tony Hawk, Lance Mountain, and Mike McGill are all sitting around a sink using their hands to do tricks with a finger-size skateboard. They look simultaneously bored and excited. To me, that is growing up in the suburbs.

Skateboarding led me to punk rock, and I quickly abandoned skating for drumming. I wasn't very good at that either, but I could fake it pretty well. I was never that nihilistic variety of punk kid. I've still never done a drug harder than weed, and I was always far away from the pit (slam dancing seems so macho and jocky, the offensive suburban stuff that I got into punk to *avoid*). So when the vegetarian siren called (via Millions of Dead Cops, Conflict, and Beefeater records), I jumped on board with enthusiasm.

Eventually, I found *The New Farm Vegetarian Cookbook*. Nearly every punk kid I'd meet on tour had a ratty-looking copy of the book in his or her kitchen. The front book jacket illustrates in a very seventies *Free to Be You and Me* pictorial style all the foodstuffs that a suburban kid wanted. There was a burger, a sad-looking burrito, a slice of cheesecake, an ice cream cone. The book is packed with unappetizing black-and-white photos of soybean ephemera and hairy hippie folk and their offspring, everyone obviously reeking of hummus and denim. The cookbook was the work of an "intentional community" (*What does that even mean? That's so cool!*) in rural Tennessee who were living off the grid and making their own food. They were future primitives. Raising little bearded babies.

My friend Christian had a signature recipe from the book: a vegan chocolate tofu pie filling that he'd pour into a store-bought Keebler piecrust (coincidentally, vegan) and top with semisweet chocolate chips. It was absolutely his thing. If you made one, his feelings would be hurt and you'd be in for it, à la Larry David: *I see you made the chocolate tofu thing, eh? Niiiiiice. Cool, cool. When, uh . . . when did you learn how to make that, huh?*

It was a tofu and chocolate pudding, really. Melt the chocolate and blend it with silken tofu in your mom's three-setting Osterizer: easy. The chocolate resets in the fridge and turns into a sliceable pudding straight from a diner dessert case. We all found it horribly impressive.

When I first arrived at Del Posto, Ladner said he wanted to devise a completely vegan tasting menu. At the time, I don't think he cared much about vegans or vegan food, but at heart the man is a student of hospitality and his guests were beginning to ask for it regularly. Best to have things ready for them.

Of course, I used the *New Farm* chocolate tofu pudding for the first Del Posto vegan dessert. Of course I did. And it worked perfectly. Rather than pour it into a crust, I smeared it on a plate, free-form, fine-dining style. The tofu-chocolate synergy firms up quite nicely, and even without a ramekin or mold to contain it, it allows you to torch the top like a crème brûlée and it keeps its shape. So you get that astonishingly satisfying super-thin crunch of burned sugar. Which plays very well with the bitterness and sweetness of the chocolate.

I always do a wavy smear, like a skateboard ramp—a ramp primed for any future primitive with a toy finger board who happens to stumble in.

Yield: 2 servings

Silken tofu one 1-pound container (453 grams)
Salt ¼ teaspoon (1 gram)
Pure vanilla extract 1 teaspoon (4 grams)
Dark brown sugar 2 tablespoons (25 grams)
Bittersweet chocolate, very best quality, chopped 2 cups (264 grams)
Granulated sugar for sprinkling
Croutons (page 132) for serving (optional)

1. In a blender, combine the tofu, salt, vanilla, and brown sugar and blend until smooth.

2. In a medium microwavable bowl, melt the chocolate in the microwave in 20-second intervals until it is completely smooth. Take care not to burn the chocolate. (If you don't have a microwave, use a double boiler.)

3. Add the melted chocolate to the tofu mixture and blend until fully incorporated. Pour the brûlée into ramekins and set in your refrigerator for about 1 hour.

To serve: Smear an irregular chocolate pudding wave onto a plate and sprinkle with granulated sugar. Using a propane torch, melt the sugar into a crackly crust as you would for crème brûlée. Garnish with croutons if you want. Alternately, just eat this as a pudding.

MOLTEN CHOCOLATE CAKE

Molten chocolate cake is an outstanding but justifiably maligned dessert. It doesn't have to, but most of the time it completely sucks. In a busy restaurant, it's rare you'll be served a fresh-baked version. More often than not, you'll get an hours- or even days-old specimen. Chefs think the MCC is corny, a cop-out, aiming for the lowest common denominator. But customers love it. You have to serve it straight out of the oven for it to transcend its cornball status.

For the opening menu at Orsone in Friuli, Italy, my team and I brought the cake out of retirement. We did it intentionally *wrong*, without the creamy core: Sorry, folks, it's baked through. It's also not intact. It's a fudgy lump with a crisp cookie hat. It looks like a cupcake with the top sabered off. I once did a short stint at a Ritz-Carlton and I can hear my French pastry chef bosses there bellowing in broken English: *"Eet separated, eez wrong! Make eet again! Will you be a shoemaker your whole life? Make eet nice or make eet twice."* It's better this way, François.

Yield: 6 cupcake-size cakes

Bittersweet chocolate, very best quality, chopped ½ cup (130 grams)
High-quality unsweetened cocoa powder 2½ tablespoons (14 grams)
Powdered sugar 2½ tablespoons (14 grams)
Salt 2¼ teaspoons (9 grams)
Granulated sugar ⅔ cup plus ¼ cup (120 grams plus 43 grams)
Unsalted butter ⅓ cup, or ⅔ stick (80 grams)
Eggs 3, separated
Bread Crumbs (page 133) 1 cup (70 grams)
Olive Oil Gelato (page 216) 1 scoop

1. Preheat the oven to 350°F. Spray the insides of a 6-cup cupcake tin with nonstick cooking spray and set aside.

2. In a medium microwavable bowl, melt the chocolate in the microwave in 30-second intervals, stirring in between to ensure that the chocolate doesn't scorch. (If you don't have a microwave, use a double boiler.) Set aside to cool.

3. In the bowl of a stand mixer, using the paddle attachment, combine the cocoa powder, powdered sugar, and salt at medium speed. Add ⅔ cup of the granulated sugar and the butter. The batter will look very grainy. Add the egg yolks and continue mixing until the batter is creamy and well incorporated, about 5 minutes.

4. Transfer the batter to a medium bowl and, with a rubber spatula, mix in the cooled chocolate. Set aside until ready to use. Clean the bowl and whip attachment of the stand mixer.

5. In the clean bowl of the stand mixer, using the whip attachment, combine the egg whites and the remaining ¼ cup sugar on medium speed until you have stiff, shiny peaks.

6. Sacrifice a scoop of meringue to the batter and, using a rubber spatula, incorporate well. This will lighten the batter up and prepare it for the remaining egg whites. Gently fold in the remaining egg whites.

7. Fill the cupcake cups two-thirds of the way with batter. Bake for 11 minutes. The cake will look like a soufflé; the top will be thin and crunchy, and the inside will be soft, moist, and collapsed.

To serve: Separate the cookie-like top from the fudgy moist center. Roll the fudgy bottom in the bread crumbs. Put the cookie back on the bread crumb–covered bottom and serve with a scoop of olive oil gelato.

See page 215.

See page 136.

PROFILE IN COURAGE:

Claudia Fleming

Born: Saturday, April 11

Occupation: Pastry chef and co-owner, The North Fork Table & Inn and The North Fork Food Truck

Status: Committed

Notable Quote: "You want *me* to count that clusterfuck?"

Shoe size: 7

Lunch food: I don't eat lunch.

Beverage: Vodka and grapefruit

I Heart NY: More than anywhere I've ever been

First time: Makes the greatest impression

Accomplishments: Finishing the NYC marathon

Ambition/future plan: Continue makin' tasty eats

Brad Kintzer is the chocolate maker behind TCHO, among my favorite brands of chocolate in the world. Having studied as a botanist before becoming a chocolatier, he knows more about the production of the stuff than anyone.

CIOCCOLATA, SCHOKOLADE, COKOLADA, CHOCOLAT, CHOCOLATE

by Brad Kintzer

Although chocolate eclipses nearly every other food and drink in global appeal, we know embarrassingly little about it. The fact is today our depth of understanding of how to control the quality of chocolate is decades behind other well-researched foods and drinks, such as wine, beer, and cheese. The level of our collective ignorance is dizzying.

Rather than focusing on what *makes* chocolate good (and what makes it better), laboratory and social scientists have historically been interested in figuring out what it is about this beloved foodstuff that short-circuits people's emotional control systems. (They tend also to ignore the horrific conditions under which it is usually produced.) A few inadequately comprehensive theories still prevail:

Chocolate is a deep-rooted comfort food. Its distinctive aromas and flavors teleport us back to the deep recesses of our earliest memories of chocolate.

Chocolate is romantic neuroscience. Buried in every bite are complex cocktails of naturally occurring psychotropic chemicals, including phenethylamine, or PEA, the same chemical that surges when we fall in love.

Chocolate is sensual. The fat used in making chocolate—cocoa butter—has immensely unique melting properties that allow the silky, slow delivery of cocoa's +/-800 kaleidoscopic flavor notes.

Chocolate saves. Some say our bodies subconsciously crave the staggeringly high quantities of heart-healthy polyphenols and other micronutrients that can be found in darker chocolates.

Chocolate is a happy amphetamine (see page 47). Society's growing dependence on sugar, the most common bedfellow of cocoa, plays a massive role in our relationship with chocolate.

Scientists concede that all these factors, along with several others, contribute to our understanding of—and obsession with—chocolate. But none of them help us unlock the ingredient's secret powers. Fortunately, the approach for getting to the bottom of pivotal questions regarding chocolate is already established: We need only follow the examples set by producers of wine, beer, and cheese to get real answers about how to understand and make better chocolate.

Wine, for example, has long had its genetic varietals meticulously mapped out and they are readily available for farmers to plant. Winemakers can search geographic overlays of latitude, soil nutrient composition, temperature, sun exposure, and other variables of their specific planting site, then order up the clones or root stock that they know will grow best and yield the best fruit.

By contrast, the genetic taxonomy of cacao is only slowly being sorted out. (For the uninitiated, *cacao* refers to the bean as it grows on the cacao tree. *Cocoa*, on the other hand, is the ingredient created after the cacao bean has been processed.) New varietals were recently discovered and categorized in cacao's native Amazon basin and Central America. Who knows what flavors, yields, and other contributions to the world of chocolate these and other undiscovered varietals can and will make? It is likely they will be enormous.

Winemakers also have the luxury of being able to scroll through designer yeast and microbial cocktail catalogs for precise and repeatable fermentation results. Fermentation of cacao, like wine, is the key to unlocking the complexity and balance of flavor. But cocoa's fermentation mechanism, how it drives flavor, is just beginning to be fully understood. Most of the world's cocoa fermentation is done by making simple cocoa piles that are then covered by banana leaves and left to sit—worlds away from the thousands of glycol-cooled fermentation tanks throughout the pristine wine-making region of Napa Valley.

One of the principal hurdles to improving chocolate quality and innovation is that cocoa, unlike grapes, is typically grown thousands of miles away from where it is made into its finished form. There is a massive disconnect between those who are growing cocoa (Southern Hemisphere) and those who are buying it and making chocolate (mostly in the Northern Hemisphere). Closing these huge geographic, technological, cultural, and socioeconomic (another essay entirely) gaps is the key to a lot of future chocolate innovation and quality improvement.

Most people are shocked to learn that many cacao farmers have never tasted any form of chocolate. One unique and rare way of clearing cultural and quality hurdles is by teaching cacao farmers how to make and critically taste their own chocolate made from their own cocoa. It is always a mind-altering experience when cacao farmers learn the process through hands-on training: When they begin connecting the dots, seeing how what they do on the farm level directly impacts the cocoa quality and how that quality is directly linked to price premiums, they become exponentially more driven toward delivering it. They are eager to learn how to improve their cocoa, and this kind of change can yield only good things for chocolate lovers.

Led by millions of loyal buyers, fine chocolate is only now undergoing its own age of enlightenment.

CHOCOLATE TREE

I was not the first person to pour tempered chocolate into ice to create a "tree." I wasn't even the second or third. Maybe eighty-eighth or something. It's like that old *Saturday Night Live* skit where Steve Martin goes to heaven and asks Saint Peter to reveal the one fact that will shock him more than any other, and Saint Peter says, "Oh, I can't tell you. You couldn't handle it." So Steve asks, "OK, what about the eighty-eighth?"

"Professional wrestling is real."

On a busy weekend at Del Posto, we plow through a ton of these trees. We ornament them with a few different kinds of chocolate candies and whisk them out to tables celebrating weddings, anniversaries, birthdays. Or maybe to a table that didn't like their lamb, or had to wait to be seated. Chocolate trees exist to punctuate or save the night.

But chocolate trees are also huge pains in the ass. They're difficult to construct and annoying to transport. They're messy to eat, too—which I actually love. Chef Cesare Casella once deliberately flipped one over at his table, raining chocolate everywhere, and then proceeded to punch the lopsided base, smashing it into pure chaos all over the linen. It was hilarious.

Dead.

Building them during dinner service is a tightrope affair. Each one is unique and you have to find the right nooks and crevices in which to stuff the candies and shards to make the tree look alive. In the past I've had cooks who built really bad trees that had zero personality—trees with a bunch of chocolate junk just leaning against it. One fellow in particular built trees that literally looked stoned and exhausted. This drives me insane. It's the one thing that sends me running around the kitchen like a psychopath: *Make it look alive! Make it look scary! Make it look like it's jumping off a cliff!*

Roger Rodriguez, a former sous-chef and chocolatier, used to be in charge of pouring kilo upon kilo of chocolate into ice to keep our trees in stock. On Sunday mornings (Roger's Monday), he'd arrive refreshed from a relaxing Friday and Saturday off and often say, "How many fucking trees did you guys sell last night?! It's straight up deforestation in here."
Yield: However many weird-size trees you decide to make

Chocolate, very best quality, chopped into
    small pieces 3½ cups (450 grams)
Big bowl of irregularly crushed ice chunks

Alive.

156

1. In a microwavable bowl, zap 3 cups of the chocolate in the microwave in 30-second intervals, being careful not to burn the chocolate. If you burn it, believe me, you will know—it'll smell really bad. (If you don't have a microwave, use a double boiler.) Bring it up to 120°F and then add the remaining ½ cup chocolate. The addition of the chopped chocolate will cool down the microwaved mixture. Let it come down to 81°F.

2. Reheat the chocolate in the microwave gently in 5-second spurts to bring it back up to 85°F. At this point your chocolate will be in temper and you can pour it over the ice, making sure to drizzle it into the crevices. Working quickly, make free-form shapes inside the cracked ice. The chocolate will set as soon as it hits the ice.

3. Allow the chocolate to rest in the ice for 15 minutes. Gently remove it, using a paring knife to pick out any remaining pieces of ice. Allow the chocolate to drain upside down until completely dry. Store, tightly wrapped in plastic, in a cool, dry area, for up to two weeks.

To serve: We put all sorts of other weird and complicated chocolate pieces and candies in ours and there are no real rules (see the opposite page). Decorate yours however you'd like.

Roger tempering the chocolate sans microwave.

Elephants fucking on your dad's grave.

CARAMELIZED CHOCOLATE GELATO

This is not chocolate gelato for a ten-year-old's birthday party. Unless you *hate* the kid. In that case make him a sundae with this.

I can tell you that my Strawberry Gelato (page 212) is all gloss and rainbows and newborn puppies stumbling around on the beach on the best summer day. But this stuff is dark and bitter, brooding, a gelato that resides in the Norwegian forest wearing matte-finish corpse paint, black fading into gray. That's why it's in this section, far away from those other, friendly gelatos.

Caramelizing the sugar has two effects: It helps the gelato stay stretchy and smooth and it makes the gelato taste *less* sweet (which is a bit odd because we are *adding* sugar). I toss in two types of cocoa powder to make it feel a little chalky—the way a Fudgsicle tastes a little chalky. Except this is the mean *Rosemary's Baby* Fudgsicle made by the weird neighbors. *Yield: 1½ quarts*

Water ½ cup (118 grams)
Sugar 1 cup (200 grams)
Whole milk 1 quart (1,000 grams)
Heavy cream 6 tablespoons (100 grams)
Milk chocolate 6 tablespoons (50 grams)
Bittersweet chocolate, very best quality, chopped 1 cup (125 grams)
Dextrose 1 tablespoon (25 grams)
Low-fat milk powder ⅓ cup (25 grams)
Light cocoa powder ¼ cup (25 grams)
Dark cocoa powder 5 tablespoons (38 grams)
Salt to taste

1. In a small saucepan over medium-high heat, combine the water and sugar, stir until dissolved, then leave the sugar alone and allow it to darken in color (caramelize). When the sides of the pan become dark, swirl the caramel to mix it in—do not stick any type of utensil in it or you will probably ruin the process.

2. Whisk the milk and cream into the caramel. (This stuff is hot. There will be steam. Be super careful.) When the milk and cream are incorporated into the caramel, bring the mixture to a boil, or wait until the caramel is melted, about 2 minutes.

3. In a large bowl, prepare an ice bath.

4. In another large bowl, combine the milk chocolate and dark chocolate and pour in the hot milk–caramel infusion. The chocolate will melt very quickly. Allow the mixture to sit for a few minutes and the hot caramel will do the work for you.

5. Add the milk powder, light cocoa powder, dark cocoa powder, and salt, and combine using an immersion blender.

6. Set the bowl in the ice bath. Let the mixture cool, cover the bowl with plastic wrap, and refrigerate for at least 3 hours. If you have time, place the mixture in an airtight container and refrigerate overnight.

7. Spin the gelato in an ice cream machine according to the manufacturer's instructions. Or use the dry-ice method in your stand mixer (see page 210).

CHOCOLATE COATING

This coating is so simple and so perfect I find myself trying to build recipes around it. The cocoa butter makes it like Magic Shell, hardening the instant it hits something frozen. *Yield: 3 cups*

Bittersweet chocolate, very best quality, chopped 2 cups (250 grams)
Unsweetened chocolate, 100%, very best quality, chopped ⅓ cup (50 grams)
Cocoa butter 1⅓ cups (300 grams)
Extra-virgin olive oil 1 tablespoon (15 grams)
Salt to taste

In a large microwavable bowl, melt the chocolate and cocoa butter in the microwave in 30-second intervals, making sure it doesn't burn. (If you don't have a microwave, use a double boiler.) Whisk in the olive oil and salt.

To serve: This is used with Tartufo al Caffè (page 165), Bastoncino (page 217), and Free-Form Caramelized Chocolate Truffles (page 163). If you'd like, create your own uses for it.

Sloane Crosley is the author of I Was Told There'd Be Cake, *which came out in 2008, the year I started at Del Posto. It's a funny book of essays that I've read eight times. Sloane and I are on the board of directors for the Housing Works bookstore in SoHo, and we're always the two who somehow get out of every board meeting with a poor excuse like "I'm moving that day" or "I have band practice." She is currently writing a novel.*

TASTE BUDS by Sloane Crosley

Taste buds look like ball sacks. They really do. Bud sacks. And your mouth is just covered in them.

The sweet ones are right up front, in the tongue's luxury box seats. So now when someone says they have an amazing story or a factoid that was "on the tip of my tongue," you can go ahead and assume they're thinking of something or someone pleasant. I shouldn't know anything about taste buds. I shouldn't know how they work or what they look like. You, a total stranger, should be able to trick me into believing that all taste buds are shaped like Elvis's profile. Alas, I have seen too much.

I became entranced with taste buds during freshman year of college, when I attended an Intro to Chemistry lecture. (Let the record show that after being formally "introduced," chemistry and I instantly started seeing other people.) In trying to educate a bunch of would-be bohemian liberal-arts students about chemical bonds, the professor told us a story about a guy he knew who had developed a chemical compound for an artificial sweetener. Apparently, the team of chemists behind this now-famous sweetener made it *too* perfect. The flavinoids or enzymes or what have you imitated brilliantly the compound that we all know as sugar. Too brilliantly. More brilliantly than nature intended.

As early trials for this sugar in drag began, the artificial sweetener was dosed onto the taste receptors of a group of volunteer schlubs. (Who signs up to eat fake sugar? What personal life events had to be canceled in favor of sucking chemicals off a Popsicle stick? Come to think of it, that doesn't sound so bad.) The volunteers apparently got more than they bargained for. Instead of simply recognizing the delightful presence of "sweet" and moving on, the sweetener locked into their taste buds. These people had the taste of sugar lodged on their tongues for weeks. Weeks of tasting nothing but sugar.

Years after my Intro to Chemistry class, the "miracle fruit" (a berry) became trendy for temporarily altering the taste of everything consumed in its wake. There were *Wall Street Journal* and *New York Times* articles on the subject. You say you want to turn "making lemons into lemonade" from an expression to a reality? The miracle fruit is the way to go. It's the real deal, despite the silly name. But unlike with the artificial sweetener, the effects are short-lived. They pass quickly, and then you're back to being you. Your tongue is your tongue. Eggplant tastes like eggplant again.

When the miracle fruit became popular, I remembered the volunteers who taste tested the too-perfect sweetener. I remembered the sympathy I felt for them. What would happen to me if day after day I tasted nothing but sweetness? Would I start punching people at random? Would I rip mustard greens from the ground and gnaw at them psychotically, roots and all? How long before I started eating paprika and rocks for breakfast? I don't know.

What I do know is that I love sugar. I love the time it spends with me when I consume it. I love that it generally leaves me wanting more. Whatever's going on with my tongue, I have "sweet teeth" lining both sides. I love sugar so much that even knowing what I know, I *still* wouldn't mind trying the faulty sweetener. Especially if it were presented as a "would you rather" scenario. Would you rather be condemned to weeks of tasting bitter, sour, or sweet? Or, God help us all, "earthy"?

Maybe the correct answer—the austere answer—is bitter. Maybe that's the key to maintaining sanity under these hypothetical conditions. But I don't fantasize about bitter. Bitter didn't send me to the college library to look up taste bud diagrams. Rather, I fantasize about a meal of sweets, about a steak made of chocolate ganache with lavender marshmallow grizzle and a salad of caramel strings drizzled in honey and garnished with whipped cream and cookie dough that crumbles over onto a helping of mashed key lime pie and poached pears that dissolve on the tongue. Suck on *that*, bud sacks.

FREE-FORM CARAMELIZED CHOCOLATE TRUFFLES

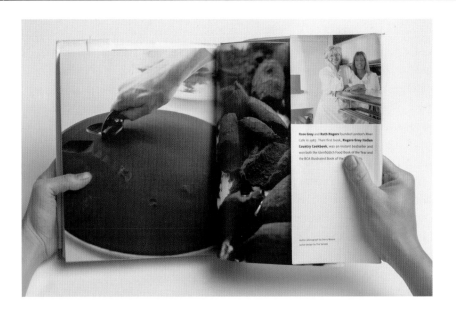

Pastry chefs spend a lot of time thinking about chocolate. I don't. In the food pyramid of my mind, chocolate is the smallest quadrant. I love it, but in reasonable portions, kind of like the thrash band Slayer. I can usually get only halfway through *Reign in Blood* before I'm like, "OK, OK, I get it. Next." And that record is only twenty-nine minutes long.

When I started at Del Posto, I had planned on putting some fancy molded chocolates on the cookie plate. This meant acquiring polycarbonate molds, which are expensive and hard to keep clean (chocolate is greasy!). Plus tempering chocolate is a scientific skill that requires exacting attention and lots of boring stirring—not my favorite thing to do. But when chocolate is perfectly tempered, it sets and has a very pleasing snap—if spread on acetate or molded in polycarbonate plastic, it takes on the shiny surface of the mold. It is what is known as *good chocolate work*, and accomplishing it is a badge of honor for most

every pastry chef in the world. Some of us don't get that badge.

When I approached Ladner with my perfectly tempered chocolate bonbons, he glanced at them deadpan and flicked one into his mouth. Without looking up from his phone, he said, "Fuck, it's sweet. And can you make it less shiny? Looks fucking industrial," and then went back to some very serious business on his mobile device. This was a huge relief. I had made only ten tiny pieces and it had taken all morning. I possess neither the skill nor the desire to make that kind of chocolate work into a daily routine.

I remembered a free-form chocolate truffle recipe from one of the River Café cookbooks that was rustic, totally don't-give-a-shit Italian, and completely beautiful. I combined that aesthetic with a caramel ganache recipe I had and I was done. These are the least shiny chocolate candies in New York City, for sure. *Yield: At least 24 truffles*

Sugar 2 cups (400 grams)
Heavy cream 1½ cups (357 grams)
Bittersweet chocolate, very best quality,
    chopped 3 cups (940 grams)
Unsalted butter ¼ cup, or ½ stick (57 grams)
Salt to taste
Natural unsweetened cocoa powder 1 cup
    (86 grams)

1. Place a large heavy saucepan over high heat for 20 seconds. Add the sugar. It should start smoking and caramelizing immediately. Swirl the pan to avoid hot spots until the caramel is almost black. (But not quite! Your smoke alarm might go off, but it's OK.) Remove the sugar from the heat and add the cream. Be careful: It will bubble up violently.

2. Return the mixture to low heat and cook, stirring constantly, until you have a caramel sauce, about 2 minutes.

3. In a medium bowl, combine the chopped chocolate and the warm caramel and emulsify using an immersion blender. Add the butter and blend until shiny. Go easy: You can overmix it at this point. Add the salt, stir, pour the mixture into an air-tight plastic container, and refrigerate for at least 4 hours, preferably overnight.

4. Use your finger to pull out irregular shapes and toss the truffles in the cocoa powder.

To serve: Serve immediately or store in a sealed container for up to 1 week.

TARTUFO AL CAFFÉ

A *tartufo* dessert is traditionally a ball of hazelnut gelato stuffed with syrupy dark amarena cherries and coated in chocolate. It is meant to mimic a black truffle, but it's a bit too perfect. A truffle is bumpy and awkward, with divots and holes. In comparison, a typical tartufo seems mass produced.

I hate doing things the perfect way, so I set out to make a tartufo that actually looked like a truffle. Lidia Bastianich, another of my bosses, had been gently encouraging me to put a coffee dessert on the menu, and so far I had been shooting blanks. This was my opportunity.

I wanted to make a *semifreddo* (an Italian frozen mousse) flavored with ground coffee beans. I've never been an avid coffee drinker—the stuff actually makes every part of my body, from my brain to my heart to my joints, feel insane. So I did what any new employee would do. I asked the chef.

Before Del Posto, Ladner was the chef and menu mastermind at Lupa, Manhattan's phenomenal West Village restaurant where I had my first tartufo. An encyclopedia of all things Lazio—the Italian region where Rome resides—he began telling me about Sant' Eustachio Il Caffè, in the heart of the city, right around the corner from the Pantheon. The Pantheon as a structure is crazy. I was bummed to find that it's now a church. It's a pagan monolith, un-churchlike in every way. In any case, Sant' Eustachio is Ladner's favorite joint in Rome to grab an espresso and he waxed poetically about the baristas and how their stations are guarded carefully by pieces of cardboard so snoopy customers can't wit-

ness their cup work. He spoke slowly and methodically, describing in detail Sant' Eustachio's otherworldly *crema,* the frothy head on espresso. I don't give a shit about coffee lore, but I was completely rapt. Ladner has enviable storytelling talents.

We ordered some Sant' Eustachio beans in from Rome to flavor our semifreddo. It pleased the conceptual quadrant of my brain to no end. The semifreddo was excellent. We poked and prodded the frozen base quickly, making a massively irregular shape rather than a perfect globe. We dipped it into a Magic Shell–like chocolate and set the tartufo, just like a real truffle. It was fun, and there were no molds in sight. My inner Italian grandma beamed.

A few years later, when I finally got to visit Rome, I went sightseeing at the Pantheon at the crack of dawn, well before the mobs of tourists descended. It was quiet and peaceful. I sought out Sant' Eustachio through the pretzeled streets, found the counter, and drank a supremely frothy espresso. I was psyched. I walked across the street, bought a map, and returned to Sant' Eustachio to study it. I sat on one of the empty patio chairs for a half second to figure out the route to Campo dè Fiori. The barista came outside, pointed at me, and told me with a very efficient Italian-style hand motion and violent twisting of his lips to *get the fuck out . . . now.*

(Note: These take 2 days, owing to freezing times.)
Yield: 15 to 20 tartufos

STEEPED COFFEE CREAM

Espresso, absolute best quality, ground
   ¾ cup (83 grams)
Salt to taste
Zest from ½ lemon
Heavy cream 1⅓ cups (333 grams)

1. In a small saucepan over medium heat, combine the coffee, salt, lemon zest, and cream and bring to a boil, whisking occasionally. When the mixture starts to boil, remove it from the heat.

2. Let the coffee cream cool to room temperature on the countertop, then transfer it to an airtight container and refrigerate overnight.

TARTUFO MOUSSE

Steeped coffee cream, strained (above)
Heavy cream 1⅓ cups (333 grams)
Egg whites 6 (166 grams)
Sugar ⅔ cup plus 1⅔ cups (133 grams plus
   325 grams)
Egg yolks 11 (200 grams)
Chocolate Coating (page 160)

1. Get a baking sheet into your freezer somehow and let it get good and cold.

2. In the bowl of a stand mixer, using the whip attachment, combine the steeped coffee cream, heavy cream, egg whites, and ⅔ cup of the sugar at medium speed until you have stiff peaks. Transfer the mixture to a separate bowl, cover with plastic wrap, and refrigerate until needed. Rinse out the bowl and the whip attachment.

3. In the bowl of the stand mixer, using the whip attachment, combine the egg yolks and the remaining 1⅔ cups sugar at medium speed until the egg yolks are pale and shiny. Fold the yolks into the coffee whipped cream with a rubber spatula, cover with plastic wrap, and freeze overnight.

4. Wearing latex gloves, grab a big scoop of the frozen coffee mousse and mold it with your hands into a free-form lump, about 1½ inches around. Place it on the frozen baking sheet in your empty freezer, and continue until all the mousse is formed. Freeze for 1 hour. Dip each tartufo in the chocolate coating, reserving the rest for serving, and freeze overnight.

CURED LEMON

Lemon 1
Sugar 8 teaspoons (33 grams)
Salt 1 teaspoon (4 grams)

1. Spray a baking sheet with nonstick cooking spray, attach a piece of parchment to it, and place it in the freezer.

2. Trim the ends off the lemon and cut it in half lengthwise. With the sharpest knife you have, cut the thinnest pieces of lemon flesh you can, like slices of prosciutto.

3. In a medium bowl, combine the sliced lemon, sugar, and salt and coat with your fingers. These will store for 1 day.

FOR SERVING

Croutons (page 132)

To serve: Put some of the reserved chocolate coating on a plate and top with a tartufo. Add some croutons and a couple irregular slivers of cured lemon on top. Eat straight away.

See page 25.

BAND TOUR FOOD DIARY: SKULL KONTROL

Zzzzz Skull Kontrol, 2000

By the time I joined Skull Kontrol, I'd started drinking alcohol, and our tour in 1998 was my first as a non-teetotaler. I have to admit, it changed the whole dynamic. In the past, with Young Pioneers, for example, if we played at a bar (a rarity), we would all give our drink tickets to Marty, the bass player. The night always ended with Marty blacked out in a fetal position in the back of the van.

On one tour, Skull Kontrol did the entire country in two and a half weeks. That's beyond fast. By the time we had arrived in a new town, we were more concerned with beer than food—at that pace, it's not really possible to be food vigilant. Our guitarist, Andy, was obsessed with Taco Bell, so we ate there a lot. At least Taco Bells are easy to identify from the highway, so it wasn't especially time-consuming. We had a thousand Veggie Delite sandwiches from Subway, in Colorado, say, or Wyoming. To this day the yeast-and-soured-pickle smell of Subway inspires in me both nostalgia and nausea. We became expert navigators of Flying J truck stops near the truck driver showers and the convenience store auto-parts sections, neither of which was known for having stellar produce. It all sounds negative, but it wasn't at all. With Skull Kontrol, there was also a marked increase in the number of females attending the shows. It had everything to do with Kim Thompson, our radical bass player. Understandably, these ladies would storm the stage after shows to talk to her; she's still the best.

One morning, as we sat in our sleeping bags eating spaghetti pomodoro on his living room floor, Corey Rusk, of Touch and Go Records, asked if he could put out a Skull Kontrol record. The details were discussed as I admired his professional-style kitchen (lots of stainless-steel surfaces). It was 1998 and I'd still never stepped foot in a professional kitchen. We eventually did two records with Corey, but the band was already winding down.

It was in this era that I'd started wearing a threadbare Joy Division shirt inside out. Don't ask. I have no recollection of why. It was 1998.

After our final show, in the summer of 1999, we drove straight from Chicago home to DC. It was during an intense summer heatwave, and it was sixteen hours of no fun and lots of gummy bears, pretzels, and Dr Peppers from the gas station. We arrived back in DC and went straight to the Raven Bar and Grill, our favorite Mount Pleasant spot. There was no grill. They didn't serve food. Which sums up Skull Kontrol's relationship to food nicely.

A few months after Skull Kontrol split up, in September 1999, I got my first real kitchen job at Galileo in Washington, DC. Arriving at my interview in a suit, carrying a faked résumé with content that would have been of no use for anyone (I said I worked at the University of Maryland food co-op making tofu and sprouted bean sandwiches), I talked my way into the job. Laurie Alleman-Weber, the pastry chef at the time, took a massive leap of faith and I signed on to work for seven bucks an hour. I was twenty-seven years old. It was technically my first real job. I finally had an occupation.

Walking into the Galileo kitchen, I knew instantly that I was going to be a cook for the rest of my life. It was as if a higher force tapped me on the shoulder and said, "Fuck it, man. Here you are." My initials are BOH—in restaurant terminology "back of house," where the kitchen staff resides. Back then I had no business being in a fine-dining kitchen. But I took the job as performance art. I never spoke to anyone in the kitchen about playing in a band. The cooks and chefs were of the old school variety, and I was a painfully quiet and shy weirdo, there to learn the ways of the fine-dining kitchen. And at the time, unless I had been in Pearl Jam or Alice in Chains (or some other cookie-cutter hair outfit), none of the staff would have given a shit anyway.
(Continued on page 192.)

CHOCOLATE-COVERED HONEYCOMB

This goes in the cookie box at Del Posto. If it is even the slightest bit humid outside, it won't work. (Don't try.) I learned to make this in Los Angeles, at Campanile, where during family meal the entire kitchen left for a smoke break, even the dishwashers (dishwashers are usually way too smart to be smokers). It was weird. That was the first time in my career where the smokers outnumbered the nonsmokers. The perfectly airy chunk of honeycomb has a slightly smoky quality, like a campfire—and maybe, to me at least, the alley behind Campanile at 4:30 p.m.

Yield: 1 big blob of honeycomb, about a baking sheet's worth

Sugar 1½ cups (300 grams)
Water ¼ cup (60 grams)
Corn syrup ½ cup (82 grams)
Baking soda 1 tablespoon (13 grams)
Bittersweet chocolate, very best quality, chopped 1½ cups (200 grams)

1. Line a baking sheet with a Silpat and set aside.

2. In a medium deep-sided saucepan over medium-low heat, mix the sugar, water, and corn syrup, making sure there's no sugar on the sides of the pot (otherwise it will crystallize). Cook until it reaches a light caramel, tan but not brown, about 15 minutes.

3. Whisk in the baking soda for 1 second. The caramel will bubble up to the top of the pan. Remove from the heat and, in a single motion, pour the bubbling caramel mixture onto the prepared baking sheet. The bubbles create the aerated, textured interior of the honeycomb. Let it cool completely, undisturbed. If you touch it or even look at it for too long, it will collapse and be ruined.

4. Using a paring knife, break the honeycomb into as many irregular chunks as you can while maintaining the airy, holed structure. There will be a lot left over—throw it out or eat it.

5. In a small microwavable bowl, melt the chocolate in the microwave in 30-second intervals, stirring in between so it doesn't scorch. (If you don't have a microwave, use a double boiler.)

6. Using a fork, gently dip the chunks of honeycomb into the chocolate to coat and return them to the baking sheet to cool. Store in an airtight container in the freezer for up to one week. The honeycombs will last for only 1 day at room temperature before they start to crack. After 2 days, they'll stop being crunchy, so eat them in a day if you aren't freezing them.

To serve: There's not all that much you can do to present this. It is its own beautiful thing. Put it on a plate and share.

TORTA CAPRESE

Torta Caprese is an Italian brownie, named for the island of Capri, and this is a very traditional version. It's easy as hell, but like everything else in this book, it requires really nice chocolate. It relies on walnuts and the superpowers of egg whites for structural support.

Torta Caprese is also naturally 100 percent gluten free, making it perfect for Passover or for that friend who is not eating gluten for whatever *very* real or totally imagined reason. *Yield: One baking sheet of brownies*

Bittersweet chocolate, very best quality, chopped 1½ cups (200 grams)
Walnuts, chopped 1¾ cups (200 grams)
Sugar ¾ cup plus ¼ cup (150 grams plus 50 grams)
Salt 2 teaspoons (8 grams)
Unsalted butter ⅔ cup, or 1⅓ sticks (155 grams), melted
Eggs 4, separated

1. Preheat the oven to 325°F.

2. In a food processor, pulse together the chocolate, walnuts, ¾ cup of the sugar, and the salt until you have chunks of chocolate and walnut that are not huge but not totally obliterated either. You don't want a paste. Avoid that.

3. Transfer the chocolate mixture to a large mixing bowl. Add the butter and mix well with a rubber spatula. Add the egg yolks and stir to combine. Set this chocolate mixture aside.

4. In the bowl of a stand mixer, using the whip attachment, beat the egg whites on medium speed, slowly adding the remaining ¼ cup sugar and beating continuously until the whites have a meringue-like texture. Do not overwhip.

5. Fold the whites gently into the chocolate mixture and pour the batter onto a baking sheet. Bake until golden, 20 to 25 minutes, or until a toothpick inserted into the center comes out clean.

6. Let the cake cool in the pan and cut it into chunks. This also freezes beautifully, and will last for up to 2 months. Just thaw and serve.

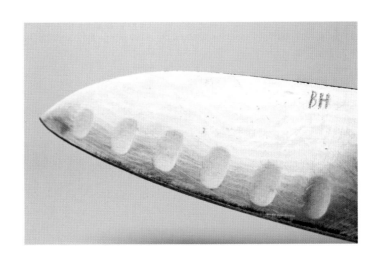

5. SEEDS & NUTS

Nut allergies make me very nervous. As the pastry chef at a highly regarded Italian restaurant in New York City, guests rely on me not to kill them. Sending a guest to the hospital at the final stage of his or her meal is the ultimate act of un-hospitality. That's the opposite of my job description. It's my nightmare.

In Italian cooking there are different kinds of nuts and seeds everywhere: sesame, hazelnuts, almonds, walnuts, chestnuts galore. Sicilia is all about sesame seeds. I am in love with their versatile nature: I can use them whole, chopped, ground into paste, sliced . . . usually roasted, but sometimes raw. They pair wonderfully with extra-virgin olive oil and browned butter. Salt them heavily and you have an umami bomb ready to go. Caramel and honey love them as much as I do.

In the winter, when fruit is scarce, I turn to nuts and seeds to help break open the menu, and then, just as I'm getting cozy, I see that a guest with a nut allergy is due and I get really freaked out. If you have a nut allergy, please skip to the next chapter. I'm sorry. I know you can't help it. It's just . . . Oh God. Just, please . . . move along. For me?

SESAME ANISE STICKS

Sesames are the anarchists of seeds. They have no gods, no masters. They are occasionally pummeled into submission for tahini, sure, but mostly they do their own lawless thing. And as a coating . . . well, maybe they stick, maybe they don't.

A Big Marty's hamburger bun, something widely available on the East Coast, has hundreds of sesame seeds grafted to the top of it. They aren't toasted or anything, but somehow they never fall off, not even as you bite into the bun. How many sesame seeds are consumed by humans annually, and how many end up on the floor of the kitchen or car, do you think?

Here is a variation on the classic NYC Italian bakery sesame cookie, only smaller. Not a monster Stella D'oro breakfast snack kind of thing, but a single bite. Something you could buy at Court Pastry Shop in Brooklyn.

I like to crush up anise seeds, incorporate them into the dough, and then fleck the cookie with whole sesame seeds before baking. The pummeled anise seeds never had a chance, and the sesame yearns for your floor mats. Anise is licorice-y. You hate licorice? Give it a chance.

Yield: Depends on the size of the cookie cutter

Unsalted butter ½ pound, or 2 sticks (227 grams)
Sugar ¾ cup (150 grams)
Egg 1 (50 grams)
All-purpose flour 2½ cups (275 grams)
Salt ½ teaspoon (2 grams)
Baking powder ½ teaspoon (2 grams)
Anise seeds, toasted and ground 2 tablespoons (18 grams)

Whole milk as needed
Sesame seeds, toasted, for dredging

1. Preheat the oven to 350°F.

1. In the bowl of a stand mixer, using the paddle attachment, combine the butter and sugar at medium speed until creamy. Add the egg and combine. Add the flour, salt, baking powder, and anise seeds and combine.

2. Transfer the dough to another clean bowl and cover with plastic wrap. Refrigerate the dough until it becomes firm and is easier to work with, about 30 minutes.

3. With a rolling pin, roll out the dough to ¼-inch thickness. Cut the dough into the shapes of your choice, dip them into milk, and dredge them in toasted sesame seeds. Bake for about 12 minutes, until golden brown. Transfer to a cooling rack and let cool for a few minutes. These will keep in an airtight container for a few days.

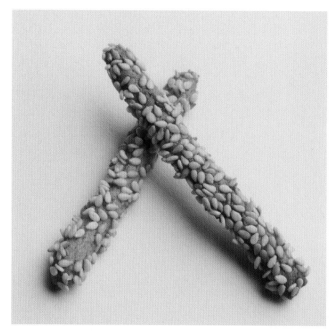

CANDIED NUTS WITH A LOT OF SALT

Candied nuts are usually done dragée style, which is a complicated French method taught at culinary schools that makes everything too sweet for my taste. The technique that follows, on the other hand, will change your life. I learned it at Campanile and it involves deep-frying. Do not be frightened. It works with walnuts, hazelnuts, and, most important, pecans. The pecan version will make you the hero of Thanksgiving. Your Ziploc bag filled with salty nuts, delivered to the family gathering, will make a mockery of that shitty pecan pie your aunt waited in line two hours to buy at the bakery at the eleventh hour.

Yield: 2 to 4 servings

Hazelnuts, pecans, or walnuts 2 cups (weight will vary by nut)
Sugar 2 cups (400 grams)
Water 2 cups (474 grams)
Cayenne pepper 1 teaspoon (4 grams)
Salt to taste
Peanut oil for frying 1 quart (864 grams)

1. In a medium deep-sided saucepan over low heat, combine the nuts, sugar, water, cayenne, and salt and stir together until the mixture becomes sticky and starts to thicken. Drain the liquid and set the nuts aside.

2. In a separate medium deep-sided saucepan over high heat, bring the peanut oil to 350°F.

3. Deep-fry the nuts for 2 minutes. Test one: Split it in half and if it looks slightly toasted on the inside, it is done.

4. Drain the nuts on a paper towel on top of a cooling rack. Salt liberally from high above while the nuts are stilling blazing hot, stirring with a rubber spatula to ensure an even coating.

177

CHAMPAGNE VINEGAR AND ALMOND CARAMELS

One of the first things I teach new cooks at Del Posto is the sniff test, which is where you stick the lower half of your face into one of the reusable plastic containers we use to store all our prepped food and take a whiff. At an Italian restaurant it is highly likely that these containers will reek of onions and garlic, even after going through the insanely hot dish-sanitizing machine. I love onions. I love garlic. But a cake or cookie or candy sealed in a smelly container is not delicious. Don't let a tainted rogue plastic container ruin all your hard work.

These caramels, spiked with vinegar and studded with dark, toasted almonds, are one of my favorite candies to make. They are a little tricky and require a thermometer, but it's worth the effort. Once, someone (who I will not name) made a big batch of these and then packed them all into a plastic container that I swear to you smelled like a hundred *tacos al pastor* with extra raw onion. *Into the trash.*
Yield: One baking sheet of caramel

Almonds, toasted and chopped 1 cup
    (140 grams)
Sugar 1⅔ cups (340 grams)
Glucose ¾ cup (285 grams)
Whole milk 1¼ cups (315 grams)
Heavy cream ⅔ cup (140 grams)
Vanilla bean ½, scraped
Champagne vinegar 1½ cups (366 grams)
Salt ½ teaspoon (2 grams)
Unsalted butter 2½ tablespoons (35 grams)

1. Preheat the oven to 200°F. Spread the almonds onto a baking sheet and place them in the oven to stay warm. Line a second baking sheet with a Silpat, spray with nonstick cooking spray and set aside.

2. In a medium saucepan over medium heat, combine the sugar, glucose, milk, cream, vanilla bean scrapings, and vinegar. Bring the mixture to a rolling boil, whisking occasionally, until you have a thick, bubbly mixture that is light amber in color, about 20 minutes.

3. Remove the mixture from the heat, add the salt, whisk in the butter, and add the warm almonds. Stir to incorporate.

4. Pour the nutty caramel onto the prepared baking sheet and, using a spatula, spread it evenly. Let it cool and set, about 1 hour.

To serve: Remove the cooled caramel from the baking sheet and cut it into ½-inch strips using a paring knife. Cut these strips in half to form cubes. Serve as candy.

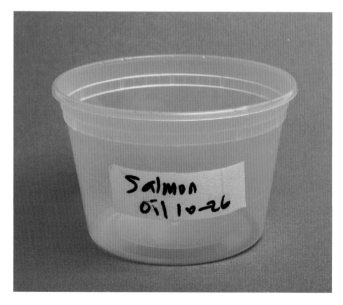

BEST QUITS

Cooks quit jobs all the time, both for reasons unknown and laughably obvious. Sometimes there's a special flourish. These are the best I've seen at DP.

VERONICA: Walked out in the middle of a busy Valentine's Day service. I found her in the hallway sobbing. *I . . . I . . . can't take it anymore!* Through the tears she asked if it was OK if she still used me as a job reference. *Yeah, totally. No problem. Don't cry.*

CLINT: Disappeared mid-prep on a Sunday afternoon. Vanished. An Irish exit. Whisps of his knife work still visible in the atmosphere. Months later, he showed up at a big event at Del Posto as a helper for another chef. We locked eyes. *Chef! Do you want me to leave? No, dude, stay. It's cool. Stay.*

MARSHALL: Brought on as an "extern" (stupid restaurant jargon for "intern") during a busy December. Disappeared for a week right around Christmas, then e-mailed me a few days after to say he'd been in the hospital for hernia surgery. He didn't have a phone or any way to contact the restaurant. The day he returned, I found him hoisting forty-pound boxes of tangerines over his head. Cried when I asked him to leave.

SHELDON: Scheduled to work a lunch shift. A few days prior, he'd asked for a raise and I had agreed to a small one. *That's all?! What is this place, résumé candy?* I smiled and said with my eyes, *Yes, my son, it is résumé candy.* He showed up late to his lunch shift and didn't set up the station. He told everyone how much he hated me and how I was a bad person. There were tears. Rather than taking the dignified exit where you quit and wreck a bunch of shit on the way out, he quit and sat down a few seconds later with puffy red eyes and had morning family meal. Cereal, milk, maybe some reheated pizza. Not even *good* family meal.

OLGA: Faked an injury via the pastry department phone. Her partner in crime, good and loud for all to hear: *Oh my God! You fell down the stairs!? You're in the hospital?!* I never saw Olga again at DP, but a year later I found her assisting another chef at an outside event I was asked to attend. Seemed fine. No leg braces, no canes. Full neck rotation. Healed well. The human body is extremely resilient.

McGILLICUDDY: A total tough guy. Built like a brick house. Very muscled, but a terrible cook. Thought he was great, though, despite the others running circles around him. Arrogant but with nothing in the talent bank. One day he brought in a made-in-his-apartment Albert Adrià–style microwave sponge cake flavored with ramps and asparagus: *It reminds me of spring, green, and of the soil.* He was fascinated with modern techniques, but had serious issues scooping a ball of ice cream. He stayed for three months and then quit to go work at one of those restaurants (now shuttered) where everything gets cooked in a plastic bag.

See page 197.

Brooks at a trade show in Washington, DC, circa 1999.

BRUTTI MA BUONI

The literal translation of this classic cookie from the Piemonte region is "ugly but good." I have been making variations of it since my very first Italian restaurant job, and it really does sum up my philosophy of Italian cooking: Who cares if it's ugly, as long as it tastes great? Ladner once described an especially haggard-looking dish made by the great Italian chef Marc Vetri: "Holy shit, the plate looked like a murder scene—totally sloppy, a complete mess, garbage to look at. But when I tasted it . . . Jesus! It tasted so incredible, like a three-hundred-year-old Italian grandma had produced it. You could literally taste the years of experience." That is everything as far as I'm concerned.

The key to this cookie is gently toasted, very high quality hazelnuts. The austere goal is a crunchy hazelnut meringue cookie. I should note that this recipe is highly susceptible to humidity. If it is raining outside, or the middle of a muggy summer day, or if it's overcast and old snow is melting into gray curbside slush, you should pick a different recipe. If you live in Las Vegas, you can make this 24-7, 365 days a year. In LA there's that one day a year when it rains—don't make these that day.

Yield: Depends on the size of your meringue "splats"

Hazelnuts 1 pound (454 grams)
Egg whites 7 (210 grams each)
Sugar 2½ cups (500 grams)
Ground cinnamon ½ teaspoon (1 gram)
Pure vanilla extract ½ teaspoon (2 grams)
Salt 1½ teaspoons (6 grams)

1. Preheat the oven to 325°F.

2. Place the hazelnuts on a baking sheet in a single layer and toast for 8 minutes, stir, and cook until they darken in color and become golden, another 10 to 12 minutes. Let the nuts cool on the sheet completely.

3. Lower the oven temperature to 300°F. Line a separate baking sheet with parchment or a Silpat and set aside.

4. Place the cooled nuts in a food processor and pulse until you have a fine powder. You don't want the nuts to become pasty, so be sure to watch them carefully as you grind them.

5. In a large bowl, whisk together the egg whites while slowly adding the sugar. Place the bowl over a pan of simmering water and continue to whisk until the sugar dissolves, the egg whites are hot, and the meringue is smooth and shiny.

6. Add the cinnamon, vanilla, salt, and nut powder and fold gently with a silicone spatula.

7. With a spoon, create splats of meringue batter on the reserved baking sheet. Bake for 20 minutes, or until lightly golden and set.

8. Immediately after you've removed the cookies from the oven, use your index fingers and thumbs to pinch the cookies into ugly little lumps—this will expose the chewy center slightly and turn the edges of meringue into crunchy peaks. Let cool on the pan for at least 5 minutes. Store in an airtight container for up to 5 days.

Photo: Ben Clark

WRANGLER
BRUTES

3733 SENECA AVE. LOS ANGELES, CA 90039

THE SWEET BLOOD OF THE LAMB

by Katie Parla

Thanks to my lapsed Catholic parents, as a youth I was never obligated to engage in the cannibalistic ritual of transubstantiation. Now, in spite of residing less than a mile from the Vatican, I have successfully avoided the literal consumption of Jesus Christ for more than three decades.

The Catholic infatuation with sacred and symbolic blood and flesh may not be appealing when it happens at the altar, but at the table it can have exciting consequences. I am referring to holiday-based sweets that evoke—or even contain—these elements. Omnivorous nonbelievers can have all the fun and flavor without the requisite reverence and somber ritual.

In early November, bakeries in Italy produce *ossa dei morti* (bones of the dead), biscuits eaten on November 1 (All Saints Day) and 2 (Day of the Dead). In one variation, a thin, off-white tibia-shape pastry shell envelopes the "marrow," almond paste enriched with butter. These bone biscuits are eaten by Italian Catholics in remembrance of dear, departed relatives. And what better way to pay tribute to grandma then to eat a sweet symbol of her skeletal remains?

In January and February, the annual pig slaughter produces the slick and savory blood, which is main component in *sanguinaccio dolce,* a sort of chocolate pudding consumed during Carnevale. The blood of freshly slaughtered pigs is heated with milk, cocoa, and sugar (variations incorporate cinnamon and/or citrus zest), thickened, then served warm with a side of *savoiardi* (ladyfingers) for dipping. The blood pudding's savory and sweet notes give way to an iron-tinged, metallic finish. Dense and caloric, sanguinaccio dolce provides sustenance before the lean Lenten period (see Note).

And after those forty days of fasting, Italian Catholics celebrate the Resurrection with prolonged Easter feasting. No paschal table is complete without an almond-paste lamb. Molded into various sizes, this lamb is no ordinary newborn: It is the sugar-rich Lamb of God. Jesus Christ. Regardless of the shop where it is made, the animal's pose is uniformly awkward, with painted-on facial features that are consistently dopey. The occasional variation includes a fancy bow tie or streamers and other inedible embellishments that must be plucked before the almond-paste lamb head is devoured.

The Lamb of God and its sweet symbolic counterparts may not be exclusive to the confessed and indoctrinated, but I think JC would approve.

Note: The commercial sale of pig's blood was banned in Italy in 1992, but during Carnevale, sanguinaccio dolce can still be found in traditional homes, where it is made with black market blood, or that gathered for personal use during home slaughter.

Photo by Katie Parla.

Italian Nonna Clogs.

BRUTALLY ITALIAN ALMOND CAKE

In Italy, I'm never too impressed by desserts served at the end of a meal. Even in the fancier restaurants, the final courses always seem to be missing something. Salt? Acid? Inspiration? The reason is probably simpler: In Italy, sweets are ubiquitous. You eat dessert all day long in Rome. Gelato for breakfast? Sure, the café where you get your coffee probably has twenty flavors and they might be left over from last night, but screw it, get a cup of *bacio* at 8 a.m. Just try to ask Italians for scrambled eggs or (gasp) a frittata for breakfast. They will usher you right out of the country. *Here, eat this sweet pastry stuffed with apricot jam. Have a coffee, too. Now go.* Cookies, cakes, Kinder candy bars . . . all to be eaten throughout the day in Italia. By the time dinner's through, a chunk of cheese or a bowl of grapes is, like, just fine.

This is a simple almond cake. Something you might see for sale by the slice at a bakery in Florence, right beside those jam crostatas with warbly lattice tops and a stack of crunchy meringues the size of footballs. The sliced almonds on top of this cake become very dark in the oven. That perfume, that nearly black, toasted-almond aroma, that's Italy, too.

Yield: One 8-inch cake

Almonds, skin on ⅔ cup (93 grams)
Sugar 2 tablespoons plus ¾ cup (25 grams plus 150 grams)
Unsalted butter ⅔ cup, or 1 stick plus 2⅔ tablespoons (170 grams)
Eggs 2
All-purpose flour ⅔ cup (80 grams)
Baking powder 1¼ tablespoons (13 grams)
Salt 1 teaspoon (5 grams)
Sliced almonds ½ cup (54 grams)
Simple syrup (see page 7) 1 tablespoon (10 grams)

1. Preheat the oven to 350°F. Grease an 8-inch round springform pan with butter, line with parchment, and set aside. Or use an 8-inch ring mold and make a bottom with aluminum foil.

2. In a food processor, grind the skin-on almonds with 2 tablespoons of the sugar into a coarse powder.

3. In the bowl of a stand mixer using the paddle attachment, combine the butter and the remaining ¾ cup sugar on medium speed until light and fluffy. Add the eggs, one at a time, making sure the first is incorporated before adding the second.

4. In a medium bowl, combine the flour, baking powder, and salt. Add them slowly to the batter and incorporate fully.

5. Pour the batter into the prepared pan. Bake for 15 to 20 minutes.

6. Meanwhile, in a small bowl, add the sliced almonds and simple syrup and toss. Add the nuts to the top of the cake, reduce the oven temperature to 325°F, and bake for 10 to 15 minutes, until the top is golden brown and toasted.

7. Let the cake cool in the pan before serving.

To serve: By the slice, accompanied by a single shot of espresso in the afternoon.

PROFILE IN COURAGE:

Christina Tosi

Born: Scorpio

Occupation: Cookie maker extraordinaire

Status: Certified crazy lady

Notable quote: "Don't take yourself so seriously."

Shoe size: 9, but I can morph my foot into a 6½ to 11, when the occasion arises.

Lunch food: Cookie dough and a bag of chips, in that order

Beverage: Fizzy water

I Heart NY: And am terrified I'll never leave.

First time: I wore jeans was in eighth grade. Kicking and screaming. That's how cool I was/am.

Accomplishments: Making my parents proud while proving my parents wrong

Ambition/future plan: Certified crazy *old* lady; diabetes enthusiast; embarrassing mom of either too many children, or pups, or both; maintaining an ever-loving fear of the dark

SAFFRON WEDDING COOKIES

I set out to make a version of those dry, crumbly Mexican wedding cookies that explode in your mouth. But I wanted to incorporate saffron and to shape them into half-moons: *mezzalunas.* I was feeling very Apician or Turkish or something. Saffron, as we all know, is expensive. Don't get too hung up on it. Between Kalustyan's and Penzeys mail order, you'll be fine. Don't buy saffron threads at a Whole Foods, because that's a sucker move. Saffron has a hint of a metallic, nearly doctor's office scent about it. But so do pomegranates, and they are delicious.

Think of this as a special-occasion cookie. Like for a wedding. Maybe even a Mexican wedding. Do they serve Mexican wedding cookies at Mexican weddings? I really have no idea. I know they are served at typical Italian American weddings. That's one thing I do know. Been to plenty of those.

Yield: A lot of cookies

FOR THE SAFFRON COMPOUND BUTTER (MAKES MORE THAN YOU NEED, DELIBERATELY)

Water ½ cup (118 grams)
Unsalted butter 1½ pounds, or 6 sticks (680 grams)
Saffron threads 1 teaspoon (1 gram)

1. In a small saucepan over high heat, bring the water to a boil. Add the saffron (like you are making tea), remove from the heat, and let it steep for 5 minutes.

2. In the bowl of a stand mixer, using the paddle attachment, cream the butter on medium speed until softened. Add the saffron tea (water and threads) and mix until smooth.

3. Refrigerate, wrapped in plastic wrap, for up to 2 weeks. Freeze indefinitely (within reason, c'mon).

FOR THE SAFFRON COOKIE DOUGH

Saffron compound butter ¾ pound, or 3 sticks (340 grams)
Sugar ½ cup (100 grams)
Almond flour, toasted 1½ cups (144 grams)
All-purpose flour 3¼ cups (405 grams)
Salt 1 teaspoon (4 grams)

1. Preheat the oven to 325°F. Line a baking sheet with parchment paper and set aside.

2. In the bowl of a stand mixer, using the paddle attachment, combine the saffron butter and sugar on medium speed until soft and creamy. Add the almond flour, all-purpose flour, and salt and mix until thoroughly combined. Refrigerate covered for 1 hour.

3. Tear off balls of dough about the size of small apricots. Shape each into a half-moon and place on the prepared baking sheet. Chill in the refrigerator for 1 hour.

4. Bake the cookies for about 9 minutes until *just* golden. Don't overbake or you will lose the yellow saffron hue you worked so hard to achieve.

5. Allow the cookies to cool on the sheet. Store in an airtight plastic container for up to a few days.

BAND TOUR FOOD DIARY: WRANGLER BRUTES

Wrangler Brutes began in 2001 and was a bicoastal band for two years. I was working at Tosca in DC. I had been hired as the pastry chef, but that was ridiculous because I had no clue what I was doing. I relocated to Los Angeles in 2003.

Wrangler Brutes did a lot of touring, and we'd do small jaunts up and down the West Coast regularly. We ate In-N-Out grilled cheese sandwiches with fries stuffed inside. We shopped at Whole Foods all the time. On Young Pioneers tours we boycotted Whole Foods, claiming it corporate and therefore not to be tolerated. Wrangler Brutes didn't care. We were always about the gag. We put out our first album on a mass-produced cassette knowing that, in 2003, not many people had the means to play it. We had it shrink-wrapped, just to be assholes. Between songs, Sam, the singer, had taken to reading fake fan letters (one entirely in Aramaic) and closing our set with a speech from *Henry V* while wearing a wig. Before we had a name for the band, he booked us a show in Tijuana, Mexico. Andy, our guitarist, peed everywhere compulsively, and at a show in Indianapolis, Indiana, where we were paid fifteen dollars after being told to lower our volume for the set, Andy blanketed the stage in a torrent of urine as we packed up our gear. (Sam later took us aside to express his disgust.) Cundo, the bass player, made a habit of befriending skinheads. There was a lot of amusing dysfunction.

We did manage to tour Japan, although it was after we officially broke up. It was the first time I'd ever been out of the country, and it was a food awakening. We went nuts. Our chaperone and tour manager Katoman took us out for breakfast and lunch each day and for a postshow snack every night. It was incredible. *Okonomiyaki* (a seafood pancake thing), raw octopus *izakaya* style, (Japanese pub food, basically) and takoyaki (octopus doughnuts) with BBQ sauce, mayo, and shaved bonito that were so hot they scorched the mouth and had everyone doing that air-sucking thing that doesn't work at all. (You just look like an idiot.) I'd never had anything like this stuff before. I was completely blown away. I think about it still.

And then everything changed.

I didn't play music for four years. I was back in DC by 2005. I worked a lot. I had two full-time pastry chef jobs: Komi and Tosca. I *almost* knew what I was doing at this point, so I figured *why not just do it double*? But I missed the drums every day. *(Continued on page 239.)*

SPEZZATA DI CASTAGNE WITH RED WINE PLUMS AND YOGURT SORBET

On the branch, chestnuts are massively photogenic, entombed in a sea urchin–like shell. On the streets of midtown Manhattan in the winter, they are roasted curbside, along with exhaust fumes and the wool-clad crush of humanity. In Milan, sweetened chestnuts are pureed and then pressed through a potato ricer to make a weird Play-Doh–like spaghetti twirl that tops the very classic yet very ditzy Monte Bianco dessert, which is beloved in pastry shops all over Japan and Korea. Chestnuts taste like it's cold out. They get me all worked up.

I admit, they are difficult to peel. A tough skin harbors the creamy nugget inside, and it's something you're just going to have to deal with. The word *spezzata* means ripped or torn, and that's what we do to the insides of the chestnut—the *castagne*. Then we pair the cake (also ripped and torn) with red wine plums and finish with a scoop of yogurt sorbet. I love this sorbet: It is bright and spry, acidic and white. It brings the whole damn thing together quite nicely.

Yield: 6 small cakes

CHESTNUT PUREE

Frozen chestnuts, thawed 2¼ cups (400 grams)
Extra-virgin olive oil to taste
Salt to taste
Orange zest to taste

1. Preheat the oven to 350°F.
2. In a large bowl, add the chestnuts and season with olive oil, salt, and orange zest. Transfer the nut mixture to a roasting pan and cook in a single layer until soft, 8 to 10 minutes.

3. In a food mill or food processor, pulse the roasted chestnuts until there is a very thick puree, almost like a paste. You can add a little olive oil to keep it pliable. Season the chestnut puree with salt and set aside.

CHESTNUT CAKES

Whole milk, warm ¼ cup (60 grams)
Sugar 1½ teaspoons plus ¾ cup (5 grams plus 150 grams)
Active dry yeast 1¼ teaspoons (5 grams)
Eggs 3, separated
Chestnut puree 1½ cups (340 grams)
Bread Crumbs (page 133)

1. In a medium microwavable bowl, zap the milk in the microwave for 30 seconds. (The milk should be warm; if it's too hot, it will kill the yeast you are about to add.) Add 1½ teaspoons of the sugar and the yeast and stir once to dissolve. Let the mixture sit for 10 minutes.

2. In the bowl of a stand mixer, using the whip attachment, combine the egg yolks and ¼ cup of the remaining sugar on medium speed until pale yellow, about 3 minutes.

3. Add the chestnut puree to the yeast mixture and combine. Fold in the yolk mixture and set aside. Clean the stand mixer bowl and whip attachment.

4. In the clean stand mixer bowl, using

the whip attachment, beat the egg whites on high until they aren't getting any taller and have reached stiff peaks. Reduce the speed to medium and slowly add the remaining ½ cup sugar. With a rubber spatula, gently fold the egg whites into the chestnut mixture.

5. Spray a 6-cup cupcake tin with non-stick cooking spray and sprinkle the bottom of each cup with some of the bread crumbs. Fill each cup halfway with batter. Bake for exactly 16 minutes. The cakes will double in size, like soufflés, and then fall when removed from the oven. It's OK; this is how it's supposed to be.

6. Allow the cakes to cool in the tin and separate them from the sides of the tin with a butter knife. Gently remove when ready to use.

STEAMED CHESTNUTS

Fresh chestnuts 2½ cups (454 grams), steamed or boiled in their shells
Salt to taste

Freshly ground black pepper to taste
Extra-virgin olive oil 1 to 1½ tablespoons (13.5 grams to 20 grams)
Zest of 2 tangerines
White wine vinegar 2 teaspoons (9 grams)

1. Cut the chestnuts in half while still warm. Remove the meat, tear it into large pieces, and add it to a small bowl.

2. Season the chestnuts with salt and pepper. Dress with the olive oil, tangerine zest, and vinegar and toss to combine.

FOR SERVING

Red Wine Plums (page 26)
Yogurt Sorbet (page 58)

To serve: Tear a chestnut cake into pieces, put it on a plate, and garnish with the red wine plums and some of the plum syrup. Sprinkle the crushed chestnuts over the dish and finish with a scoop of yogurt sorbet.

WARNING:
Scene
Rapers!

FUCK

Born Again$ †

→ THEY ARE NOT PUNK! AND DON'T LET THEM TELL YOU OTHERWISE

FUCK THEY'RE GREED. AND GAURANTEE!
(AND THE SHOWS THAT FILL THEY'RE POCKETS.)

ONCE A POWERFUL EDUCATION NOW WHAT!

THEY SELL VERMIFORM© OFF TO DUTCH

EAST TO MAKE MONEY OFF OUR SCENE!

DON'T LET THE D.Y.I. SCENE BE CORUPPTED BY THIS

SENSELESS SELLING OF HARDCORE!

SPEAK OUT!

NOW.

PUNK NEEDS NO KING! NO LEECH! NO PROFIT! NO THANKS!

OR

BORN AGAINST
BILL CLINTON
DAVID KORESH
NIRVANA
MTV
COLUMBUS

ALL SHIT IN THE SAME
PILE!

NEXT BIG PRODUCT, NEXT BIG THING

I STEAL AND SMASH EVERYTHING

"Think about the farm worker every time you eat"—Vinyl matrix inscribed on the Man Is the Bastard side of Born Against/MITB split 8 inch, 1995

Fregolotta is a type of cookie that is studded with almonds. You don't even need a mixer to make it. You do it with your hands in a bowl, like a grandma would—which makes sense since I stole most of the recipe from Lidia Bastianich. On paper, it's so simple. It doesn't even have any butter in it. But despite its simplicity, getting it right is a fine and studied art. When I think of deceptively uncomplicated recipes like the one for fregolotta, I think of the early 1990s and of the late great power violence band Man Is the Bastard.

Whenever Young Pioneers, Born Against, or UOA were on tour, we'd visit them in Claremont, California, right outside LA. We'd play a show with them and then crash—but the Man Is the Bastard guys would finish playing and go straight to work at a local bakery. They did the overnight shift. In the morning, we'd wake up, head to the bakery, and get croissants or whatever. They'd all still be working from the night before. It was beyond impressive.

The bakery was called Some Crust, which is just so California. It's still around. Man Is the Bastard's whole vibe was also completely Southern Californian, but I guess a lot of people think of them as being scary because their imagery and music were so antiauthoritarian and bleak. But I never saw them that way. What stood out to me was their connection to the punk band with the most renowned work ethic of them all: Black Flag. You play a show and then you go and work until dawn at the bakery. No complaining. That approach really struck a chord with me. So I stole it.

I find Man Is the Bastard inspiring. They were so much more than just a band, and their live performances are burned into my subconscious. Now, nearly twenty years later, when I'm working on a new dish and it's getting overly busy or complicated, I think about how they would approach it. Their song "Puppy Mill," a condemnation of dog breeding that sounds like terrifying bleats isolated in empty space (an emulsion!) with the lyric "cuteness kills," gets stuck in my head a lot when I'm making ice cream.

Many of the recipes I develop are like their songs, which are almost stupid in their simplicity. But I keep in mind that this is their genius disguised: Those guys are practiced, experienced musicians. That's what it takes to make that simple, perfect music, even if the song's just forty-five seconds long. Fregolotta, too. It takes time and focus to get it right. Anybody can grab cream, nuts, orange zest, and flour and crush them together. But being able to take that thing and make sure it isn't too thick is an art. Like most good things, a fregolotta has got to have space between the notes.

*upside-down.

198

FREGOLOTTA

At most three- and four-star restaurants in Manhattan, everything is very contained and formal. It generally is at Del Posto, too, but there are times when we like to let things be a little bit messy, a little bit out of control. So when we serve fregolotta, we smash it on the table and the pieces fly everywhere. It's an Italian good-luck gesture. We bring out some cookies in hand-painted jars that a little old lady in Umbria made for us. We flip the jar upside down and drop the fregolotta so that it shatters all over the nice linen. It's a Lidia thing—she calls it "confetti-ing the table."
Yield: 6 large cookies

All-purpose flour 1 cup (125 grams)
Zest of 1 orange
Sugar 1 cup (200 grams)
Egg yolks 3
Heavy cream ¼ cup (60 grams)
Almonds 30, toasted

1. Preheat the oven to 325°F. Line a baking sheet with parchment paper and set aside.
2. In a large bowl, whisk together the flour, orange zest, and sugar.
3. In a separate bowl, whisk together the egg yolks and cream.
4. Slowly add the egg mixture to the flour mixture and combine by hand until you have a crumbly, textured dough.
5. Using a 4-inch ring mold, portion the dough out onto the prepared baking sheet, making sure to leave ½ inch between each. Press 5 toasted almonds into each cookie. Remove the ring molds. Bake for 12 minutes, or until golden. Remove to a rack to cool.

6. When the cookies are cool enough to handle, transfer them to parchment sheets, being careful not to break them.

To serve: Smash on a table and invite everyone to eat the shrapnel.

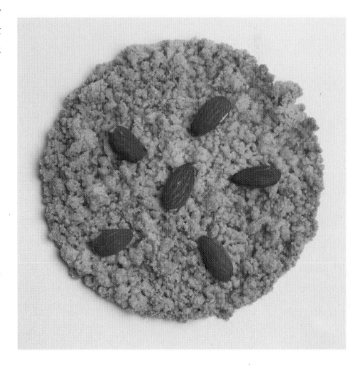

TWO PEANUT BUTTER AND JELLY SNACKS THAT CONTAIN NEITHER

Faustino, a cook-comedian-dishwasher at Tosca in DC during my time there, once made me a plate with a single uncooked baby shrimp, a nasturtium leaf, and a dot of ketchup smeared into a Nike swoosh. He looked me straight in the eyes and said, "Check it out, Pan Blanco. White people food." Early on he named me Pan Blanco. *White bread*. It stuck because it's true. A suburban dude from the outskirts of Baltimore, white bread is who I am. Totally.

Pork *baos*, also known as steamed buns, got extremely popular in New York in the late 2000s. They'd obviously been around forever in Taiwan, but all of a sudden the dining public was losing its collective marbles over them in Manhattan. The reason: the bun. It was identical to Wonder Bread. The filling was inconsequential. Like a peanut butter and jelly sandwich.

Peanut butter and jelly is an American icon, a member of the family, the drunk uncle who shows up to Thanksgiving half in the bag already—amusing but tough in large doses. The following two snacks are my attempt to keep it in the family while still maintaining the character of the immortal PB&J (or in the case of the Apples and Dulce, its cousin, the caramel apple). They are more suggestions than recipes. Springboards. The approach is a bit grandmotherly. They're good for both passing around at a party or eating in your underwear, standing at the kitchen counter at 3 a.m.

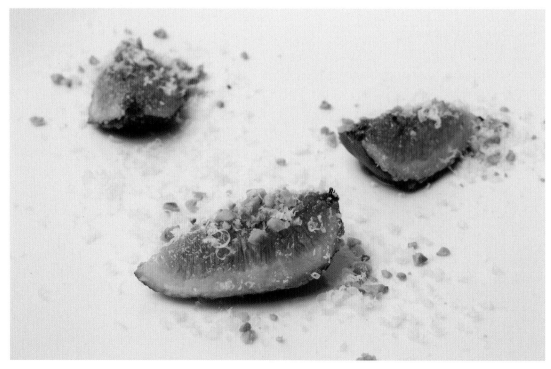

FIGS AND PARMIGIANO WITH HAZELNUTS

Yield: 2 servings

Figs 6, halved lengthwise
Turbinado sugar ¼ cup (50 grams)
Extra-virgin olive oil to taste
Salt to taste
Freshly ground black pepper to taste
Parmigiano-Reggiano a large chunk
Hazelnuts, toasted and crushed, to taste

   1. Preheat the broiler or a toaster oven to 500°F.
   2. On a baking sheet, place the figs, cut side up, and sprinkle with sugar. Broil for 30 seconds. Rotate the baking sheet and broil for another 2 to 3 minutes—you're set when the sugar has melted and the figs are engorged.
   3. Transfer the figs to a plate and drizzle with olive oil, a little salt, and pepper.

   To serve: Using a Microplane, blanket the figs with grated Parmigiano and top with the crushed hazelnuts. Serve immediately.

APPLE WITH DULCE AND SESAME SEEDS

Yield: 2 servings

Honeycrisp or Granny Smith apple 1, unpeeled, sliced into 12 pieces
Dulce de leche one 10-ounce can
Sesame seeds a handful, toasted
Maldon salt to taste
Extra-virgin olive oil to taste

   1. Smear each apple slice with a bit of dulce de leche.
   2. Coat the dulce completely with toasted sesame seeds. Sprinkle with a few grains of salt and drizzle with olive oil.

   To serve: Eat it.

6. DAIRY

"I drink milk, I drink milk, I drink milk, I drink milk, and I don't care what people say"—"I Drink Milk," Teen Idles, 1980

I grew up surrounded by vegan and vegetarian propaganda. In the late 1980s and through the 1990s, vegetarianism was an unavoidable by-product of punk rock. I'd taken to it eagerly. And then eventually it turned into *sort of* vegetarian, which is where my diet resides these days.

Milk is delicious, and milk *aged* is cheese. As Mario Batali is fond of saying, "Cheese is milk made immortal."

I was allergic to the stuff as a kid. I grew out of it and had my first real helping at a preteen pizza party at a Baltimore Blast indoor soccer game. I've still never had an actual glass of milk, Christoph Waltz style, but now I'm completely obsessed with the stuff. I had better be. As a pastry chef, I traffic in dairy.

I suggest you start a relationship with a dairy farmer. You'll be able to find one at your local greenmarket. Buy her cream, her milk. It will be more expensive, but you are going to use dairy sparingly anyway, so that won't be an issue. Get good, weird cheeses from your local monger. I guarantee the folks who run your neighborhood shop are fanatical cheese nerds and will let you sample lots of stuff. I'm not trying to turn you into an elitist with the little boutique food shops, or torch your kid's tuition fund in the process. Really, I'm not. Just get the good stuff and cherish it.

PASTRY CREAM

Don't eat too much of this. It's meant to be the filling for something small, like a doughnut (see page 137) or a cream puff. It's really just a vanilla pudding, but it's the richest vanilla pudding you have ever had. Even as the filling for a regular-size éclair you're going to feel pretty clobbered and in need of a nap if you eat the entire thing. Naps are good, though. I have no problem with naps. If you plan to smoke pot and do some cooking, make something else. Don't make this. You will eat it all and wake up angry and in pain.

Yield: 1 quart

Whole milk 2⅔ cups (650 grams)
Vanilla bean 1, scraped
Egg yolks 7 (126 grams)
Cornstarch ⅓ cup (40 grams)
Sugar ¾ cup (150 grams)
Unsalted butter 3 tablespoons (42 grams)

1. In a medium saucepan over medium heat combine the milk and vanilla bean scrapings and bring to a boil.

2. In a small bowl, whisk together the egg yolks, cornstarch, and sugar.

3. Add a little of the warmed milk to the egg mixture to temper. Add the rest of the egg mixture to the milk mixture and return to a full boil for at least 2 minutes, to cook out the cornstarch flavor.

4. In the bowl of a stand mixer using the paddle attachment, combine the cream mixture and butter on medium speed. When the bottom of the mixer bowl is cool to the touch, the cream is done. Store in an airtight container for up to 1 week in the fridge.

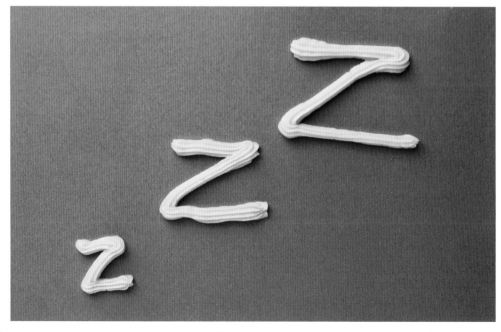

CORN CREAM AND PIT CREAM

For the opening of the new Bastianich restaurant Orsone in Fruili, I had a real piece-of-shit gelato machine. As someone who puts ice cream on nearly every dish, I was crippled by this thing, which was one part stoned fat kid and two parts giant middle finger. It worked, but only when it wanted to, and then only with a massive chip on its shoulder.

My deputy Annie and I made flavored whipped creams rather than deal with that goddamn Carpigiani Quartetto machine (the name rankles my neck hairs still). It was summer, and we had amazing Italian apricots and not-so-hot Italian corn on the cob. For all the polenta consumed in Northern Italy, you would think you could find nice fresh corn. I found only weird, starchy garbage.

We placed the apricot pits on a dish towel and cracked them with a frying pan: It's not a fast method, but it's really fun, ominous, and gratifying. We extracted the bitter almond inside and used it to make a whipped cream. Excellent. It has a strong marzipan flavor, with a slight burn on the back end that feels illicit. We named it "pit cream" because all the official terms for what we were doing were French and boring. *Hey, Annie, your pit cream doesn't taste enough like nuts.* We were working eighteen-hour days, and the low-hanging-fruit comedy lobes of our brains were perpetually engorged.

The corn was inedible. It tasted like corn, but the kernels refused to break down as you chewed. So we stripped the cobs and soaked them in cream to make a corn stock. The cobs looked like chicken bones or chicken necks floating in the pot. But they infused the liquid with a beautiful corn flavor: a perfect match for blackberries.

On the second day we were open for service, an American tourist at the bar requested an Irish coffee. We had only the corn cream ready and whipped, so we went with that. The bartender didn't return with a complaint, so I gather it worked out just fine. Not that I recommend using it in Irish coffees, or drinking Irish coffees at all.

CORN CREAM

Yield: 1½ cups

Heavy cream 2 cups (500 grams)
Corn cob 1, stripped of kernels
Powdered sugar ¼ cup (30 grams)
Salt to taste

1. In a medium saucepan over low heat, warm the cream. Add the corn cob, bring to a boil, and remove from the heat. Let the milk infuse on your countertop for 1 hour.

2. Strain the mixture through a chinois or fine-mesh strainer into a clean bowl and refrigerate until chilled, about 1 hour. Meantime, place an empty mixing bowl in the freezer until it is very cold.

3. Transfer the cold corn cream to the cold mixing bowl, add the powdered sugar and salt, and whisk until fluffy.

PIT CREAM

Yield: 1½ cups

Apricot pit nuts about 12
Heavy cream 2 cups (500 grams)
Powdered sugar ¼ cup (30 grams)
Salt to taste

1. Fold the apricot pits in a sturdy kitchen towel and whack with a frying pan to break them open. Inside the pit there is a nut that looks kind of like an almond. It has a soft white flesh. Remove the flesh parts and discard the exteriors until you have ¼ cup (50 grams). This is a labor of love. (Don't eat these kernels, by the way. They are poisonous.)

2. In a medium saucepan over low heat, warm the cream, add the pit nuts, and bring to a boil. Remove the mixture from the heat and let the pit nuts infuse the cream on your countertop for 2 hours.

3. Strain the mixture through a chinois or fine-mesh strainer into a clean bowl and refrigerate until chilled, about 1 hour. Meantime, place an empty mixing bowl in the freezer until it is very cold.

4. Transfer the cold pit cream to the cold mixing bowl, add the powdered sugar and salt, and whisk until fluffy.

To serve: Use either the pit cream or the corn cream with the Polenta Shortcake with Blackberry Compote (page 118)

ZABAGLIONE, BOTH WAYS

Del Posto is an extraordinary place to work. I bow and kiss the metal grates of the employee entrance ramp before every shift. All restaurants have something unique about them—usually it's some variety of dysfunction. But Del Posto stands out as unique in one outrageous way. Instead of having a single visionary chef on board, Del Posto has three: chefs Mark Ladner, Mario Batali, and Lidia Bastianich. To say nothing of the force that is Joe Bastianich, the dude who makes sure we have a roof. I tell my staff often that our bosses are the four most important and influential people in the United States in terms of pushing Italian food forward—probably even the world. They are all fully, unapologetically Italian in every possible way, which means that inherently they'll have different visions from time to time, if not minute to minute (it's an excitable culture, as you've probably heard). It's my job to make sure each of those visions is taken into consideration to produce a unified whole when it's my turn.

Take zabaglione. It's easy to make: very simple, very Italian. You need to finesse it, but it'll always be a straightforward pleasure that screams *Italia!* It has a beautiful whiff of Marsala.

Mario digs it fluffy and puffy, whisked vigorously and gently simultaneously (*not* easy) so the result is a whipped cream–like cloud, airy and voluptuous. Lidia likes it almost completely without air, creamy, like an anglaise or hollandaise. Pourable. Her version is equally sexy, made with a rubber spatula in a calculated figure-eight motion with your wrist. It requires mother-like patience.

Both zabagliones are great. I'm not going to argue with either of them. It's like, what's better: Black Flag or the Misfits?
Yield: About 2 cups

Egg yolks 6 (108 grams)
Marsala ¼ cup (59 grams)
Sugar ¼ cup (50 grams)
Salt to taste

MARIO STYLE

1. In a medium saucepan, bring 3 cups of water to a simmer over medium-low heat.

2. In a medium heat-safe bowl, whisk together the egg yolks, Marsala, sugar, and salt. Place the bowl on top of the simmering water and whisk gently until you have a ribbony, frothy mixture. Keep moving the bowl around as you whisk. You don't want scrambled eggs. You want an unset custard.

LIDIA STYLE

1. In a medium saucepan, bring several cups of water to a simmer over medium-low heat.

2. In a medium heat-safe bowl, whisk together the egg yolks, Marsala, sugar, and salt. Put your whisk down. Grab a rubber spatula.

3. Place the bowl on top of the simmering water and stir the yolks in a figure-eight motion with the spatula until you have a creamy, mayonnaiselike sauce. Keep moving the bowl around as you stir. You *still* don't want scrambled eggs.

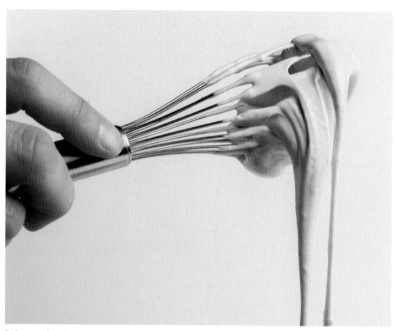

Mario Style.

Lidia Style.

GELATOS

It is impossible to make restaurant-perfect gelato at home. In the same way you can't make a pizza in your home oven that competes with the ones made inside your favorite pizza joint's 900-degree wood-burning oven. It's a hardware issue.

Still, gelato is *at least* several hundred years old. Fancy machines didn't invent it. The art of the technique will come in more subtle ways, and with time and patience. It will always be tricky coaxing ingredients into a beautiful gelato, but that's exactly why we want to make gelato. Make sure everything is *very* cold when you churn. Hell, if you're using a "freeze the chamber" machine, clear everything out, run an extension cord, and stick the machine *in* the freezer.

BASIC GELATO

This is where you'll begin for most all of your gelatos. Flavoring gelatos can be tricky, so I've also put together several recipe modifications to illustrate the techniques I use most often.
Yield: 1½ quarts

Egg yolks 5 (90 grams)
Whole milk 2 cups (500 grams)
Heavy cream ⅓ cup (75 grams)
Condensed milk ¼ cup (80 grams)
Nonfat milk powder ¼ cup (25 grams)
Dextrose 2 tablespoons (25 grams)
Sugar ⅓ cup (75 grams)
Honey 1 tablespoon (20 grams)
Salt to taste

1. In a large bowl, prepare an ice bath.
2. In a medium deep-sided bowl, using a rubber spatula, stir the egg yolks until they are a cohesive liquid. Do *not* use a whisk!
3. Add the whole milk, cream, condensed milk, milk powder, dextrose, sugar, honey, and salt, and combine using an immersion blender for about 1 minute.
4. Set the bowl in the ice bath. Let the mixture cool, cover the bowl with plastic wrap, and refrigerate for at least 3 hours. If you have time, place the mixture in an airtight container and refrigerate overnight.
5. Spin the gelato in an ice cream machine according to the manufacturer's instructions. Or use the dry-ice method in your stand mixer (see page 210).

MINT GELATO/PARSLEY GELATO/ BASIL GELATO

Yield: 1½ quarts

Fresh herb of choice 1 bunch chopped
Whole milk 2 cups (500 grams)
Egg yolks 5 (90 grams)
Heavy cream ⅓ cup (75 grams)
Condensed milk ¼ cup (80 grams)
Nonfat milk powder ¼ cup (25 grams)
Dextrose 2 tablespoons (25 grams)
Sugar ⅓ cup (75 grams)
Honey 1 tablespoon (20 grams)
Salt to taste

1. In a medium saucepan over high heat, bring 3 cups of water to a boil. Blanch the herbs in the water for 45 seconds, take them out, and put them in a bowl of ice water. Drain the herbs.

2. In a medium deep-sided bowl, add the drained herbs and 1 cup of the whole milk and puree using an immersion blender. Strain the puree through a chamois and set it aside.

3. In a large bowl, prepare an ice bath.

4. In a medium deep-sided bowl, using a rubber spatula, stir the egg yolks until they are a cohesive liquid. Do *not* use a whisk!

5. Add the cream, condensed milk, milk powder, dextrose, sugar, honey, salt, herb puree, and remaining 1 cup whole milk, and combine using an immersion blender for about 1 minute.

6. Set the bowl in the ice bath. Let the mixture cool, cover the bowl with plastic wrap, and refrigerate for at least 3 hours. If you have time, place the mixture in an air-tight container and refrigerate overnight.

7. Spin the gelato in an ice cream machine according to the manufacturer's instructions. Or use the dry-ice method in your stand mixer (see below).

THE DRY-ICE TECHNIQUE

Let's talk briefly about the dry-ice method not made famous by the genius Heston Blumenthal. (We all should have made this famous by now.) It is the method I would use if I didn't have professional-grade equipment available to me and wanted high-quality gelato.

Dry ice is not the exclusive domain of twitchy TV hazmat chefs. I've tried every gelato method and the dry-ice technique is pound for pound the best. It's uncomplicated. It's cheap. It's quick. Getting dry ice might be a hassle, but everything's at least a little hassle unless you love doing it. I promise you'll love this. You've also already added dry ice to your shopping list to make Ladner's Philadelphia Bellini (page 44). Here it is:

Buy the dry ice, in pellets if you can. Don't touch it, and *Jesus Christ, don't let your child touch it.* Put a few cups of dry ice (4 or 5 golf ball–size chunks if you can't get pellets) in the middle of a kitchen towel and fold the towel over several times. Smash the dry ice with a heavy pot until it is a powder (no chunks larger than a Grape-Nut). Measure out 1 cup of powdered dry ice. Add this to your gelato mix inside your stand mixer, spin for 2 minutes with the paddle attachment, and put the gelato in a prechilled airtight container in the freezer overnight.

SAGE GELATO

Yield: 1½ quarts

Fresh sage leaves 2 cups (64 grams)
Whole milk 2 cups (500 grams)
Egg yolks 5 (90 grams)
Heavy cream ⅓ cup (75 grams)
Condensed milk ¼ cup (80 grams)
Nonfat milk powder ¼ cup (25 grams)
Dextrose 2 tablespoons (25 grams)
Sugar ⅓ cup (75 grams)
Honey 1 tablespoon (20 grams)
Salt to taste

1. In a medium saucepan over high heat, bring 3 cups of water to a boil. Blanch the sage in the water for 45 seconds, take it out, and put it in a bowl of ice water. Drain the sage and place it in a medium bowl.

2. In a medium saucepan over medium heat, bring the whole milk to a simmer, pour it over the sage, and let it steep to however sage-heavy you want your gelato to taste—2 to 3 minutes. Strain the mixture through a chinois or fine-mesh strainer and let the sage milk come to room temperature.

3. In a large bowl, prepare an ice bath.

4. In a medium deep-sided bowl, using a rubber spatula, stir the egg yolks until they are a cohesive liquid. Do not use a whisk!

5. Add the cream, condensed milk, milk powder, dextrose, sugar, honey, salt, and the sage milk, and combine using an immersion blender for about 1 minute.

6. Set the bowl in the ice bath. Let the mixture cool, cover the bowl with plastic wrap, and refrigerate for at least 3 hours. If you have time, place the mixture in an airtight container and refrigerate overnight.

7. Spin the gelato in an ice cream machine according to the manufacturer's instructions.

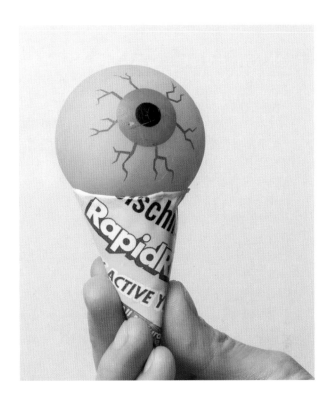

Or use the dry-ice method in your stand mixer (see opposite page).

YEAST GELATO

Yield: 1½ quarts

Whole milk 2 cups (500 grams)
Active dry yeast ⅛ cup plus 1 tablespoon (36 grams)
Sugar ⅓ cup (75 grams), plus a pinch for the yeast
Egg yolks 5 (90 grams)
Heavy cream ⅓ cup (75 grams)
Condensed milk ¼ cup (80 grams)
Nonfat milk powder ¼ cup (25 grams)
Dextrose 2 tablespoons (25 grams)
Honey 1 tablespoon (20 grams)
Salt to taste

1. In a medium saucepan over medium-low heat, warm the milk to 100°F. (You definitely need to use a thermometer.) Whisk in

the yeast and the pinch of sugar and remove from the heat. Allow the yeast to bloom in the warm milk for about 20 minutes, or until it gets frothy.

2. Return the yeast mixture to the stove over high heat and bring to a boil to kill the fermentation of the yeast. Strain through a chinois or fine-mesh strainer and set aside.

3. In a large bowl, prepare an ice bath.

4. In a medium deep-sided bowl, using a rubber spatula, stir the egg yolks until they are a cohesive liquid. Do not use a whisk!

5. Add the sugar, cream, condensed milk, milk powder, dextrose, honey, salt and yeast mixture and combine using an immersion blender for about 1 minute.

6. Set the bowl in the ice bath. Let the mixture cool, cover the bowl with plastic wrap, and refrigerate for at least 3 hours. If you have time, place the mixture in an air-tight container and refrigerate overnight.

7. Spin the gelato in an ice cream machine according to the manufacturer's instructions. Or use the dry-ice method in your stand mixer (see page 210).

STRAWBERRY GELATO

Yield: 1½ quarts

Hulled strawberries 3 cups (400 grams)
Sugar 2 tablespoons (25 grams)
Juice of 1 lemon
Salt to taste
Egg yolks 5 (90 grams)
Whole milk 2 cups (500 grams)
Heavy cream ⅓ cup (75 grams)
Condensed milk ¼ cup (80 grams)
Milk powder ¼ cup (25 grams)
Dextrose 2 tablespoons (25 grams)
Sugar ⅓ cup (75 grams)
Honey 1 tablespoon (20 grams)

1. In a medium deep-sided bowl, combine the strawberries, sugar, lemon juice, and a small pinch of salt and let the berries break down, or macerate, for at least 30 minutes.

2. Puree the macerated strawberries using an immersion blender and strain through a chinois or fine-mesh strainer. Add 2 table-spoons of the pulp and seeds back into the strained puree and set aside.

3. In a large bowl, prepare an ice bath.

4. In a medium deep-sided bowl, using a rubber spatula, stir the egg yolks until they

are a cohesive liquid. Do not use a whisk!

5. Add the whole milk, cream, condensed milk, milk powder, dextrose, sugar, honey, and strawberry puree, and combine using an immersion blender for about 1 minute.

6. Set the bowl in the ice bath. Let the mixture cool, cover the bowl with plastic wrap, and refrigerate for at least 3 hours. If you have time, place the mixture in an air-tight container and refrigerate overnight.

7. Spin the gelato in an ice cream machine according to the manufacturer's instructions. Or use the dry-ice method in your stand mixer (see page 210).

RICOTTA GELATO

Yield: 2 quarts

Ricotta (Calabra brand is preferred and
    widely available) 6 cups (1,500 grams)
Simple syrup (see page 7) 3 cups (1,000
    grams)
Honey ½ cup (170 grams)
Salt to taste

1. In a large bowl, prepare an ice bath.

2. In a medium deep-sided bowl, combine the ricotta, simple syrup, honey, and salt using an immersion blender for about 1 minute.

3. Set the bowl in the ice bath. Let the mixture cool, cover the bowl with plastic wrap, and refrigerate for at least 3 hours. If you have time, place the mixture in an air-tight container and refrigerate overnight.

4. Spin the gelato in an ice cream machine according to the manufacturer's instructions. Or use the dry-ice method in your stand mixer (see page 210).

RICOTTA STRACCIATELLA

This is chocolate-laced ricotta gelato. You'll notice that I turn to it often.
Yield: 2 quarts

Bittersweet chocolate, very best quality,
    chopped ½ cup (156 grams)
Ricotta Gelato (above)

1. Place a large metal bowl in the freezer.

2. In a small microwavable bowl, melt the chocolate in the microwave in 30-second intervals, stirring in between to ensure that the chocolate doesn't scorch. (If you don't have a microwave, use a double boiler.) Set aside.

3. Transfer the ricotta gelato to the frozen bowl and, using a spoon, drizzle the chocolate over it in an irregular pattern. Fold the gelato over onto itself—don't be gentle—and continue until you've run out of chocolate and there are shards of chocolate mixed throughout.

To serve: This is used with Eggplant and Chocolate (page 98), but can, in fact, be served a thousand ways.

OATMEAL-INFUSED GELATO

I served this dish to Fergus and Margot Henderson, the awesome husband-wife chef duo from London, when they were dining at Del Posto. I figured oatmeal gelato was the most British thing on the menu then (I was thinking UK and porridge. You know, they eat loads of porridge in England, don't they? And drink hot tea?) and I was excited to present it. At the time, I knew all about Fergus, but nothing about Margot. When I went to the table, I shook Fergus's hand furiously and smiled. "Oh man, it's so cool to meet you, I'm such a big fan. This is oatmeal-infused gela—" I hadn't finished when Margot let out a loud *harrumph*. She held out her hand. Ashamed, I shook it. I learned that oatmeal gelato ain't especially British. More important, I learned that you do not accidentally disrespect Margot Henderson. She will have your ass.

Yield: 1½ quarts

Old fashioned oats 4 cups (205 grams)
Whole milk 2 cups (500 grams)
Egg yolks 5 (90 grams)
Heavy cream ⅓ cup (75 grams)
Condensed milk ¼ cup (80 grams)
Nonfat milk powder ¼ cup (25 grams)
Dextrose 2 tablespoons (25 grams)
Sugar ⅓ cup (75 grams)
Honey 1 tablespoon (20 grams)
Salt to taste

1. Preheat the oven to 350°F. Line a baking sheet with parchment.

2. Spread the oats across the baking sheet evenly and toast until they are very dark but not burned, stirring occasionally to prevent scorching, about 10 minutes.

3. In a medium saucepan over medium-low heat, bring the whole milk to a simmer and then remove from the heat.

4. Add 2 cups of the toasted oats to the milk and steep for only 5 minutes.

5. Strain through a chinois or fine-mesh strainer, discard the oats, and return the milk to the saucepan. Reheat the milk to a simmer. Remove from the heat and add the remaining 2 cups oats and infuse a second time, again for only 5 minutes. Strain through a chinois or fine-mesh strainer, discard the oats, and let the oat milk chill for two hours.

6. In a large bowl, prepare an ice bath.

7. In a medium deep-sided bowl, using a rubber spatula, stir the egg yolks until they are a cohesive liquid. Do not use a whisk!

8. Add the cream, condensed milk, milk powder, dextrose, sugar, honey, salt, and oat milk, and combine using an immersion blender for about 1 minute.

9. Set the bowl in the ice bath. Let the mixture cool, cover the bowl with plastic wrap, and refrigerate for at least 3 hours. If you have time, place the mixture in an airtight container and refrigerate overnight.

10. Spin the gelato in an ice cream machine according to the manufacturer's instructions. Or use the dry-ice method in your stand mixer (see page 210).

CASHEW GELATO

Yield: 1½ quarts

Raw cashews 4 cups (570 grams)
Whole milk 2 cups (500 grams)
Egg yolks 5 (90 grams)
Heavy cream ⅓ cup (75 grams)
Condensed milk ¼ cup (80 grams)
Nonfat milk powder ¼ cup (25 grams)
Dextrose 2 tablespoons (25 grams)
Sugar ⅓ cup (75 grams)
Honey 1 tablespoon (20 grams)
Salt to taste

1. Preheat the oven to 350°F.

2. On a baking sheet, spread the cashews out in a single layer and toast until very dark, checking on them after 20 minutes. You really want these cashews to toast, basically until they look burned, but they're not.

3. In a medium saucepan over medium heat, bring the whole milk to a simmer.

4. In a medium heat-safe airtight container, add all but a handful of the hot cashews and pour in the hot milk. Let the nut-milk mixture cool, cover, and then store overnight in the fridge to infuse milk with *molto* cashew flavor.

5. In a large bowl, prepare an ice bath.

6. Strain the milk through a chinois or fine-mesh strainer and discard the nuts.

7. In a medium deep-sided bowl, using a rubber spatula, stir the egg yolks until they are a cohesive liquid. Do not use a whisk!

8. Add the cream, condensed milk, milk powder, dextrose, sugar, honey, salt, and cashew milk, and combine using an immersion blender for about 1 minute.

9. Set the bowl in the ice bath. Let the mixture cool, cover the bowl with plastic wrap, and refrigerate for at least 3 hours. If you have time, place the mixture in an air-tight container and refrigerate overnight.

10. Roughly chop the reserved toasted cashews, add to the chilled mixture, and spin the gelato in an ice cream machine according to the manufacturer's instructions. Or use the dry-ice method in your stand mixer (see page 210).

OLIVE OIL GELATO

Yield: 1½ quarts

Egg yolks 5 (90 grams)
Whole milk 2 cups (500 grams)
Heavy cream ⅓ cup (75 grams)
Condensed milk ¼ cup (80 grams)
Nonfat milk powder ¼ cup (25 grams)
Dextrose 2 tablespoons (25 grams)
Sugar ⅓ cup (75 grams)
Honey 1 tablespoon (20 grams)
Extra-virgin olive oil ½ cup (93 grams)
Salt to taste

1. In a large bowl, prepare an ice bath.

2. In a medium deep-sided bowl, using a rubber spatula, stir the egg yolks until they are a cohesive liquid. Do not use a whisk!

3. Add the whole milk, cream, condensed milk, milk powder, dextrose, sugar, honey, olive oil, and salt, and combine using an immersion blender for about 1 minute. You want to give this a larger dose of salt than normal: It will bring out the olive oiliness of the olive oil.

4. Set the bowl in the ice bath. Let the mixture cool, cover the bowl with plastic wrap, and refrigerate for at least 3 hours. If you have time, place the mixture in an air-tight container and refrigerate overnight.

5. Spin the gelato in an ice cream machine according to the manufacturer's instructions. Or use the dry-ice method in your stand mixer (see page 210).

BASTONCINO

Piero, the suave, stressed-out maître d' at Del Posto—*I need that table back, please, Bello. Please, I need it, dio cane*—came up with the name for these. *Bastoncino* translates into "stick." You don't have to put these desserts on lollipop sticks, but they're pretty cute and you can find the sticks easily (you can buy them at any craft store). These are olive oil gelato lollipops that are dipped in chocolate and then rolled in salted and olive oil–fried bread crumbs. Early on I had doubts that the frozen bread crumbs would work. But they are so good, and they stay very crunchy. Someone once told me they reminded him of a Choco Taco from Taco Bell, which I did not take as an insult in any way.

Yield: Lots of little lollipops

Olive Oil Gelato (opposite page)
Chocolate Coating (page 160)
Bread Crumbs (page 133)

1. Place two parchment-lined baking sheets (any size) in your freezer overnight.

2. Using a spoon, scoop free-form ice cream balls onto your frozen baking sheets, working as quickly as possible. Stick a lollipop stick into each one. Return the sheets to the freezer for 30 minutes.

3. Have your chocolate coating ready at room temperature and still fluid. Place the bread crumbs in a wide shallow bowl.

4. Dip each ice cream ball fully into the chocolate, and while the chocolate is still setting, dip the ball into the bread crumbs. Place the chocolate-covered balls back onto the frozen baking sheets and into the freezer to set again.

To serve: Go for it.

217

Nicholas Coleman knows a lot about olive oil. He is an olive oil expert. I use a lot of extra-virgin olive oil, and sometimes Nick wanders into DP and we drink different oils and talk. He has perfectly groomed facial hair, goes by "Nicky Oils." He works in New York City at Eataly, a food emporium owned by the Bastianiches and Mario Batali. He strong-armed his way into the job. He strong-armed Mario Batali and Joe Bastianich. I cannot explain how insane that is.

ON REGIONAL ITALIAN OLIVE OILS
by Nicholas Coleman

Class A extra-virgin olive oil is, after salt, the most fundamental ingredient in the culinary world. It is the king of the Italian pantry and the backbone of the Mediterranean diet. Few foods are as versatile or as useful to the home or professional cook. Olive oil pairs well with vegetables, beans, bread, pizza, pasta, cheese, soup, salad, seafood, meat, poultry, and yes, dessert.

A wide variety of boutique Italian-grown, single-estate oils has enriched the olive oil market over the past few years. How best to pair these oils with the appropriate cuisines and courses requires an understanding of their individual virtues.

Oils vary greatly in character from country to country and region to region—there are, in fact, often distinct differences evident within the same olive grove from one season to the next. Like wine, all olive oils are not created equal. Key determinants include the age and health of the trees, the olive cultivars, the timing of the harvest, the soil, the growing season weather patterns, the altitude, how quickly the olives are brought from tree to mill, and, most important, as with wine making, the skill and diligence of the grove's caretaker.

Italy, generally, can be divided into three olive oil production zones: northern, central, and southern. Each region has its own distinctive flavor profile.

Due to the region's typically late harvest, oils produced in Northern Italy tend to be buttery, mellow, and delicate, with soft undertones of sweet almonds or toasted pine nuts. These oils generally finish with a slight nip of black pepper and pair best with dishes in which the oil's flavor is intended to subsume, not overpower, the other ingredients, making them ideal for finishing basil pesto, eggs, or raw fish.

Central Italy produces oils that tend to have strong aromas of freshly cut grass and bitter herbs, ending with a pungent, lingering black pepper finish that slowly trails off in the back of the throat. The cause of this intense peppery sensation—considered an attribute of high-quality olive oil—is oleocanthal, a natural phenolic compound that has both anti-inflammatory and antioxidant properties. This style of oil is best utilized where the intent is for the oil to cut through and brighten up the dish, pairing well with red meat, cannellini beans, or a simple tomato soup.

Oils produced in Southern Italy, where primarily green olives are harvested early, tend to be fruity and vibrant, with hints of green apple skin or green tomato vine, ending with a robust, peppery finish. These oils will be quite assertive when used as a finishing oil and can add to the food a pleasing fruity, zesty element. These oils pair well with grilled seafood, Caprese salad, or eggplant caponata.

A variety of approaches can be applied to pairing oil with a specific dish. One is to consider how the food is prepared: Is it raw? Baked? Grilled? Fried? Each method produces a different food "weight" that better corresponds with an oil's particular intensity. For example, a grassier, more robust oil would be a better choice for a seasoned grilled steak than for a raw preparation, such as steak tartare.

It is also helpful to think regionally. If, for example, the goal is to re-create an authentic Tuscan dish, then the most accurate result will be achieved using a high-quality Tuscan oil. If the goal is to re-create a Sicilian dish, use Sicilian oil.

When choosing oil, the three most important pieces of information to look for on the label are the harvest date, olive cultivars, and the region from which it originates.

Unlike many wine varieties, olive oil does *not* improve with age, so freshness is a key quality component. Check the date. In addition, different olives will have varying organoleptic properties (taste, color, aroma, feel, etc.), and knowing the cultivars of which the oil is composed is crucial. There is a saying: "What grows together goes together." Be sure the olives from which the oil in the bottle is produced come not only from one country, but from a specific, localized region within that country.

Most important, when choosing oil, be sure to smell and then taste it—on its own, independent of other foods—so that you can experience and then analyze its viscosity and flavor profile. This will trigger ideas about what it pairs best with. There are no firm rules here. It is very personal. With eyes closed, listen to your palate.

Finally, no single oil can solve all your culinary conundrums. Have a variety of oils on hand. At minimum, one each of the three above-mentioned types, indicated by region: a delicate finishing oil that won't overpower basic flavors, one robust finishing oil to cut through stronger food, and one more affordable (but clean-tasting) extra-virgin olive oil for cooking.

PEANUT BUTTER MASCARPONE WITH BEJEWELED BANANAS

I have never served this at Del Posto. Ladner despises bananas. But it is absolutely a killer at home, or at a restaurant where the chef won't murder you for using bananas.

You have to use Skippy or Jif for this. The recipe is engineered for their massive sugar content. Let's face it: Peanut butter, in the best American sense, is a dessert. How it ever became a bagged-lunch mainstay is ridiculous. It's the Nutella of the USA.

Cheap, mass-produced peanut butter mixed with elegant, imported Italian mascarpone cheese is wrong in every way. Somehow it works. I blast the bananas in the broiler until they look like deformed jewels, top them with salty and sweet croutons, and serve in a very small portion. It's Fat Elvis goes to the Veneto.
Yield: 4 servings

Mascarpone 1 cup (225 grams)
Peanut butter 1 cup (258 grams)
Salt 1 teaspoon (4 grams)
Bananas 2, cut into ½-inch slices
Turbinado sugar 2 tablespoons plus 1 table-
    spoon (50 grams plus 25 grams)
Croutons (page 132)

1. Preheat the oven to 500°F.
2. In a medium bowl, mix together the mascarpone, peanut butter, and salt, being careful not to overmix—the mascarpone will split. You'll know if it does, because it will look gross.
3. On an unlined baking sheet, space out the bananas evenly, sprinkle with 2 table-spoons of the sugar, and place under the broiler until the sugar is bubbly and the bananas lose their shape, about 1 minute, maybe less.

To serve: Surround a scoop of the peanut butter cream with the bananas, top with the remaining tablespoon sugar, and finish with some croutons.

"Brown food is brown and it is beautiful." —Chris Bianco

BREAKING UP WITH PANNA COTTA

Oh man, gelatin: It is creepy stuff, for sure. It's made out of animal bones, sometimes pigs, sometimes fish. So it's not even vegetarian, which makes Jell-O sort of evil to me. There are other plant-based hydrocolloids that do similar gelling duties, but there is always something off about them. They lack the melt-in-your-mouth quality gelatin provides. And it makes sense, I guess, since gelatin is gunk from a once-living animal that melts at body temperature.

Don't get me wrong, I have a long-standing relationship with Haribo gummi bears, which are one of the greatest foods on the planet and gelatin achieving its ideal. But for Christ's sake, why do so many pastry chefs use so much gelatin? They *rely* on the stuff. They *worship* it! Is it all about control? I prefer being slightly out of control. I like food that struggles to support its own structure. Messy stuff, awkward stuff. That's my version of Italian.

So I broke up with panna cotta a few years ago.

Some dessert menus in NYC are basically *all* panna cotta, just with gussied-up nomenclature. But here's the thing: If it's a gelatin-stabilized mousse or crème or custard or *cremeux* or whatever, then it is panna cotta.

Ladner has no real beef with panna cotta. (He did, however, warn me against pairing a panna cotta with a sorbet: *Are you kidding me? It makes no sense texturally!*) After all, a panna cotta flavored with nothing is the most Italian thing in the world. Celebrate the cream! The cow! This fucking cow! It is so beautiful! Look what it gives us! (Adam Nathanson, the guitarist from Born Against and Young Pioneers, once said to me, "You ever looked at a cow's face close up? Cows are cool, man.")

But the epidemic of flavored panna cottas was killing me: mango, passion fruit, strawberry, buttermilk, crème fraîche, "vanilla bean." It was an irresponsible reliance on gelatin—way too much gelatin. It's all bouncy, unnatural textures. Gels. The only gels I want to eat are made by Wylie Dufresne. So panna cotta and I, we split up. Said our good-byes. Collected our belongings from each other's apartments, erased our numbers from speed dial, and walked away.

Then a couple years later, I had a panna cotta at Franny's, a fantastic, *honest* restaurant in Brooklyn. Its panna cotta is molded in a cup but plated as a freestanding thing. The panna cotta is set with the bare minimum of gelatin and it bells out on the plate, shapeless. A blob. Like Pizza the Hut from *Spaceballs*. It comes drizzled with aged balsamic vinegar and, goddamn, it is a thing of beauty: simple, jiggly, super sexy, very Italian. Food meant for eating. I mopped the plate.

So I went crawling back to panna cotta. It was in April. A spring romance. We hung out in the park and watched the sun come up. We walked around New York City in the rain and planned a trip to Easter Island together. *Wouldn't that be rad? Have you ever been there? Me neither! Dude! We gotta do it!* These days you will find panna cotta on the menu at Del Posto year-round.

BROWN BUTTER PANNA COTTA

I started the band Oldest with Mick Barr in 2009 as a two-person project. Mick's guitar playing is complicated, and I play drums like a caveman. Our songs take months of rehearsing before they're ready to be recorded. With C.R.A.S.H., my other current band, the songs can be written and played live within hours. Brown butter panna cotta is like an Oldest song.

My sous-chef Kim Janusz is 100 percent responsible for this technique and recipe. It's her thing. I watch in awe when she makes it. It is by far the most complicated recipe in this book. But then Scotty, another cook at Del Posto, made this recipe in the tiny, generator-powered kitchen of a beach house in Maine. He said it came out perfectly, and he did it with the added handicap of having his one-year-old son strapped to his chest during the process. So give it a shot.

Day 1

Unsalted butter ½ pound, or 2 sticks
    (226 grams)
Heavy cream 2 cups (476 grams)
Salt ½ teaspoon (2 grams)
Whole milk, cold 2 cups (488 grams)

1. In a large pot over high heat, combine the butter, cream, and salt. The mixture will boil up and then drop. Once it goes down, begin stirring it constantly with a heat-resistant spatula. It will thicken and then break—stir it constantly, otherwise it will "butterscorch." ("Breaking" is the milk solids separating from the fat.) When the solids have turned dark brown, your pot is smoking, your fire alarm is screaming, and the neighbors have alerted the authorities, it is ready.

2. Remove the mixture from the heat and add the cold milk . . . carefully.

3. Into a heat-resistant container, pour the brown butter milk and let it cool on your countertop. Don't touch it. Walk away. Once the milk is cooled, cover it tightly and refrigerate overnight. (Seriously, don't touch it.)

Day 2

Remove the brown butter milk from the fridge. If you did this right, there will be a thick layer of fat over the top of the milk. Run your knife around this fat and then lift it right off. Beneath the fat is the infused milk with its solids. It should be golden in color.

NOW YOU'LL NEED

Unflavored gelatin 4 sheets
Heavy cream 2⅓ cups (562 grams)
Light brown sugar ½ cup (100 grams),
    packed
Salt to taste

1. In a medium bowl filled with ice water, add the gelatin and let it bloom, 3 to 5 minutes. Wring the water from the gelatin and place it in a bowl.

2. In a medium saucepan over medium heat, warm the skimmed brown butter milk, the cream, and brown sugar. Do not let it come to a boil. Add the gelatin and cook until it is melted.

3. Strain this mixture through a fine-mesh strainer back into the original bowl,

pressing it through the strainer with a spatula to get out all the flavor in the milk solids. Cover tightly and refrigerate overnight.

Day 3 (I know!)

1. Remove the final layer of fat off the top of the milk. Under this is your delicious, perfect, really fat-free panna cotta.

2. Using a double boiler, melt the perfect, delicious panna cotta down again and then portion it into your containers of choice.

3. Cover tightly and refrigerate until the panna cotta is set, at least 3 hours, but preferably overnight.

To serve: Serve your hard-won brown brown butter panna cotta with whatever acidic fruits are seasonally available and shards of the Pasta Frolla (page 136). Add a touch of Maldon salt and a drizzle of good olive oil and you are done. Serve immediately, savor success.

REGULAR PANNA COTTA

Yield: About 3 cups

Unflavored gelatin 4 sheets
Whole milk 1 cup (250 grams)
Heavy cream 2½ cups (600 grams)
Sugar ¾ cup (145 grams)
Salt a pinch

1. In a medium bowl filled with ice water, add the gelatin and let it bloom, 3 to 5 minutes.

2. In a small saucepan over medium heat, warm the milk, cream, sugar and salt, stirring occasionally until the sugar dissolves completely.

3. Squeeze the water out of the gelatin and add it to the cream mixture, stirring gently until it dissolves. Remove the mixture from the heat and let it cool slightly. Portion the mixture into containers of your choice.

4. Cover tightly and refrigerate until the panna cotta is set, at least 3 hours, but preferably overnight.

To serve: As simply as possible.

HAND-PULLED STRACCIATELLA WITH STRAWBERRY QUICK JAM AND CROUTONS

I try to mention strawberry shortcake as often as possible. I hope you share my deep appreciation for this classic. The following variation on strawberry shortcake will confuse your friends, because it feels like a salad. And I get no greater thrill than when someone says of one of my dishes, "You know what, man? I don't know what to even call this . . . Is it a dessert? Is it a salad? I really don't know. It's just like, um, a thing."

I use Caputo Brothers mozzarella curd. It has a lovely and slight tang that recalls genuine burrata from Campania and can be found at online retailers. But I know of fancy restaurants in NYC that use Polly-O curd and people still flip out. Everyone goes nuts over freshly made mozzarella.

Yield: Serves 8

Caputo Brothers Mozzarella curd, thawed one 1-pound container (453 grams)
Water a kettle's worth, heated to 190°F
Salt large pinches
Heavy cream 1 quart (952 grams)
Strawberry Quick Jam (page 37)
Fresh strawberries, cut up, for serving (optional)
Croutons (page 132)
Freshly ground black pepper to taste
Extra-virgin olive oil to taste

1. Into a large heat-safe bowl, dump out the mozzarella curd and cover with the hot water. Liberally season with 3 large pinches of salt and let the curd sit for a minute to soften.

2. You need to stretch the cheese. Lift out of the water and let it drip and stretch slowly back into the bowl. With a wooden spoon, hold the curd down as you pull pieces out and over the edge of the bowl, using the spoon to drag it back into the water. Do this over and over, lifting and dropping and stretching. You want a curd that is smooth, but not completely without bubbles—one you can pull apart into stringy cheese.

3. In a medium bowl containing the cream, add the cheese strings and season with salt to taste.

To serve: Place some strands of stracciatella in a shallow bowl and top with a few blobs of strawberry jam. Add some cut up fresh strawberries if you have them. Top with a few croutons, a pinch of pepper, a drizzle of olive oil, and a sprinkle of salt.

CREAM CHEESE CRUST

By far one of the easiest recipes in this book, cream cheese crust, despite the goofy-sounding name, is a powerhouse, a superhero. It is an integral component in the Eggplant and Chocolate (page 98), and works for all varieties of baked fruit tarts. It puffs slightly but remains crunchy, and it requires about 1,000 percent less effort than a batch of classic puff pastry, which for me rarely if ever delivers on the effort-to-result space-time continuum.

I use Philadelphia brand cream cheese because I prefer its texture and think it tastes better than the generic stuff. Plus I am a sucker for iconic packaging, and that silver cardboard box just screams, "I will fuck up the bad guys." And even though there is not a single NYC deli or bagel place that uses Philadelphia cream cheese, this recipe *feels* like New York to me. It is versatile, resilient, full of character, cocky, smirking, and a total sweetheart.

Yield: One baking sheet of dough

Unsalted butter ⅓ cup, or ⅔ stick (85 grams), softened
Cream cheese ½ cup (113 grams), softened
Egg yolk 1 (18 grams)
All-purpose flour 1½ cups (188 grams)
Salt ½ teaspoon (2 grams)
Almond spread (page 100)
Turbinado sugar as needed

1. Preheat the oven to 450°F.
2. In the bowl of a stand mixer, using the paddle attachment, combine the butter and cream cheese on medium speed. Add the egg yolk and mix to incorporate. Add the flour and salt and mix until the dough just comes together.
3. Pat the mixture into a ball, put it in a bowl, and refrigerate for 30 minutes.
4. Between two sheets of parchment, roll the dough out to ¼-inch thickness. Refrigerate for another 30 minutes.
5. Rip the dough into irregular shapes, like Africa or Brazil but not Tennessee or Argentina. Smear a thin layer of almond spread onto each dough shape, top with your topping of choice, and bake until golden and slightly charred around the edges, about 8 minutes.

To serve: This is used with the Eggplant and Chocolate, but it works well as a universal pie or tart crust.

Cali Thornhill-DeWitt is a Los Angeles–based artist. More than twenty years ago he lived in the neighborhood where Del Posto currently resides. He has a Born Against tattoo that spans both wrists.

THE WEST SIDE OF LOWER MANHATTAN BEFORE DEL POSTO

by Cali Thornhill-DeWitt

When I moved to the corner of Ninth Avenue and 14th Street in 1991, just around a bleak Manhattan corner from where Del Posto now sits, the neighborhood was a different animal. The Meat Market, as it was known then, was mostly a ghost town. During the day, guys in large trucks from all over the city came to buy meat in bulk on behalf of restaurants. Once night fell, the area was overrun with transvestite prostitutes, crack dealers, and cast outs from a world-famous S&M dungeon called The Vault. Everywhere there were trash cans full of animal parts dyed blue to deter the local homeless. It was a cinematic dead zone, a zombie thrill under every pile of garbage.

Being new to town and with little to no financial resources, moving my life into a meat locker seemed like a pretty good option. It didn't *resemble* a meat locker—it *was* a meat locker. There were no windows, but there was a huge refrigerator door and a drain in the center of the room for liquid runoff. A few large leftover hooks hung from the ceiling, and it came prefurnished with an ancient butcher block that was stained deep from decades of use. It was attached to a welder's shop, and the welder and I shared a kitchen and bathroom.

One night I was outside haggling with a young gentleman over the price of his crack rocks. He handed me a suspicious little packet that I tore into and checked for authenticity. He was poking me in the stomach and mumbling muted threats as I discovered he had just handed me some dried-up ragweed. As I launched into an outraged diatribe demanding my money back, I noticed that thing he'd been jabbing into my stomach was a .45 automatic.

So he got my eight dollars or whatever my bullshit life savings was at that moment. But it was clear he was freaked out by my aggressive teenage death-wish vibe, and that gives me some satisfaction still.

I lived in the meat locker with my "girlfriend," a pro at relieving lonely middle-aged men of their money. She was young and beautiful and the most manipulative person I have ever met. One evening, we were in our usual position: no money, no food, no drugs. She decided to walk across the street to The Vault and see what, if any, opportunities existed. Thirty minutes or so later, she was back with three leather dykes, who had agreed to instruct her in the correct way to whip someone. That someone was me.

So there I was, a naked teen (I had boxers on when they started but those rascals quickly whipped them to my ankles), up against the wall of my live-in meat locker being thrashed by three strangers—three strangers who were at that same moment getting their bags rifled through. I cannot remember exactly how the night ended, but we were richer after they'd left than we were when they came. This was not an uncommon night in the meat locker. The Meat Market may have appeared deserted and ominous, but it was also an end-of-the-world playground for perverts and creeps.

For a good three to four months I was very, very itchy in that meat locker. Thinking back, it began almost as soon as we moved in—itchy and often covered in mysterious rashes. I told friends living elsewhere that NYC was an itchy town. Eventually, I went to a free clinic, where the doctor looked at me from several feet away and said, "You have scabies. And measles."

A little more than twenty years later, I was sitting in Del Posto, a block or so from my former meat locker. I ate a hundred-layer lasagna. I was presented with an apricot sorbet that took something like six weeks to prepare. I was eating a meal that had all my pleasure centers on high alert. My bloodstream was flooding with dopamine. I was eating the best meal of my life so far, and I would talk about it for months to come.

For reasons probably inexplicable to most, I miss the danger that used to exist in what is no longer the Meat Market but the Meatpacking District. It was like living in an unbelievable cartoon then, and was probably far weirder before I ever got there. Now it's a place where you can drop thousands at Diane Von Furstenberg and Alexander McQueen, and walk the High Line in complete safety, day or night. Where there are blocks-long lines of rich young socialites at midnight on a Tuesday, waiting to get into a club, while time marches forward and the past becomes unrecognizable.

COCA-COLA SAUCE

Two of my idols are chefs Gabrielle Hamilton of Prune, in New York City, and Nancy Silverton of Pizzeria Mozza, in Los Angeles.

Many years ago I moved my ass three thousand miles to California to work for Nancy at her restaurant Campanile, earning next to nothing, just to learn her food. Many of the recipes in this book are rip-offs masquerading as homage. She is a genius. Gabrielle, too. She just rules. She can cook me a branzino garnished with a blanket of raw parsley, get me to eat grilled cow tongue, or write an essay that makes me question my very existence. She is a true multitalent, a hyphenate, like John Waters or Galileo or Dave Grohl.

This sauce is inspired by both chefs equally.

I read once that Gabrielle is a big fan of Coca-Cola, which struck me as being among the best things I'd ever heard. Coke doesn't get a whole lot of love in the food world. But really, is there anything more refreshing than an ice-cold can of Coke? It's engineered by science to be *just that*!

When I worked at Campanile in the mid-2000s, I learned a dessert sauce that was so revolutionary to me that more than a decade later I still use it regularly. It is a champagne vinegar caramel sauce, with the vinegar taking the place of the cream in what would otherwise be a traditional caramel. It's wildly

"This is it."

refreshing. It is both caramel and acid, sticky *and* tart. Ideal when you need a jolt of acid on a dessert plate.

When we make it at the restaurant, we label it "Cham Vin," even though we use white wine vinegar, because that's the variation I learned from Nancy. Further complicating things, I call it Coca-Cola sauce because it completely captures the essence of drinking a Coke. Not surprisingly, the recipe suffers a bit of an identity crisis, like a nickname that over time evolves into something with no correlation to its real name. My former roommates Adam and Alyssa had a dog named Loretta, who we eventually began calling "Mozzarella," until finally her name was just "Cheese."

If you look on the back of a can of Coca-Cola, the main flavorings are caramel and acid. I know glass-bottled Coca-Cola is the pet of the food illuminati, but I'm not into it. Coke in a bottle, Mexican, plastic, or otherwise, lacks the hypercarbonation of the perfect canned variety. And please, do not ever talk to me about Diet Coke. It is the absolute fakest, most vile-tasting swill on the planet. If you don't want sugar, then drink fucking water. A few years ago when I saw that one of my favorite chefs did a series of Diet Coke commercials, my heart sank into my shoes. I am the last person on earth to cry "sell-out!" because I have recently realized that there is no such thing, *and* I wholly approve of and applaud Andrew W.K. doing those absurd KitKat commercials. It's just that Diet Coke is reprehensibly gross.

In Naples you eat pizza and drink Coke. When my friend Cali, who doesn't drink, came to Del Posto, the bartender paired his serving of Ladner's hundred-layer lasagna with a glass of Coca-Cola on crushed ice. It was a perfect pairing. El Bulli's Ferran Adrià once said of the American love of the sweet-and-savory combination: "A burger with ketchup and a Coca-Cola is your national treasure." Coke is it, man. Coke is it. Here is the sauce.

Yield: 1 quart

Sugar 4 cups (800 grams)
Water ½ cup (118 grams)
White wine vinegar 1 pint (478 grams)
Unsalted butter 1 cup, or 2 sticks (227 grams)
Salt 1 teaspoon (4 grams)
Juice from 1 lemon

1. In a heavy saucepan over medium-low heat, combine the sugar and water until it is the consistency of wet sand and is a slightly blond caramel in color. Be sure there is no residual sugar on the sides of the pan.

2. Remove from the heat and add the vinegar. The sugar will bubble and seize. Return to low heat for a few minutes longer, until all the sugar remelts. Whisk in the butter and add the salt and lemon juice.

4. Allow the sauce to cool to room temperature.

To serve: This works well with both the Polenta Crêpes (page 116) and the Buckwheat Crespelle (page 114). Or just pour it on some ice cream.

See page 61.

PROFILE IN COURAGE:

Gabrielle Hamilton (Chef-Owner, Prune, NYC)

Born: **Early morning**

Occupation: **Member of the society of the hypervigilant**

Status: **Soberly optimistic**

Notable quote: **"This is not our last supper."**

Shoe size: **It's the footprint that matters.**

Lunch food: **Buttered toast**

Beverage: **Negroni**

I Heart NY: **Except when I'm driving**

First time: **Better than expected**

Accomplishments: **Regular brushing and flossing**

Ambition future plan: **To keep Prune alive and relevant long enough that my sons can have jobs as busboys!**

CANNOLO STILE LIBERO: THE FREE-FORM CANNOLI

Everyone loves a good cannoli—or at least the *idea* of a good cannoli. But lucking onto a good one is extremely rare, like finding a first pressing of the Misfits' "Cough/Cool" 7-inch, or a Shamrock Shake at McDonald's. Most Italian bakeries have shitty cannoli. There, I said it. Taking one for the team here: The majority of cannoli are greasy, thick-skinned, and filled with corrosively sweet ricotta paste. One bite and you are done.

A good chunk of the Italian nationals who work or have worked at Del Posto come as front-of-house employees: captains, back waiters, sommeliers, bartenders. Rarely do we get Italian cooks. Together they represent the different regions of Italy: Sicily (Denis, the hilarious class clown), Calabria (Piero, the ur-maitre d' whose coif reveals the weather outside), Tuscany (Allesandro, the arrogant prick I love to hate), Lazio (Andrea, "I'm not Italian, I'm *Roman*. I have history, fuck these jerks"), Lombardia (Elisabetta, always smirking in a charming way), Friuli (Sbrizzo, the teddy bear with a bad attitude), and of course Long Island (Russo, loves golf, wife-beater undershirts, and hockey). They all have a bone to pick with one another.

When I ask them for Italian language advice for menu descriptions, it's a regionally linguistic free-for-all. Denis claims that anything north of Naples is a total backwater. Daniel, from the North, claims that Denis is a stupid southern hick all hopped up on garlic and almonds. Russo wonders if anyone caught last night's game at the Nassau Coliseum. It gets heated.

I love the idea of a great cannoli, too. But when I set out to make Del Posto's version, I was quickly sucked into trying to deconstruct it. Sbrizzo, in a lightbulb moment, dubbed it *cannolo stile libero*: the free-form cannoli. I already had a ricotta stracciatella gelato, so that was going to be the filling. I rolled the cannoli dough out really thin, like a pasta dough (in fact, use a pasta machine if you have one), so it would cook bubbly and crisp, but would still barely be there. We cut the cannoli dough into tortilla chip–like shards, fried them, and pushed them onto an irregular blob of the gelato. In the iconic words of Mario Batali on just about every episode of *Molto Mario*: "Take it to the plate."

Yield: 5 servings of cannoli "chips"

All-purpose flour 1½ cups (187 grams)
Sugar 2 tablespoons (25 grams)
Salt ¼ teaspoon (1 gram)
Extra-virgin olive oil 2 tablespoons (27 grams)
Red wine vinegar 1 teaspoon (5 grams)
Red wine ½ cup (117 grams)
Peanut oil for frying 1 quart (864 grams)
Ricotta Stracciatella (page 213)
Powdered sugar for dusting

1. In a food processor, combine the flour, sugar, and salt and pulse to incorporate.

2. In a bowl with a spout, whisk together the olive oil, vinegar, and red wine. With the food processor still running, slowly add the wine mixture to the flour mixture, checking to make sure they are incorporating. Once the dough comes together and begins to circle around the food processor blade, it is ready.

3. Turn the dough out onto a floured surface and knead it for about 2 minutes, or until you have a smooth ball. Wrap it in plastic wrap and refrigerate overnight.

4. In a deep-sided saucepan over high heat, bring the peanut oil to 350°F. Line two baking sheets with parchment and set aside.

5. Cut the dough into quarters and run each quarter through a pasta machine to get it as thin as possible, dusting liberally with flour as you go and storing the rolled dough on the reserved baking sheets. Cut the sheets of dough into small chips, about the size of Tostitos. Deep-fry until golden and blistered, 4 to 5 minutes.

6. Transfer to a paper towel–lined cooling rack to cool. These will keep in an airtight container for up to 5 days.

To serve: Adorn a scoop of ricotta stracciatella with some cannoli chips and dust with powdered sugar. Serve right away.

BAND TOUR FOOD DIARY: OLDEST/C.R.A.S.H.

By 2009, I was dying to play drums again. I'd also been slightly busy with a move to New York and getting a job at a little joint called Del Posto. I started Oldest (as in nothing *older*) with Mick Barr around this time. It was our no-pressure band. Just recording, no live shows. At the time of this writing, we still have not played a live show. A good chunk of our practices and recording have put us in the Woodhaven neighborhood in Queens. Our snack of choice varies: the Dunkin' Donuts waffle egg and cheese sandwich (Mick: *Hey, it's new!*), Sal's Pizza on Jamaica Avenue (so old school it feels and tastes like 1975), and the Thai place that got shut down by the NYC DOH (bummer). Lots of Bustelo coffee for Mick and supermarket-brand seltzer water for me.

I formed C.R.A.S.H. in 2011. It's a fun project—loud, ridiculous—that yet again has me flying back and forth between the East and West Coasts to practice and play shows. C.R.A.S.H., well, we don't take ourselves too seriously. I once organized a show for us at what used to be Lung Shan restaurant in San Francisco. We played with the doors open, out onto the street, at 3 p.m. on a Sunday afternoon—to nobody. We played two more shows later that same day and people came to watch, but they were nowhere near as fun.

One weekend in LA in November 2013, we played two shows. One was in a Dumpster cage downtown with the doors shut, so the crowd was forced to stand on benches outside and look down in at us. The second was a guerrilla show in the seating area of our favorite Iranian ice cream shop, Mashti Malone's, in West Hollywood. It was busy, and as we played customers queued up with their fingers plugging their ears and bought clone cones anyway. We made zero dollars that weekend.

We have one vegan member and the rest of us will eat anything. I force these guys to go to expensive bakeries when we play San Francisco, and we had a band meeting once at Pizzeria Mozza in LA. But for the most part we just eat lots of tacos. It's Los Angeles. It doesn't make a lot of sense to do otherwise. Our entire set takes thirteen minutes.

TIRAMISÙ

Tiramisù is a classic Italian dessert that isn't classic in any way. Some say it's been around since the late 1960s, and others say it was first made in the 1980s. The subject is as laden with conspiracy theories as a Bob Dylan biography or the Stanley Kubrick NASA footage.

Tiramisù translates to "pick-me-up." And it is so true: espresso, sugar, a little booze, cheese. Best served in a small portion. At Del Posto we sometimes do a version that is only slightly larger than a shot glass. "Impossibly small" we call it on the menu. Although we pride ourselves on hospitality, giving our guests whatever they want, we refuse second servings. "Can I have another?" *Nope. That's all you need.*

Here is the easiest and most delicious version of tiramisù I have eaten (and I have eaten thousands). Good, freshly brewed espresso is key, so even if you have to go to some lame corporate coffee store to get some, you should. Same goes for the cheese: Get the best imported Italian mascarpone you can find (I prefer Galbani). Don't worry that it is sloppy—if you're able to serve a perfectly sliced piece of tiramisù, it's probably gross. You should need to spoon it. If you don't want to make the sponge cake, buy quality imported *savioardi* at the same Italian market where you got the mascarpone. No one will know. Cool? *Yield: About 3 cups*

TIRAMISÙ CREAM

Mascarpone 2 cups (450 grams)
Sugar ½ cup (100 grams)
Egg yolks 4 (72 grams)
Heavy cream 2 tablespoons (30 grams)
Dark rum 2 tablespoons (28 grams)
Salt to taste

In the bowl of a stand mixer, using the whip attachment, combine the mascarpone, sugar, egg yolks, cream, rum, and salt on slow speed, gradually increasing the speed as the mixture becomes stable. Whip until you have a very fluffy cream, but don't overwhip. Mascarpone curdles and separates with heavy agitation.

TIRAMISÙ SPONGE CAKE

Eggs 9 separated
Sugar 2 cups (400 grams)
Water ¼ cup (59 grams)
All-purpose flour 1 cup (125 grams)
Cornstarch ½ cup (64 grams)
Salt to taste

1. Preheat the oven to 375°F. Line two baking sheets with parchment and set aside.

2. In the bowl of a stand mixer, using the whip attachment, combine the egg whites on slow speed. Slowly add 1 cup of the sugar, gradually increasing the speed to create a stable meringue. Scoop the mixture into a separate bowl and refrigerate until ready to use.

3. In the still-messy bowl, add the egg yolks, water, and the remaining 1 cup sugar and whip on high speed until you have a fluffy, ribbony mixture.

4. In a large but shallow mixing bowl, add the egg yolk mixture and the reserved egg white mixture and combine gently using a rubber spatula. Be nice. Streaks are fine. The more you manipulate this, the less fluffy it will be later.

5. Sift together the flour, cornstarch, and salt and gently combine them with the eggs until you can't see any flour. Using a large spatula, distribute the batter onto the two baking sheets *very gently*. Don't get all speed metal and go crazy smearing the batter everywhere. Think Barry White.

6. Bake for 7 to 10 minutes, until the tops of the cakes are golden brown and still soft to the touch. Let the cakes cool completely in the pans.

FOR ASSEMBLY

Espresso, freshly brewed, cooled 3 cups
Natural unsweetened cocoa powder, very best
 quality, to finish

To serve: In a fancy shallow serving dish, spread a thin layer of the tiramisù cream. Add a layer of cake. Using a plastic squirt bottle, soak the cake completely with the cooled espresso. Add another layer of tiramisù cream, another layer of cake, more espresso. Don't be stingy with the espresso, OK? Finish with a last layer of cream. Spoon a few tablespoons of cocoa powder into a double layer of cheesecloth, pull it into a fist-size ball, and gently shake the cocoa onto the finished tiramisù until fully blanketed. Serve immediately, or hold in the refrigerator for no longer than 8 hours.

Home made sponge cake or store-bought Savoiardi ladyfingers.

BOIL THE CAN, YOU MADE A BOMB

"A boiled can of sweetened condensed milk is like sex in a tin."—Chef April Bloomfield, 2008

Explosions are not cool. I don't get my rocks off from fireworks. I couldn't care less, and (no kidding) July Fourth is my birthday. My friend Speck throws an Independence Day party every year at her apartment in Brooklyn Heights. I usually stay inside and go through her records while everyone else crams onto the balcony to watch the fireworks. This annoys Speck immensely. I tell her I slept through the application process for the let's-blow-shit-up gene. Not interested.

The label on a can of Eagle Brand Sweetened Condensed Milk says in very clear writing: DO NOT BOIL THIS CAN. It's there for a reason. Canned sweetened condensed milk is an explosive in negligent hands.

We used to make dulce de leche at Del Posto by boiling big number 10 cans of Eagle Brand milk in a huge stockpot. Dulce de leche is an amplified caramel sauce. It's sexy, gooey, absolutely delicious.

Once, Dulce (that was her name; I'm not making this up) dropped a can in a huge pot, covered it with water, cranked the flame to high, and went downstairs to tackle some prep work. Cooking the contents of the can into dulce de leche takes a long while and requires that you constantly replace the water that evaporates.

It was an early Saturday morning. The first shift of cooks wasn't due for several hours. Dulce forgot about the milk.

The number 10 can bobbed along for a bit before all the water completely evaporated. The flame, still maxed, turned the stockpot black, and then an ominous electric pink. I didn't witness this, but Ladner did. He was in the kitchen early that morning, preparing to teach a rare Saturday-morning cooking class. I was asleep (see I Sleep Through Cooking Classes, below).

The first thing Ladner did when he arrived was get two giant pasta boilers rolling. A few feet away, Dulce's science experiment was throbbing and groaning impatiently on the pastry line. Ladner didn't notice.

But at some point he must have smelled the burning metal. Beside him was in effect a pipe bomb, not all that far from exploding molten caramelized milk and shrapnel everywhere.

In an act of MacGyver/head chef brilliance, he pulled the pot *gently* off the heat. He slowly, terrifyingly, poured some of his boiling pasta water over the engorged can. He told me later that the pot was almost soft to the touch. Even though he was adding fast-boiling water, the can hissed and sputtered.

Had the can exploded, it would have destroyed that part of the kitchen and maimed anyone nearby. The mess of dripping black caramel would have been impossible to clean. A disaster.

So, please: Buy premade dulce de leche at the supermarket. That's what I do. It's just like boiling it yourself. It really is. It's in a can or jar. It is sold at the Western Beef near Del Posto, so there is a good chance your local store will have it, too. It's the same exact thing. Only it's made in the safe environs of a commercial facility.

No explosions. They freak me out. Please. Not interested.

I SLEEP THROUGH COOKING CLASSES

A few days after Del Posto was awarded four stars in *The New York Times,* I was scheduled to teach a cooking class to ten paying guests as part of a food festival. I was a no-show. I slept through it.

It is a fireable offense at any other restaurant, and it *should* have been at Del Posto. I awoke to eighty-three missed phone calls and a text message history that grew increasingly desperate before dropping off entirely. I wear that day as a cloak of shame. Now, if I have to be anywhere before 9 a.m. (the airport, a doctor's appointment, a Department of Health test), I stay up all night. I have no choice. I cannot relive that. I'm shuddering even typing this.

NANCY IS A GENIUS

As the founder of La Brea Bakery in Los Angeles, the opening pastry chef at Spago, the mastermind behind the desserts at Campanile, and the pizza crust genius of Mozza, Nancy Silverton has shaped how Americans look at flour, water, salt, and yeast in a way very few, if any, others have. That artisanal loaf of bread at the Vons or Safeway near your house? Nancy is responsible for that. I often refer to her as the Ian MacKaye of bread. Her influence is everywhere, and the people who *know*, they just know.

When Nancy opened Pizzeria Mozza in 2006, I had just moved back to Washington, DC, after serving two years in LA. My first year in LA was spent laboring over minute-long Wrangler Brutes songs and paying the bills with terrible jobs. During year two, I worked under Nancy and her sergeant at arms at Campanile, pastry chef Dahlia. The experience permanently altered my approach to food. The menu changed every day based on the seasonal availability of fruit, and we used top-quality everything. We had a bible of Nancy's desserts, and we rotated them constantly. Presentation was a distant second to flavor. Plates were often messy, and maybe some sauces ran a bit. Nothing was overworked or unnatural looking, and we plated everything with our hands. Tweezers would have been booed off the stage.

The signature dessert at Pizzeria Mozza is a butterscotch budino—a pudding, basically, topped with chewy and salty caramel and slightly sour whipped crème fraîche for acid balance. Those neon-gold hard candies your grandfather has in a jar on his coffee table are all most people know of butterscotch. But this was real, simple butterscotch, in a pudding that relied on actual butterscotch made from scratch. It was revolutionary.

I'd already moved to New York when the dish debuted. I hadn't tasted it. But it didn't matter. I knew what it was by what I'd read and heard about it. It's especially easy to know with Nancy. I had to steal it.

My first few attempts were miserable failures. I didn't have the recipe, so I tried to channel Nancy and Dahlia. Shitty. *Did they use cornstarch on the stove top? Was it a baked, egg-set custard?* Nope. Too runny, not butterscotch-y enough. Just plain boring. Then the *Los Angeles Times* published the actual recipe. *Fucking yes!*

I still couldn't do it. I have a hard time following recipes. So I did my own thing (though still completely thieved), and it worked. It's been on our menu for five years. Thanks, Nancy!

BUTTERSCOTCH MASCARPONE SEMIFREDDO WITH MILK JAM AND SBRISOLONA

The butterscotch is straightforward: dark brown sugar, butter, vanilla, salt, a little booze. As I whip some eggs, I gently fold in the butterscotch, creating a flavored zabaglione. Instead of combining this with a straight whipped cream, as you would to make a simple semifreddo, I mix mascarpone with some cream—but carefully. Mascarpone is trouble if overworked. So we have our two foamy things: Fold the butterscotch zabaglione into the whipped mascarpone and freeze. The result is homey, very Italian, and a little bit funny. The other components are not as confusing as they sound, either. Plus you get to use instant polenta again in the sbrisolana.
Yield: 8 cup-size portions

BUTTERSCOTCH MASCARPONE SEMIFREDDO

Mascarpone 1½ cups (125 grams)
Heavy cream 1½ cups (90 grams)
Dark brown sugar ⅔ cup (141 grams), packed
Browned butter 2 tablespoons (28 grams)
Light rum 2 tablespoons (28 grams)
Vanilla bean ½, scraped
Salt to taste
Egg yolks 8 (144 grams)
Dulce de leche for serving
Sbrisolona (page 122)
Fresh fruit for serving

1. In the bowl of a stand mixer, using the whip attachment, combine the mascarpone and cream at medium speed. Transfer the mixture to another bowl and refrigerate.

Clean the bowl and whip attachment of the stand mixer.

2. In a small saucepan over medium heat, combine the brown sugar, rum, vanilla bean scrapings, and salt and bring to a boil, stirring occasionally, until you have a thick butterscotch. When the sugar mixture is dark and smells just about burned, remove it from the heat and set aside.

3. In the clean bowl of the stand mixer, using the whip attachment, beat the egg yolks on medium speed. Add the browned sugar mixture and whip until the bottom of the mixer bowl is cool to the touch. Fold in the mascarpone mixture gently.

4. Pour this semifreddo batter into a freezer-safe container and chill overnight in the freezer. This will keep in your freezer forever if stored properly.

DULCE "MILK JAM"

We're not doing the condensed-milk can trick, remember? (You will most likely die.—Sous-Chef Kim) (This is not a joke.—Brooks)

Buy a can or jar of dulce de leche from the store. Call it milk jam.

To serve: Smear milk jam on a plate, add a spoonful of sbrisolona, and spoon about 1 cup of the semifreddo on top. Garnish with sharp, acidic fruits, cut to your liking: cherries, blood oranges, tangerines, plums, or peaches.

YOGURT DATES

In most fancy restaurants there is a distinct tension between the savory side of the kitchen and the dessert station. Line cooks often think of the pastry people as three-fifths of a cook: effete, overly sensitive, possessing no knife-sharpening skills. Pastry cooks see the line cooks as knuckleheads lacking finesse who reek of testosterone and raw meat. At Del Posto there is very little of that attitude. Ladner would never allow it.

At Komi, in DC, I worked alone, producing and plating every dessert. An army of one. Then I hired Brallan (pronounced *Brian*) and he helped me make doughnut dough and lollipops. One of the signature savory courses at Komi was a hot mascarpone-stuffed date throttled with olive oil and sea salt. Holy Jesus, it was delicious. It was our enemy.

When it came time for me to present desserts to a table, guests would often say, "May I just have another stuffed date as my dessert?" Tensions rose, guns were drawn, lips curled into scowls. But only for me, of course. The line cooks doled out high fives and applauded victoriously every time. So years later, when I needed a new item for the cookie box at Del Posto, I had no problem co-opting the date as a dessert. Give the people what they want, you know?

My variation involves labneh, a strained yogurt. Instead of serving the dates whole, I cut them into a cross-section so they look like a Goetze's caramel cream candy.

Yield: 3 servings

Dates 6
Labneh 1½ cups (430 grams)
Salt to taste
Fresh lemon juice to taste
Freshly ground black pepper to taste
Extra-virgin olive oil for serving
Coarse sea salt for serving

1. In a medium saucepan over high heat, bring a pot of water to a boil. Add the dates and cook for 10 seconds to loosen the skin. Remove the skin from the dates using a paring knife. Remove the pits from the dates using a pair of pliers. Don't damage the flesh.

2. In a small bowl, mix together the labneh, salt, lemon juice, and pepper. Place the mixture into an ordinary piping bag and fill the cavity of the date. (You can even snip the corner off a Ziploc bag and use that as your piping tool.)

3. Line the dates in a single layer on a plate and refrigerate until the filling is firm, about 1 hour.

4. Preheat the oven to 400°F. Line a baking sheet with parchment and set aside.

5. Slice each date lengthwise into 3 pieces and place on the prepared baking sheet. Bake until the dates caramelize, about 1 minute.

To serve: Drench the dates in olive oil and coarse sea salt and serve as fast as you can.

See page 239.

S'MORES: WARM LA TUR WITH CHARRED BREAD AND CHOCOLATE–OLIVE OIL SAUCE

Campfire time! This is it. The last recipe. Grab the kindling.

This dish is the bastardization of fondue, a cheese course, and s'mores (*all'Italiana*). It's a fun and interactive dish meant to be served family style. The La Tur, a sheep-goat-cow cheese from Piemonte, is soft and kind of barnyard-y. The bread and blackened paper deliver a dreamy charcoal-like flavor. The chocolate–olive oil sauce is not nearly as sweet as you may think and balances perfectly with the bread and cheese. It's an unexpected, conversational element. At Del Posto, we serve this as the cheese course on our tasting menu. It seems obvious, but remind your guests that they shouldn't eat the charred paper. It is neither fun nor delicious.

Wheel of La Tur cheese 1
Loaf of rustic country bread 1
Chocolate Sauce (page 100) to taste

1. Preheat the broiler to 500°F.
2. Wrap the cheese in parchment, like a birthday present, and place it in an ovenproof baking dish, seamside down (you are serving in this dish, so pick something handsome). Allow the cheese to sit at room temperature for 2 hours, or until very gooey.
3. Tear the bread into small chunks, being careful not to crush the insides as you tear it. On a grill pan over high heat, grill the bread on both sides until quite charred, longer on the crust side. (Alternatively, you can toss the chunks with a small amount of olive oil and toast them in a 375°F oven until golden brown.)

4. Place the parchment-covered cheese under the broiler, just long enough for the paper to blacken, about 10 seconds.
5. Using scissors, cut the paper top off the cheese and tear it into a jagged formation, leaving the excess burned paper attached and exposing the warmed and slightly molten cheese.

To serve: Place the baking dish on a large platter and surround the cheese with the charred bread pieces. Drizzle the warm chocolate sauce around the plate and on the cheese. Serve immediately.

Happy Birthday
Happy Birthday!
Happy Birthday!
happy birthday

ACKNOWLEDG-
MENTS

I would like to give special thanks to the following individuals without whom this book would have never existed:

To Mark Ladner, the gatekeeper *and* the key master. To Mario, Lidia, and Joe, the folks who sign my paychecks and keep the inspiration flowing. To Chris Cechin-De la Rosa, my field marshal and collaborator, who stopped showering to make sure we got this thing finished on time. To Chloe Brownstein, who compiled recipes for me and attended Smith College, a storied institution in western Massachusetts, USA. To Kim Janusz and Roger Rodriguez, my mercenary team of sous-chefs at Del Posto, for covering my shifts when I was chained in my apartment or in a PDR to complete the tasks at hand. To Jason Fulford and Tamara Shopsin for the propaganda. To Laurie Alleman-Weber for hiring me in the first place—I owe you prorated royalty checks. To the kitchen squad at Del Posto, Orsone, and Babbo at the time of this writing—Rosa, Paco, Diana, Jen, Sooji, Scotty, Rosanne, Eddie, Kelly, Rebecca, Annie, Justine, Oliver, Mateo, Tony, Melissa, Carlos, Josh, Andres, Nelson, Jon, Dana, Gio, Justin, Tyler, Maria, Jennah, Gina, and Michael. To Luis Garcia, the man who knows everything about everything at Del Posto. To Kim Witherspoon for putting me in my place; your powers cannot be contained. And to Inkwell sergeant at arms Allison Hunter.

To Jill Bialosky for remaining calm even as the demands became more and more troubling, and to everyone else at W. W. Norton who made this book possible. To Layla Gibbon for the rummaging of papers, Sameena Ahmad for the questionable intel, Eric Wareheim for the crass commercialization, Nastassia Lopez for the reactionary politics. To Cecelia Pleva for not kicking me out. To Peter Meehan for helping to get the scales of justice tipped. To Jesse Pearson for the false start and for always reminding me that Rorschach is more brutal than Born Against. To Cundo, Michelle, Dean, and Mick, the folks who make sure I get to bang on shit and not lose my shit.

CHAPTER CONTENTS

INDEX

Note: Page numbers in *italics* refer to illustrations.

WORKING PASTRY: THE FORM LETTER

The drunken email that follows got me my job. If you are looking for pastry work, you'd be smart to use it. Don't change even a word. It has a 100 percent proven track record.

From: ——————— <——————— *pastry@yahoo.com*>
　　　　YOUR NAME　　YOURINITIALS

To: ———————@———————————.com
　　DREAMJOB　　　DREAMRESTAURANT

Subject: pastry chef position at ———————————
　　　　　　　　　　　　　　　DREAM RESTAURANT

To Whom It May Concern:

Hello, this is ———————. I was the dessert chef at ——————————— *(Food &*
　　　　　　　YOUR NAME　　　　　　　　　　　　FANCY LOCAL EATERY

Wine top ten new chefs ———————————) in ——————————— from
　　　　　　　　　　YEAR YOUR FORMER BOSS WON　　　NOTEWORTHY FOOD TOWN

——— until ———. Previously, I was at ——————————— for nearly ———
DATE　　　DATE　　　　　　　　　FANCY LOCAL EATERY　　　　　　NUMBER

years (I was the opening pastry chef there), with a brief interlude in Los Angeles to work at

———————————.
JUST WRITE "MOZZA"

I began my pastry career at ———————'s infamous ——————— in ———.
　　　　　　　　　　　　FAMOUS CHEF　　　　　FAMOUS RESTAURANT　　YEAR

Both high-end fine dining *AND* ——————— desserts are in my blood. My family
　　　　　　　　　　　　　　PREFERRED CUISINE

is from ———————————————————————————————.
　　　OBSCURE BUT NOTEWORTHY REGION OF DREAM RESTAURANT'S PREFERRED CUISINE

My time at _____ was _____. I did _____%
       FANCY LOCAL EATERY   POSITIVE ADJECTIVE   NUMBER APPROACHING 100

of the dessert production, and plated every single dessert and dessert amuse that left the kitchen.

I treated dessert like a line cook, with as much ala minute preparations as time would allow.

I spent my Sundays picking up fruit at the _____, and my
       COOL LOCAL GREENMARKET BONA FIDE

Mondays experimenting in the kitchen when it was _____. We were
       INTROSPECTIVE ADJECTIVE

open _____ days a week, but I was there every day. I loved working there and I would have
       NUMBER

stayed there for years, however my _____ moved to _____.
       LOVE INTEREST   NOTEWORTHY CULINARY TOWN

I have since relocated to _____ and have been
       TRENDY NEIGHBORHOOD NEAR DREAM RESTAURANT

working at a restaurant on the _____.
       BOUGIE AREA YOU ARE SURE YOU CAN SAFELY SNUB YOUR NOSE AT

My current position is temporary and I am looking to move into a restaurant of the _____
       ADJECTIVE

quality, such as _____. I _____ believe that the _____
       DREAM RESTAURANT   ADVERB   DREAM RESTAURANT'S CUISINE

way of food is the best. Simplicity, letting ingredients shine, and comfort. That is the way I

approach desserts. I am, to put it bluntly, a _____. It is my work, my
       HYPERBOLIC SELF-DESCRIPTION

hobby, and my life. I am equally comfortable making a _____ with
       AVANT-GARDE TECHNIQUE

_____ or vacuum-compressing Granny Smith apples to turn them trans-
AVANT-GARDE INGREDIENT

luscent and green as I am crafting a rustic _____, or a classic _____, or
       APPLE RECIPE   APPLE RECIPE 2

_____. I cannot wait for the spring fruits to begin popping up at the _____
APPLE RECIPE 3   SECOND LOCAL

_____, although lately I am enamored with the _____ and
GREENMARKET BONA FIDE   ESOTERIC FRUIT 1

_____ of winter. I am a ravenous reader of culinary books, having recently finished
ESOTERIC FRUIT 2

_____ and _____'s _____
OBSCURE OUT-OF-PRINT RECIPE BOOK   EVEN MORE OBSCURE AUTHOR   MAKE UP A FAKE

_____.
BOOK NAME

In the past I have staged at ———————————— and ————————————.
                              REPUTED RESTAURANT   RESTAURANT WITH SOME STARS

And since in New York I have taken a panettone/holiday bread class with ———————————— at
                                                                        LOCAL CHEF-HERO

————————————————, and a ———————————————— class with the folks
LOCAL CHEF-HERO'S RESTAURANT   COMPLICATED TECHNIQUE

of ———————— to further my cooking skills, I have also eaten my way around the city on my
     SCHOOL

days off . . . ————————————————————, ————————————————
              RESTAURANT YOU THINK YOUR MAYBE-BOSS LIKES 1   RESTAURANT YOU THINK

————————————————, ———————————————————— , RESTAU-
YOUR MAYBE-BOSS LIKES 2   RESTAURANT YOU THINK YOUR MAYBE-BOSS LIKES 3

————————————————————, and ————————————————————
RANT YOU THINK YOUR MAYBE-BOSS LIKES 4   RESTAURANT YOU THINK YOUR MAYBE-BOSS

————. I dined at ———————————— a few years ago and had a great time. I know of the
LIKES 5   DREAM RESTAURANT

———————————— connection to Mozza in LA. Having worked at ————————————, I
DREAM RESTAURANT   RESTAURANT IN LA

also worked with ———————— and ————————.
                  LA HERO 1   LA HERO 2

I am looking for the perfect restaurant in which to work. Somewhere inspiring and motiva-

tional where innovation and tradition are of equal value. And it sounds like ————————————
                                                                            DREAM RESTAURANT

is that kind of restaurant.

I really admire Chef ————————'s approach to food. And as passionate as I am about the
                      MAYBE-BOSS

food itself, I also understand the business aspects of being a pastry chef: inventory, food costs,

staff training, overtime, working ———————— days a week, etc.
                                  JUST WRITE "7"

If you are still looking for a pastry chef, then I would love to meet with you, or come in and

do a tasting as your schedule would allow.

————————————————
YOUR NAME

Brooks Headley has been the executive pastry chef of the *New York Times* 4-star restaurant Del Posto since March 2008. He received the James Beard Award for Outstanding Pastry Chef in May 2013. Previously he spent time at Campanile in Los Angeles and Komi in Washington, DC. He lives in Greenwich Village.

See page 248.